Born in Eastbourne in 1957 and educated at Brighton and
Cambridge, Joe Bennett taught English in a variety of countries
before becoming a newspaper columnist and writer of travel
books. He lives in Lyttelton, New Zealand.

Hello Dubai

Skiing, Sand and Shopping in the World's Weirdest City

JOE BENNETT

SIMON &
SCHUSTER

London · New York · Sydney · Toronto

A CBS COMPANY

First published in Great Britain in 2010 by Simon & Schuster UK Ltd
A CBS COMPANY

Copyright © 2010 by Joe Bennett

1 3 5 7 9 10 8 6 4 2

Simon & Schuster UK Ltd
1st Floor
222 Gray's Inn Road
London
WC1X 8HB

www.simonandschuster.co.uk

Simon & Schuster Australia
Sydney

A CIP catalogue copy for this book
is available from the British Library.

ISBN: 978-1-84737-674-9

Wilfred Thesiger excerpts are taken from *Arabian Sands*,
published by Penguin Classics, 2007

Typeset in Palatino by M Rules
Printed in the UK by CPI Mackays, Chatham ME5 8TD

Contents

Contents

For Albert Arriola

Acknowledgements

I'd like to thank my hosts in Dubai and Al Ain for their generosity and kindness. And also their friends and the many others who answered my persistent questions with such tolerance and patience.

Introduction

When I was at school I hadn't heard of Dubai. If you'd asked me where it was I would have guessed Africa. I wouldn't have been far wrong. But if I'd guessed India I wouldn't have been far wrong either, or Asia, or even Europe. Dubai isn't far from anywhere. That centrality has served it well.

I hadn't heard of Dubai forty years ago because there wasn't much to hear of. It was just a hot little port on the Arabian Gulf. People had lived there for hundreds of years. They'd put to sea and traded and eaten a lot of fish, but they hadn't multiplied much because the land they inhabited was desert. Offering only dates, a bit of meat and a few sources of fresh water, the desert kept the people skinny and pinned them to the coast. Dubai, like Arabia in general, was a quiet place.

Time was, however, when Arabia in general had run the world. In the middle of the eighth century, only a hundred years after the birth of Islam, the Arabian Empire was larger than the Roman Empire had ever been. It embraced Spain and about two thirds of the Mediterranean seaboard. It had swept up through what is now Turkey. It had penetrated the Indian subcontinent. It had reached the great mountain ranges of Central Asia and had even clambered over them into what is now western China.

Arabia, in short, was the great world power and Islam was the great world religion.

The world owes much to that empire. It kept learning alive in the West. When Europe was benighted under illiterate tribal thugs, the Arab world was fostering science and philosophy, translating classical texts, importing mathematics from India and adapting technology from the Far East.

But gradually the empire declined as empires do and Arabia settled back into what looked like a terminal snooze. Then, in the twentieth century, oil happened. It happened to Dubai as it happened to much of the Middle East. Dollars rained down. If it hadn't been for oil, Dubai would still be snoozing in the sun and I'd still think it was in Africa.

The places that found oil, or had it found for them, reacted variously. Many leaders gorged on the wealth it brought, but Dubai proved wiser. Perhaps because it didn't have as much oil as others had, it foresaw a time when it wouldn't have any. So Dubai set about creating something that would endure when the party was over. The result was the city that seemingly grew overnight.

In only a few decades Dubai has become a hub of global trade and global finance. It has developed a tourism industry. It has erected buildings that everybody knows. And it has attracted people from almost every country on earth. Since 1960, Dubai's population has multiplied about twenty-fold.

And all this has been accomplished peaceably. Though it is situated in the world's most volatile region, where blood has been spilt throughout my lifetime and looks unlikely to stop being spilt any time soon, Dubai has fought no wars and suffered no terrorism. In a time of increasing tension between the Muslim world and the nominally Christian one, Dubai has somehow stood aside from the fray.

On the face of it, Dubai would seem like a model for the way ahead, but its critics are abundant and strident. As the American economic crisis spread across the world and put the wind up capitalism, there came a flood of articles about Dubai that oozed hatred. The writers, most of them British, saw Dubai as the emblem of a rotten world, a world that was imploding. Dubai was brash. Dubai was cruel. Dubai was exploitative. Dubai was a speculative bubble. Dubai, in short, was plain bloody horrible, and if the economic crisis killed off Dubai it would at least have done one good thing.

In the *Independent* Johann Hari called Dubai a city built 'on credit and ecocide, suppression and slavery.'

In the *Sunday Times*, Rod Liddle asserted that Dubai was 'a slave state' and 'not too far removed' from 'a pre-war Third World fascist theocracy.'

And Simon Jenkins of *The Times* went in for prophecy. 'The dunes will reclaim the soaring folly of Dubai,' he wrote. Dubai was 'the last word in iconic overkill, a festival of egotism with humanity denied.'

I joined the chorus in a small way myself. In a newspaper column in 2008 I called Dubai 'the spiritual home of suit man.' Suit man, I suggested, was the business-class executive with the BlackBerry and the Rolex and nothing to contribute to the world except his ability to turn one dollar into two without doing anything useful.

And on what evidence did we so despise Dubai? Well, I can't speak for the others, but I'd spent four days there one summer a few years back. During those four days, the heat was too fierce to do anything much but shift from air-conditioned hotel room to air-conditioned bar. In other words I knew next to nothing of the place. My opinion was prejudice.

That prejudice had been partly fostered by a patrician Englishman called Wilfred Thesiger. Thesiger was an oddball, a loner and an explorer. In the 1930s and 40s he made repeated treks across the sands of the Arabian Peninsula, including two crossings of the Empty Quarter, a terrifying blank on the map.

Like his hero, T.E. Lawrence, he dressed as an Arab and he travelled in the company of Arabs, the tribal nomads known generically as the Bedouin. 'Born freebooters,' he called them, 'contemptuous of all outsiders, and intolerant of restraint,' and he painted a picture of them as a heroic race; but also a doomed one, for oil had already been found in the region. Modernity was sniffing round the edges of the desert. It would seduce and destroy, predicted Thesiger, an ancient and noble way of life.

Thesiger died only a few years ago. As an old man he was invited to return to the United Arab Emirates and see the soaring new cities of Dubai and Abu Dhabi. He hated them. He described them as 'an Arabian nightmare, the final disillusionment.' It's an old man's lament, of course, for what was, for 'a vanished past . . . and a once magnificent people.' But it's a persuasive lament nonetheless. From the comfort of one's armchair and with a supermarket just down the road, it is easy to view modern Dubai as the triumph of shallow materialism over ancient nobility, of consumption over honour, of shopping over endurance.

It is equally easy to see Dubai as the purest expression of western free market politics. But Dubai isn't the West. It is Muslim. Its laws are not western laws. Its press does not enjoy the freedom of the western press, and it remains an autocracy, run by an unelected sheikh from an effectively royal family.

But the one outstanding truth about Dubai is that none of these facts and none of the criticism has deterred hundreds of thousands of people from travelling to Dubai in search of a better life. All of us know someone who's gone there. And most of us know someone who has stayed there. Out of curiosity, I followed them.

1

Let It Snow, Let It Snow, Let It Snow

Dusk in the desert. The sand's warm. It seeps into my shoes like dry water and grinds beneath my socks. How deep the desert is I cannot guess. Ribbed like a beach, and relieved only by the odd sprig of grey vegetation, it stretches away from me for perhaps fifty metres. Whereupon it becomes the sixth fairway of the Arabian Ranches Golf Club.

On the cobbled track for golf carts I empty the sand from the shoes, then set off for the distant clubhouse. As I pass a shrub, four birds erupt, plovers I think. They startle me. My spine jumps at the place where a dog has hackles. The birds screech a five-note alarm call. 'Where are you going?' it sounds like. 'Where are you going?' Well, birds, I'm going to meet Stephen for a drink.

The birds wheel in the darkening air and settle further up the fairway. The base of the shrub they rose from is coiled around with irrigation tubing.

Half an hour ago the sun set like a Christmas bauble. Now it's no more than a pinkish smear on the horizon, but the air is still warm as a blessing. It's deep mid-winter. Christmas happened just a few days back and, as in the Christian world, it's party time in Dubai. Friends of friends have already invited me to a New Year's Eve celebration. It is to be held in the desert, which I hope means more deserty desert than this. We'll eat and drink amid the limitless sands, then sleep there in tents – like Thesiger but without the hardship. I have been warned not to leave my shoes outside the tent overnight. Scorpions like to snuggle down in them, apparently.

I bet scorpions have been banished from this golf course. The place is encircled by the reason for its existence, a housing estate for ex-pats called Arabian Ranches. The houses are not ranches, and neither were they built for Arabs, but misnomers are endemic in Dubai. There are other estates here called The Greens and The Meadows, and it's hard to imagine anywhere less green or meadowy. The estates have all gone up in the last four years, built on the sands that fringe the city.

I follow the smooth track as it winds over bulldozed hummocks – their veneer of forced grass mown to different lengths as stipulated by the Royal and Ancient – and around bunkers. Dubai does excellent bunkers. Night's approach has driven all the golfers to the clubhouse, and left the course to the birds. The birds have surprised me. Already I've seen plovers, partridges, doves, mynah birds, wagtails, and numerous bright and darting things I cannot name. Have they always come here? Or have they discovered Dubai more recently as the place has greened? Have they come, like the ex-pats, for the golf courses? I don't know.

Near the clubhouse the driving range and putting greens are lit by banks of floodlights. The air resounds with the surprising and distinctive twang of metal woods. A tractor of sorts glides about the range, driven by a man in a metal cage. The machine hoovers the balls into its innards as if feeding.

More women than men are out practising, almost all of them white and middle-aged, their wide lower portions encased in three-quarter-length shorts. Despite the ballast of their butts, the women don't hit the ball very far.

I trot up the grand steps to the clubhouse. The place is mock-baronial, with a marble atrium and flunkeys in uniform. The bar is thirty feet long. Behind it stand more flunkeys in dark shirts and aprons. Their skins range from light hazel to lustrous African black, and they're all young, fresh and well groomed. On the other side of the bar, and facing them, stand men in less appealing skins. Those skins are twice as old and range in colour from sallow straw to soon-to-burst burgundy, though these men would all describe themselves as white. They wear polo shirts and they don't look happy.

I order a Stella Artois, the Belgian beer that was the cheapest available when I lived in France thirty years ago but which has since thrown foil round the neck of its bottles and, by a masterpiece of marketing, become a premium brand. It still gets you drunk but more expensively. It's a beer that seems apt for Dubai.

'I'm sorry, sir,' says the barman with a propitiatory smile, 'fifteen minutes.' He taps his watch to underline his point, then indicates a laminated notice, one of several dotted along the bar. It announces, with apologies, that the bar will not open until 6.30 p.m. in honour of the Islamic New Year.

Only then do I notice that none of the men at the bar has a drink. And they are exceptionally keen to get one. They fizz like wasps in a jam jar, glancing abstractedly at a screen showing an English football match, then back to their wrists and the cruel dawdle of time. There's an air of only just good-natured impatience.

'What do they think this is, a ██████ mosque?' The speaker is short and tubby, and his accent, Liverpudlian at a guess, turns ██████ into fooking. His plump little gut is enclosed by a shirt of a colour that I wouldn't have chosen myself. For me or for him.

I ask him how it is that the Islamic New Year differs from the Christian one, but in the circumstances it's a poor choice of question. 'Fook it,' he says and turns to the football. Ads for beer line the pitch. I hope they annoy him. The pitch is English winter mud. Many of the lithe young footballers have skins like the ones behind the bar.

One golfer ceaselessly drums his fingers on the bar top, as if doing a piano exercise. Others banter with the staff. 'Come on, mate. The cops aren't going to come in. We're all friends here.'

The youngsters behind the bar are used to accommodating these older men. They open doors for them, fuel their bellies with booze and food, agree with them at all times and on all subjects, laugh at their jokes and hope for tips. Thwarting them brings acute discomfort.

More men come in and add to the waiting throng. The pressure mounts. In the end it tells. Watched by a hundred eyes, a barman reaches up, extracts a glass from the rack and pulls the Heineken tap. By my watch it's 6.25. The tap gurgles and splutters. The froth becomes a steady stream of beer. The gates of heaven have opened and Allah chooses not to send a thunderbolt. And there's an instantaneous exhalation of breath and a change of mood. The men stir with anticipatory pleasure. They do not clamour to be served, but they get close to it. The evening has begun. And so, almost, has the Islamic New Year.

It takes a while to ease the backlog. The men retreat from the bar one by one, holding glasses of what they crave to smooth the edges of the evening, to put out the little fires of dissatisfaction. I take my Stella out to the patio, laid with tables and chairs for dining and big cushioned chairs for sprawling in and drinking. Free-standing heaters on wheels abound like tall green toadstools. They are not needed this evening. The air bathes the skin.

The floodlit practice area is more sparsely populated than

half an hour ago, the golfers whirring back to the clubhouse on their little electric carts like birds coming in to roost. A couple of stars have appeared in the night sky, or perhaps planets. I have never known the difference.

The terrace starts to fill with men and family groups, a few of them Indian or oriental, but the great majority white. The women wear what seem to me to be abnormal quantities of jewellery, but maybe I am deceived by my expectations: I'm expecting the ostentation of *nouvelle richesse*.

The villas that encircle the course are just inky shapes. The irrigated rock garden at the fringe of the patio is planted with exotic shrubs, immaculately tended. The trunks of the date palms have been clipped to neatness and wound around with strings of Christmas lights. Invisible speakers play easy-listening music, by which I mean the stuff that it's easy not to listen to, familiar, tuneful, out-of-date songs, a sort of aural wallpaper.

Stephen, my friend and host, arrives, his hair wet. He apologizes for being late.

'I decided to have a shower,' he says. 'Wonderful showers here.'

'I thought you said you weren't a member?'

'I'm white, aren't I?'

It seems that no one has ever challenged him.

I offer to fetch him a beer but, as if by telepathy, a girl appears, places a salver of crisps and peanuts on the low table and takes Stephen's order. She is from Myanmar. She's been in Dubai for eight months, she says. She is pleased to be here. Her smile is all charm.

A pair of young Indians appears, one in staff uniform, the other in the check trousers and straitjacket of a chef. They wheel a barbecue onto the patio and set up stall to make pasta on demand. And bang on cue for the Islamic New Year an Islamic moon rises. It's the thinnest sickle, gleaming and whetted. I think immediately of the curve of metal that tops the roof of every mosque in the world. And simultaneously of a knife, curved and gleaming, a knife to slit the throat of an infidel dog.

Stephen is more forthcoming than the Scouser on the subject of the Islamic calendar. It is based on lunar months, which are shorter than Christian months, so the date of the new year shifts back a bit each year. But apparently the local authorities are not above nudging it neatly onto a weekend so as to minimize disruption to business.

I know Stephen from university. After he graduated he crewed for a few years on rich people's yachts. He tells me how he loved being on watch on nights like this, calm nights with a moon. He'd sit on deck and stare up into the multitude of stars. And in the great rocking silence of a huge ocean he would sink into a reverie, a Wordsworth-like communion with a pointlessly spinning globe. And with it would come a sense of cruel beauty, allied to a sort of consoling indifference. The speech surprises me. I'd never thought Stephen was given to that sort of thing, though on reflection, I expect we all are in one way or another.

Stephen tells me how, many years ago, on just such a night in the vastness of the Indian Ocean, he was alone on deck and sunk in reverie when, whoompha, something struck him in the back. He jumped more than he has ever jumped before or since. Instinct relayed mighty immediate messages of terror through his body. The shock, he says, must have come close to killing him. On the deck beside him lay a flying fish.

We sit a long while in the sweet, luxurious evening. Stephen gives me some rudimentary lessons in astronomy, pointing out a couple of planets. Planets shine continuously, he says, while stars only twinkle. 'See there,' he says, 'that one's a planet, whereas that one next to it, that's a star.'

'Ah yes,' I say, though I can see no difference. I think I may be looking at the wrong bits.

Sprinklers pop up audibly on the golf course to ready it for tomorrow's traffic. Our Myanmari waitress keeps us supplied with European beer. On the first evening of the Islamic year 1430, the Christmas lights twinkle in the date palms. The Indian chef cooks Italian dishes. The tubby ex-pat golfers and their families sit and laugh under a sickle moon. Dean Martin sings, 'Let it snow, let it snow, let it snow.' It is 9 p.m. and twenty degrees. And we are sitting above desert.

'Welcome to Dubai,' says Stephen.

'Cheers,' I say. We chink glasses. And I wonder to myself, quite cheerfully, whether I am going to be able to make any sense of this tangled place.

2

I Love You, I Respect You

The Arabian peninsula lies between Africa and Asia. It's bounded by the Red Sea to the west, and to the north-east by the Arabian Gulf. The little rhino horn of land that protrudes into the eastern end of the Gulf is the United Arab Emirates. It consists of seven emirates, one of which is Dubai. And the Emirate of Dubai consists of the city of Dubai and a small chunk of desert.

If you drive west along the coast from Dubai you'll pass through Abu Dhabi, Qatar, Saudi Arabia and Kuwait before fetching up in Iraq. Directly across the Gulf from Dubai is Iran. In other words, Dubai is close to a lot of oil and even more volatility.

The rhino horn comes to a tip at the Straits of Hormuz, beyond which lie the Arabian Sea and the Indian Ocean. Carry on down the other side of the horn and you'll reach Oman, Yemen, the Red Sea, Egypt and eventually the Suez Canal.

Dubai sits on the Creek, a saltwater inlet that stretches inland a few miles before subsiding into salt marsh and, astonishingly, a flock of flamingos, as pink as teenage nail varnish. Beyond the flamingos lies desert – or at least it did until Dubai began to swell. A lot of the desert's gone. I fear the flamingos may follow it, but it's the non-flamingo end of the Creek that matters for the city. Without the Creek this place would never have been settled. From the very beginning the Creek has provided safe harbour for sea-going vessels and the sea has provided fish and trade.

Down by the Creek at ten in the morning, in this most futuristic of cities I meet a scene that's ancient. Moored at the wharf are a mass of chunky ramshackle wooden boats that look as old as Christ. These are dhows, big four-square blunt things. Each has an elaborate painted superstructure in a fetching state of decay. Their squat and bulbous hulls remind me of the dumpy galleons in which Europeans set sail during the sixteenth and seventeenth centuries to grab what they could of a new world.

Accommodation for the crew consists of ragged hammocks. The railings are hung with even more ragged washing. It's a scene of picturesque poverty, ripe for the tourist camera, but it clearly isn't laid on for the tourist. It's business. The dhow is a small-scale trading vessel doing what's been done up and down the gulf for thousands of years.

The decks of the dhows are heaped with stuff, arbitrary stuff in arbitrary heaps. And the wharf is heaped with even more stuff, tons of it, all higgledy-piggledy. I can walk up and touch it: huge boxes of blanched cashew kernels from India, Best Brand Tamarinds, ten-inch oval plates from the Better Home Company of China, pallets of car batteries, fish traps, air-con units, Taiwanese tablecloths, fridges in cardboard boxes, all of them stacked any old how. Someone must know what's where but it looks bewildering to me.

People abound, a few of them actively loading or unloading stuff. But most just squat on their haunches smoking, playing cards, arguing, mending a sandal, drinking milky tea from poly-styrene cups, eating rice and scraps with their fingers, or simply looking vaguely into an unfocussed distance and just being. All the people look poor. None of them looks remotely Arab. Most are from the vast Indian subcontinent: Bangladesh, Sri Lanka, Pakistan, India. They are small, skinny, dark people, wearing cotton smocks or loose two-piece pyjamas or t-shirts and dirty jeans. And all of them are men. It's a place of shouting and idling, a place of small-scale human business. I buy a cup of Lipton's tea, sweetened with both condensed milk and sugar, and sit a while under a palm in the room-temperature air, just watching, and feeling that I like all this.

A parakeet swoops between trees, a scream of luminous green, like lime juice brightly lit. Ants are busy at my feet, more industrious than the wharf but with a similar air of random activity held within an overall order. On the coarse grass of a berm there's a patch of vomit in which the ants take great inter-est. And alighting to take an intense interest in the ants is, to my surprise and delight, a hoopoe.

I know the hoopoe from the bird books I read as a kid. It was supposed to visit the UK but I doubted it. This bird was too exotic for the cloudy north. With its weird crest it belonged somewhere they worshipped odd gods. And here it is now, smaller than I expected, but every bit as bizarre. Its wings are zebra striped, its bill long and curved, but the bird is rendered distinctive by its crest. It resembles the bony protrusion on the heads of the first flying creatures, those nightmare dinosaurs with wings of skin and beaks of teeth. At the same time, that crest seems the distilled essence of Egypt, of a piece with hiero-glyphs and the sort of neck-thrust dancing that some people perform regrettably at discos. Or used to anyway. I haven't danced in decades.

A man comes by pushing a bike. He is five foot tall, swarthy, fat as the Michelin logo and wearing pyjamas. The low-slung crotch of his pyjama trousers would arouse admiration in any skateboarder. He looks perhaps forty years old. The bike looks older. The hoopoe understandably takes fright.

As I wander down the Creek the place smartens with money. Here's a cliff of glass, the Dubai Chamber of Commerce and Industry. It's everything the wharf is not: modern, rectilinear, impenetrable, air-conditioned, wealthy, security-guarded and daunting. And here are dhows that are dhows no longer. They've been refurbished, prinked and polished, permanently moored and turned into restaurants for tourists. Parodic authenticity, the hallmark of tourism the world over.

I pass swanky hotels with big cars pulling up in the *porte-cochere* and doormen in uniform rushing to their sides. The doormen are Indian, the cars European and the people who get out of them mostly Arab. The Arab men all wear the long white surgical gown known as the *dishdash*.

It's evocative garb. I am immediately reminded of London in the Seventies, when a sudden spike in the oil price made Arabs into lords of the world. The white gowns moved about Mayfair in Rolls Royces and bought everything from whores to skyscrapers with what seemed like imperious disdain. I remember there was resentment and a sort of sulky dread. Britain was slumped in terminal decline and a three-day week and it seemed that the order of the world was changing.

Beside the Creek a few tourists promenade, looking bored, looking not to have quite found the joy they expected to find when they planned this jaunt. Nevertheless they are storing in their cameras a mass of pixellated images, to be administered to friends at a later date, like soporific drugs.

And it's a pretty enough urban scene that the friends will be bored by, with the Creek glittering in the sun and the air benign, and poverty out of sight, and food and drink available at little cafes on the prom, at one of which I take a seat. Two men are playing chess. One coughs with a bubbling insistence that sounds terminal. An Indian fills a bucket from a standpipe. He has the deep-sunk eyes of a brigand and skin so dark it shines. His t-shirt says 'Desert Car Wash'. I had expected to get through life without seeing the phrase 'Desert Car Wash'.

Coffee was the signature drink of the Bedouin Arabs. When Thesiger made camp for the night, his companions would always brew coffee. Strong and bitter stuff, apparently, served in a huge elaborate pot and tiny cups. I've already seen such a pot in a souvenir shop. It had a spout like a toucan's bill. But drinkable coffee has proved hard to find. I order one now and get a plastic beaker of what I can only describe as a brown. Thin and warmish, it makes up for its lack of coffee flavour with sugar. A cat inspects me from a wall with that fixed stare they affect. Like every cat I have seen so far in this city it looks skinny and scared.

An Arab approaches in full regalia – sandals, dishdash, head cloth. As he mounts the steps to the little terrace he grabs at his crotch. He grabs meatily and unabashedly. His eye meets mine. He grins and grabs his crotch once more, whether to relieve irritation or just for the pleasant sensation, I can't tell. He smiles, broadly. 'You want tea?' he says. I have already given up on the brown.

'Thank you,' I say and the man calls like an emperor for two teas and sits on the plastic chair opposite mine. He takes off his sandals, folds one foot under himself, gives his crotch another affectionate mauling, and grins. His teeth are terrible. Broad and white at the business end, they narrow towards the gums, corroded by brown rot, so each tooth resembles an off-white miniature spade with a rotten wooden handle. 'My name Abdullah,' he proclaims.

'Joe,' I say.

'John,' he says as we shake hands.

'Joe,' I say.

17

'John,' he says.

'I'm pleased to meet you,' I say.

'John,' he says, giving me another unimpeded view of those teeth. 'I see you. I respect you. I love you.' And he lays his hand on my arm and beams.

By means of some simple questions several times repeated and rephrased I discover that Abdullah is from the Yemen. He has a wife and four children.

'I working very good,' he says with evident pride.

'Working,' he repeats when he sees me looking puzzled. He places his hands on the table to indicate a length of about a foot, then he thrusts his pelvis back and forth so that the chair legs rasp on the concrete. 'Working good, good,' and when I catch on and congratulate him, he is delighted and tells me once again that he loves me.

'Where you are sitting?' says Abdullah.

It's clearly a question, but I suspect that the obvious answer isn't the one he's looking for. I resort to my puzzled look.

'Where are you sitting? You are sitting in hotel?' he says.

'Ah, I see. No, I am sitting with friends.'

'I am sitting in Sharjah.'

Sharjah is the emirate next door to Dubai.

I ask him about his work. He either doesn't understand or doesn't work, but he has plenty to tell me about a local prostitute.

'Too expensive. No good. She want dinner. She want room. She want present. She want thousand dirham. I working very good,' and he slaps his hands together to illustrate a brisk sexual efficiency. 'All over. One hundred dirham. All over. You got telephone?'

I don't, but he gives me his number. 'You lonely you call me. How my English?'

'Your English is very good,' I say. Were he a pupil I would give him top marks for gusto.

'No book. No writing. Oh no no no, no writing. I talking, see,

18

talking everybody,' and he spreads wide his arms to embrace the linguistic world.

In Yemen, he tells me, he chews a lot of *khat*, the mildly narcotic leaf that is apparently a way of life there. Perhaps that explains his teeth. He misses khat in Dubai. Dubai has similar drug laws to Singapore. Here he has to smoke cigarettes. I offer him a Rothmans but he waves it away with theatrical disgust. 'Hot hot hot,' he exclaims, 'My God no,' and he extracts a packet of Pine cigarettes which I've never seen before. He doesn't offer me one.

When conversation dries up, in other words when he is confident that he has communicated to me all the things that I need to know about his life and in particular about his sexual potency and his forthright treatment of prostitutes, and he has learned of me only the wrong name and my current sitting position, I tell him I must be on my way. We shake hands, he repeats his love for me, I tell him I have enjoyed meeting him, which I have, and I get up to leave.

He gets up to leave too. He puts his arm in mine. I don't think he's paid for the teas.

As we stroll like lovers beside the Creek, he waves and says hi to a western man who does not wave or say hi back.

'I speak that man many time,' he says. 'Many many time. Pah! Now where going?'

I have no idea where we're going. I've planned only to wander. I know this won't be a satisfactory answer. 'The gold souk,' I say because I have seen it marked on a map.

'Long long way,' he says with alarm. He stops, grips my arm, points down the road, gives me some incomprehensible directions which I make no effort to comprehend, says, 'I love you, I respect you' with more apparent sincerity than I have ever heard from anyone but drunks, and certainly with more than I feel I've earned, releases my arm and leaves.

*

Having mentioned the gold souk to Abdullah, I feel that I may as well try to find it. And in the warren of buildings and businesses stretching back from the Creek, it takes some finding.

When Thesiger came briefly to Dubai after one of his desert treks he found a sleepy place of twenty-five thousand or so inhabitants. But it was already a place of trade and it was already cosmopolitan. 'Behind the diversity of houses which lined the waterfront were the souks, covered passageways, where merchants sat in the gloom, cross-legged in narrow alcoves among their piled merchandise. The souks were crowded with many races – pallid Arab townsmen; armed Bedu, quick-eyed and imperious; Negro slaves; Baluchis, Persians and Indians.'

An entrance arch says 'Dubai, City of Gold.' As in Thesiger's day it's a covered passageway and as in Thesiger's day it is crowded with many races. But that's about it for similarities to Thesiger's day. For in the rush to modernize over the last forty years or so, Dubai demolished most of its souks. But then the tourists started to arrive, and tourists like to shop. And they particularly like to shop in traditional markets. So Dubai rebuilt its souks.

For some reason most of the windows sport a sign in English saying 'German Spoken Here'. Every shop is a jeweller's shop. Every shop seems to have identical stock. And the cumulative effect of all that gold is numbing.

In one of the little shops all four of the assistants say 'Good morning, sir.' All four are Indian and all four have moustaches. I ask them how business is.

'Very good,' says one. His colleagues nod and smile.

'Better than last year?'

'Oh no, sir, no, sir, very worse.'

'Do you think it will pick up again.'

'Oh yes, sir, yes, sir, definitely.'

I finger a delicate golden crucifix on a chain. There are hundreds of designs to choose from.

'You want cross, sir? Very nice cross.'

'Where do you get your stock from? Is it made here in Dubai?'

'Italy, sir, most from Italy. Very good jewellery, Italy.'

Suddenly all four assistants look up. I follow their eyes. A girl is passing. She is perhaps nineteen and has the honeyed skin of the Mediterranean. She wears sunglasses, a halter top that makes much of her breasts, and a tiny pair of hot pants, white and tight, cradling the taut little rounds of the buttocks. Thesiger saw nothing like that.

3

Just Walking the Dog

I wake early. Stephen's house is silent. I cannot even hear air conditioning, though the place is the same temperature as when I went to bed. Buddy the dog is delighted to see someone up so soon. He brings me a rubber bone to biff. 'Come on, Buddy,' I say, 'we're going out.' It's what I do at home.

Hung in the hallway I find one of those spring-loaded retractable leads, and we emerge from the baronial front door into Arabian Ranches. The street's as quiet and windless as the house, the air as mild as an English spring. A slight mist hangs like stage smoke. The berms are planted with shrubs and other tuberous or wispy things, all immaculately trimmed and thriving, it seems, on just sand and irrigation. The dog fossicks down drives and wraps the lead deftly around lamp posts.

The large detached houses loom sandy-grey in the half-light. Garage doors stand open, partly because there is no need to lock them but mainly because they are too full of vehicles to close. The vehicles spill out onto the hard standing, three or four per house, big vehicles, flashy vehicles, vehicles that cost a lot. Every house has a four-wheel drive. Many have two. About one in four is a Range Rover, that most squirearchical of cars, the car for the owner of acres who doesn't have to work those acres, or for the owner of a suburban house who likes to appear to own acres. I suspect the Range Rover owners of being British. They've made their money here in the desert but they trumpet it in the vehicular language of home.

I suspect the Hummer owners of being American, and in this silent suburban street there are more Hummers than in a Schwarzenegger movie. Brute cars, bully cars, singing a song of paramilitary virility. On the rear windscreen of a yellow one there's a big red sticker: 'I Brake for Nobody'.

And all these mechanical beasts – Range Rovers, Hummers, Jeeps, Prados, Pajeros, BMWs, Audis and low-slung growly sports cars – amounting to what must be several million dollars' worth on this single street, stand beaded with moisture and silent, like sleeping animals.

The houses they sleep in front of are known as villas but they look like mansions. There are several thousand of them in this complex. Most have a pool set in an automatically irrigated garden. All have accommodation for a live-in maid. Her room is about a third the size of the garage. The houses have no external guttering. Rain, when it comes, which is rarely, just bounces off and soaks into the limitless sands beneath. But these villas have been built with a nod to the region's past. With their rounded edges, and their sandy coloured plaster and their flat tops and their pediments and balconies, and the wooden beams that protrude from their walls for no structural reason, they resemble, or at least allude to, the only local buildings that are more than fifty years old, the mud-built forts and palaces of the sheikhs. And right now, against the bleached pre-dawn sky, they don't look entirely out of place.

The reason that these buildings exist goes to the root of the nature of this place. Dubai is a sheikhdom. The Al Maktoums are the ruling family, increasingly referred to as the royal family, and they are not elected. They were never elected. They rule because they rule. The current sheikh is Mohammed. His brother was sheikh before him. His father before *him*. That man was Sheikh Rashid, universally acknowledged as the creator of modern Dubai. Further back than that we won't go for the moment.

All land belongs to the sheikh but he can and does dole out chunks of it as gifts. These gifts go exclusively to Emiratis so, until recently, there simply wasn't a real estate market. Ex-pats, which meant pretty well everybody, had to rent. However wealthy they became, however their collection of Hummers for all occasions might spill out of the garage and onto the street, they could not own that garage. As the city boomed, so rents soared. The result was wealthy Emirati landlords and grumbling ex-pat tenants. The tenants clamoured for property rights. Without them, though they might have lived in Dubai for ten or twenty years, their toehold in the sand remained only a toehold.

Every ex-pat in Dubai is here on sufferance. He's a guest with a visa. The longest visa available lasts only three years, and most visas are tied to employment. Lose your job and you lose your right to stay. And all visas can be revoked at any time by the sheikh without legal comeback. From Dubai's point of view, it's a most convenient system. You can get rid of anyone any time.

But if you allow a foreigner to buy a house then it's harder to justify hoofing him out if he loses his job. He's gone part way to becoming a citizen.

So the sheikh was faced with a dilemma. If he allowed ex-pats to own houses he would to some extent lose his power over them. Moreover he would run the risk of alienating the Emiratis. They do not elect him, but he retains power only by their consent. So he has to keep them sweet. And what better sweetener could there be than allowing them a monopoly on residential property in a booming metropolis?

But at the same time, if Dubai was to continue to boom it needed ex-pats, and if they continued to be unable to own a house then Dubai might lose out to the several other cities that were trying to imitate Dubai's success.

Around 2002 the belief grew that the sheikh would cave in and people began to trade in houses. In 2006 the sheikh caved in. He didn't grant ex-pats citizenship, but he did allow them to buy freehold property. There remains some confusion over precisely what rights this confers, and there may be horrible legal problems down the track, but the decision was like dropping a bleeding carcass into a sea of sharks.

The house in which I'm staying was bought in two minutes. Stephen's wife, Kay, was given a numbered ticket to a show day for the development called Arabian Ranches. That was all Kay knew about it. The show day was held in a downtown office because there was nothing to show. The houses hadn't been built. The land was still sand.

Kay attended only out of curiosity. When she arrived, the queue of ex-pats stretched round the block and then some.

She was tempted to turn back but her numbered ticket entitled her to jump the queue. She presented it at the door, was ushered to a desk in a thronged office and was shown three different house designs. She thought she preferred one.

The saleswoman pulled out a plan of the proposed development and asked where she would like her house built. This was all happening a little faster than Kay had expected or felt she could cope with. Nevertheless she studied the plan and pointed a tentative finger at a lot backing onto the golf course because Stephen liked golf.

'Right, Design three, Lot thirty-two,' said the saleswoman and she typed something into her computer and said that as yet Lot 32 had not been taken and she could hold it for two minutes while Kay made up her mind. If she decided to go ahead she had to pay her deposit right then. If she didn't she missed out.

Kay rang her husband. He didn't answer the phone. 'Time's up,' said the saleswoman.

Kay is a farmer's daughter from the Midlands. She is not given to whimsical purchases. But then she thought of the queue outside the office. 'I'll take it,' she said. As she wrote a cheque for a hundred thousand pounds or so, she felt queasy and guilty. This wasn't the sort of thing that a farmer's daughter from the Midlands did. But farmers in the Midlands had never seen anything like Dubai.

She left the building feeling that she might throw up. When she emerged, the first person in the queue asked if she'd bought a house. Kay said she had. The person made her an offer for it. So did the next. She could have doubled her money, perhaps trebled it, in a minute. All of which made her feel she'd done the right thing.

Every available lot in the unbuilt Arabian Ranches sold that day. And that story was replicated all over the city. It was a property boom to rival any in history. In the golf club the other night I heard tell of an Irishman who flew to Dubai one morning, bought a handful of houses off plan, sold them in the afternoon, and flew home in the evening a millionaire. The story may even be trueish.

Buddy has sunk his snout in a pile of Christmas wrapping paper overflowing from a bin. Turning over a red and black cardboard box that held a remote-controlled car far bigger than him he extracts a discarded hard-centre chocolate with tooth-marks. A gate opens just along the street. A woman and a dog. The woman's a tiny Filipina maid, the dog's a vast mastiff. The maid could sit astride the beast and ride it like a jockey. She sees me, yanks the mastiff's head, and walks swiftly in the opposite direction. Another gate opens, another maid appears, this time with a lolloping shaggy retriever. She too heads in the opposite direction when she sees us. It is obvious from the way they walk that the maids have no affection for the dogs. Walking the dog at dawn is just the first of the long day's chores.

Arabian Ranches is walled like a medieval city. To enter or leave you have to pass through one of perhaps forty checkpoints. Each has a barrier arm and a guard in a guardhouse. As we approach, the guard emerges, a brown-skinned man in a blue semi-military uniform. He observes my white skin. He observes my un-Islamic dog.

'Good morning, sir.'

I am unaccustomed to being called sir, especially when dog-walking at dawn. I am wearing old jeans and yesterday's soiled shirt. I feel a middle-class uneasiness with deference. I ask the man where he's from.

'Nepal, sir.'

'How come you're in Dubai?'

'Sir?'

'How did you get this job?'

'Security, sir, I am security.' And he smiles with a sort of eager desperation.

I don't push it, and Buddy is keen to move on. We cross the road that circles the blank outer wall of the Ranches. I release the dog. He rewards me with the unfailing joy of dogs. He exults, as little children do, in the simple delight of running. When I call him he stops in a cloud of sand and hurtles back to me for a morsel of hamburger I filched from the fridge. His flesh quivers with zest. To see him is to smile by contagion.

The half light of dawn is shifting by imperceptible stages into the full light of day. A line of pylons marches across the desert, the wires looping like mooring ropes. Some twenty kilometres away a scruffy layer of mist hangs above the city like smoke from a steam train. It'll take the heat of the sun to shift that.

Somewhere in the background I can hear the hum of early traffic on the Emirates Road.

Birds in surprising numbers flit and lilt between the irrigated bushes. Little rufous doves as delicate as vases, another hoopoe silhouetted against the pearly air, a gang of birds with blackened heads like hangman's hoods, and on the far side of a wrought-iron fence a scuttling covey of partridges. The far side of the fence is desert proper. No bushes, no irrigation, just sand and blown litter.

The dog spots the partridges. He charges. Under the wrought-iron fence he ducks, and away over a little dune. The birds burst into the air. 'Buddy,' I call, 'Buddy, come,' but he is suddenly atavistically deaf. Scared of losing him, I crawl under the fence and find him a few dunes away, nosing at a yoghurt carton. He sees me and remembers domestication.

The undulation of the sand has concealed from view the vast new housing estate. It has muffled the road noise too. I am perhaps two hundred yards from Range Rovers and air-conditioning yet I'm walking a dog in the desert. I snort with sudden laughter. The dog looks round surprised, then wags his stumpy tail. All joy is good by him.

Fifteen minutes later we crawl back under the fence and startle a work gang. Small, silent, Indian men in overalls with scarves wrapped around their heads against the mildish air, they have the beaten demeanour of prisoners. They carry shears and clippers and plastic bags of food that they hang from shrubs. Their job, day in day out, is to tend the forced vegetation on ex-pat housing estates. When Buddy approaches to sniff at one man's lunch bag, the man shies and turns away in fear of the shin-high creature. I call Buddy, say sorry and good morning, but get nothing back.

A gurgle and the irrigation switches itself on, miles of black tubing running from plant to plant and coiling round their stems. Near my feet the plug on a side-tube has popped off.

Water glugs out to be swallowed by the sand, blackening it. All of this water, every drop of it, has been drawn from the sea and desalinated.

Half a mile up the road I can see a mini-van dropping off another gang. To live here as an ex-pat is to learn not to see these quiet servants, to look past or through them, to edit them out. I haven't been here long enough.

In the fifteen minutes that I've been among the dunes, Arabian Ranches has stirred and rubbed sleep from its eyes. The path inside the ring road is now spattered with joggers, trim, gym-tautened white women in Nike footwear carrying a baby's bottle of water as they run, blonde hair tied back in a ponytail, skin tanned to a light hazel, shorts laundered and ironed by the maid. Some run in sunglasses. I see only one man running, a man with the look of a banker: pasty, whey-faced, not more than thirty, his soft little belly slopping as he goes, every stride an effort of will, his feet slap-slapping on the paving. The runners pass the workers squatting with tools among the bushes and neither species of creature seems to see the other. Both are aliens in an alien land. They have come to Dubai for the same reasons, but to opposite ends of the status scale.

As I am about to reclip Buddy's lead he catches sight of a Dalmatian with maid attached. The maid shrieks as the dogs meet and dance. She tries to haul the Dalmatian away. The dogs sniff genitals, their tails wagging with the taut and nervous etiquette of greeting that goes back millennia.

'Sorry,' I say as I clip Buddy back on.

'Thank you, sir,' says the maid, but she is acutely uncomfortable. Were she my social equal she would not have said thank you.

She's carrying a Spinney's supermarket bag with which to scoop up the Dalmatian's shit. Here on the desert fringe there are dedicated bins for dog shit, so that instead of baking in the sun and crumbling to dust within a day, the shit can fester in its own hot juices and bloom to putrescence before being collected by a minion in a truck and lugged to a place of disposal.

As I pass back through the security gate a string of 4WDs is heading the other way, each with a single male passenger bound for the city in his tank-like vehicle. And as he swings onto the Emirates Road, a multiple-laned highway that carves across the last scrubby remnants of desert between this estate and the city that is coming out to meet it, he will pass a billboard the size of a house. On it is a picture of Sheikh Mohammed, Ruler of Dubai, and the sons who are being groomed to succeed him. In block letters above the image, the words 'Our Visionary Leaders'.

When I get back to Stephen's house, the papers have arrived. Israel is attacking Gaza with its customary military ruthlessness. Hundreds of Palestinians have died and a dozen of the dead are on the front page in colour, curled foetally or stretched like starfish, the wounds that killed them centre stage, engorged and purple. The blood puddle that surrounds the corpses is turning black like irrigated sand. No newspaper in the West would print such photographs. And yet no newspaper in the West is as subject as this one to effective censorship. Every editor here knows that if you wish to remain in business there are things you just don't say, such as boo to the sheikh, and other things that you say as often as possible, such as boo to Israel.

4

Essential Supplies

Coffee *is* to be found in Dubai, but you have to go to the malls. The coffee shop Stephen's brought me to, in the atrium of a mall somewhere off Sheikh Zayed Road, is part of an American chain and could be anywhere in the wealthy world. There's low-slung padded furniture and bleached wooden tables and thirty varieties of coffee that come in disposable cups. The cup sizes are described as regular, tall and large but would be more accurately rendered as too big, much too big and swim-mable-in.

Stephen's friends that we've come to meet are all ex-pats of long standing. One's Swedish, two English, and each is the size of a couple of Filipinos.

The bulkiest of them has a handshake like a damp petal. He's a spook. He instals telecommunication surveillance equipment for anyone who pays. His most recent employer was the Libyan government.

The Swede's in telecommunications too. Soon he and the

spook are engaged in a merry conversation crammed with acronyms. CDMA and GSM are the only ones I recognize, but the nub of the conversation is how easy it is for the technologically savvy to fleece telephone companies and how easy it is for telephone companies to fleece the non-technologically savvy. 'Once you get a mobile phone,' says the spook, 'we've got you. You can't get away.'

The spook is married to an Iranian. He tells us that at a party the other night they were playing some board game and his wife was required to guess the class of object most likely to be found hanging outside someone's house. The correct answer was washing. Her guess was criminals.

The third man turns out to be an authority on horizontal drilling, which is a method of gaining access to oil reserves that you otherwise couldn't gain access to for reasons of geography or politics.

'This guy,' says Stephen, 'started the first Gulf War.'

The horizontal driller smiles modestly.

It seems that by means of his expertise, Kuwait was tapping into Iraqi oil. Saddam told Kuwait to stop. Kuwait persisted. So Saddam invaded Kuwait. Whereupon the Americans invaded Kuwait as well, led by Stormin' Norman.

'Well done,' I say to the horizontal driller, though I am unsure whether I am having my leg pulled, and if so to what length. All three men sprawl. They occupy space with a regal confidence born of wealth and certainty. And like blokes anywhere they swap stories. The horizontal driller is a rugby enthusiast, a fixture at the annual Dubai Sevens where he dedicates several days to drinking. Last year the tournament was interrupted by a ferocious thunderstorm. 'I had to ring my bloody houseboy,' says the horizontal driller, 'and get him to bring me some dry clothes.' Everyone enjoys the tale, but I suspect I am the only one who jumps at the word 'houseboy'. It sounds like the British Raj to me. But if I lived here a while

I've no doubt I'd get used to it. Indeed, I'd probably employ one.

As we leave the mall we pass an Ice Bar.

'Sixty dirhams,' says a surly Russian youth at the door when I ask whether I can just nip in to have a look. 'With complimentary juice.'

'Oh go on, I just want a quick look.'

'Nyet. Look through the window, like everybody else.'

I look through the window. It's thick, like a heavy-duty aquarium. On the other side of it is a room made of ice. All the furniture is carved from ice. There are crude ice chandeliers and a few coloured lights illuminating the icy walls. Three Asian women are inside, togged up in fur-trimmed anoraks, taking photos of each other, sipping from their complimentary juices and looking frankly bored.

Opposite the ice bar is a Lamborghini stand. Not the Lamborghini of the cars, but his brother, apparently. He's selling Lamborghini key rings and Lamborghini coffee, or at least offering them for sale. I'm the only browser. The coffee and key rings bear a logo not entirely dissimilar to the logo on his brother's preposterous cars.

'Come on,' says Stephen, 'we've got to go.'

We're going to fetch booze.

Booze is readily available in Islamic Dubai. It may not be drunk on the streets, but in the business and tourist areas, which means pretty well all of downtown Dubai, there are innumerable licensed hotels. The stuff is expensive, however, so when an ex-pat needs to restock his liquor cabinet at home he heads north-east, out of Dubai, skirts the neighbouring emirate of Sharjah, and fetches up in the little emirate of Umm-al-Qwain. The UAE isn't big.

'There she blows,' says Stephen an hour or so later.

'She' is a defunct Russian cargo plane, standing huge and

white and stark beside the road. To me it's another oddity in what is rapidly becoming a land of oddities, but to the ex-pats of Dubai this plane is a cherished landmark. It announces that they are within range of cut-price booze.

Just beyond the cargo plane we turn into the car park of the Barracuda Beach Resort. The resort has cabins and picnic areas and a swimming pool and playgrounds for the kiddies and at three o'clock on this weekday afternoon they're all deserted. The Taal Indian Night Club is padlocked. But the car park is packed. Big expensive cars circle like sharks as they wait for a space to become free. What has drawn all these vehicles is a windowless barn, the existence of which is never advertised because it doesn't need to be. Knowledge of it is part of Dubai life, a survival skill handed on from ex-pat to ex-pat.

I grab a trolley from the trolley snake, push through the glass doors and find myself standing amid walls of booze. The place is as well stocked as any liquor store in the West. Almost twice as well stocked, in fact, because it seems that for every well-known western brand there's a rip-off Indian equivalent. Here is Johnny Walker Red Label Scotch whisky at ninety dirhams a bottle alongside Indian Green Label not-quite-Scotch whisky at twelve dirhams a bottle. The red label is red and the green label is green but the designs are effectively identical.

India doesn't seem to make wine, however, or at least not yet. Here's a Cloudy Bay sauvignon blanc all the way from New Zealand. Beside it stands a display of a French red called Fat Bastard. At twenty-eight dirhams it's more than twice the price of a Jordanian red described as Wine From the Holy Land. I put a couple of bottles of each in the trolley along with slabs of Scandinavian Carlsberg and Filipino San Miguel and a bottle of something sticky for Kay. Stephen adds several cardboard casks of South African table wine and I am surprised by my own surprise. Ten years ago I bought such casks myself. They tasted all right and did the job, but somehow, gradually, I have learned to look down my nose at cask wine, to see it as the sad resort of raddled divorcees on empty afternoons. How this happened I don't know. I suppose in the end it's just a bit of agreed ersatz wisdom that's in the air of the society I inhabit, a meme of sorts, like knowledge of the whereabouts of the Barracuda Beach Resort.

I insist on paying for the trolley-load of booze. When Stephen resists, I tell him that I can't think of a nicer way to pay rent. Moreover the total cost, which is roughly what I'd pay for the same trolley-load at home, amounts to little more than one night at a tourist hotel in town. The days of cheap Dubai are long gone.

Indians wrap our booze in opaque polythene bags and insist on wheeling our booty out and loading it into the car. A couple of men in sunglasses and immaculate clothes have filled a Hummer with more freight than it would have borne in Vietnam. Two chubby British golfing types in ill-advised shorts supervise an Indian youth as he humps case after case of Grolsch into their BMW. The golfers tip him and climb aboard, each involuntarily grunting as he collapses into the low seat. The driver turns the key, the smooth as honey engine responds, and they head off for Dubai. We follow them. And at the instant we turn onto the public highway we all become smugglers. It is illegal to transport booze between emirates. If we were stopped, we'd be in trouble. A bribe might be necessary. If, and this is far more likely, we were to be involved in an accident, the discovery of a boatload of grog would make us the guilty party in the crash, regardless of fault. On the road home Stephen drives with noticeably more caution than on the anarchic streets of Dubai, and with particular circumspection as we pass through the Emirate of Sharjah. For Sharjah is dry. To explain why requires a very much potted history of the UAE. This isn't a history book, but as with anywhere in the world the present can only be understood through the lens of the past.

People have lived in these parts for thousands of years, but they saw no need to be a single country. Indeed they had no notion of countries. Everything was tribal. There were nomadic tribes, now generally known as the Bedouin, and there were tribes who formed more permanent settlements, almost all of which were on the coast. The two dominant tribal groups were the Qawasim who inhabited by and large the coastal area to the north-east of Dubai, and the Bani Yas tribe to the south-west. Dubai stands more or less on the boundary between the two tribes' territorial areas. In consequence it was much disputed.

Relevant modern history began with the arrival of Europeans in the sixteenth century. The Portuguese held much of this area for a while, and the French and the Dutch also sniffed around. Then came the British. The reason all these nations took an interest in the region was that it lay on a vital trade route. The Europeans were concerned simply with making money – a fact which the people who condemn Dubai as a mercantile monstrosity would do well to remember.

In the eighteenth century the British owned India. They ran it through the agency of the British East India Company, which conducted a lot of its trade through the Gulf, passing by here on the way to the port of Basra in what is now Iraq. The Qawasim tribe were very keen to muscle in on this trade; the British East India Company was just as keen that they shouldn't.

The company repeatedly complained to the Admiralty in London that the Qawasim were raiding British ships. A few of the reports may even have been true, but in general it seems that the locals were simply taking trade from the British by being better at it. They were expert sailors and intimately acquainted with the local waters.

Nevertheless, the company's propaganda worked and in consequence this region came to be known as the Pirate Coast. Eventually, in the early nineteenth century the Royal Navy was sent in to teach the natives a lesson. The Brits flattened a few forts, engaged in a few skirmishes, and prevailed because of the size of their guns, but they did not want to absorb the region into the British Empire. So, over the course of the rest of the nineteenth century, they made a series of truces with assorted sheikhs in the region. Essentially the terms of the truces were that the British would endorse the ruling sheikhs and even come in to bat for them militarily if required. In exchange, the sheikhs would leave British ships alone, acknowledge British interests in the Gulf, and take important decisions only after consulting with the British agent in the Gulf. Whereupon the region stopped being the Pirate Coast and became the Trucial States.

The effect of these truces on tribal politics was considerable. I am grossly over-simplifying a long and complex business, but essentially the British created royal families. Any sheikh who signed a truce with the British fixed his family at the top of his tribal tree, more or less in perpetuity, because of the backing he now had from the greatest military power on earth.

Though the local tradition of feuding didn't cease, and many a sheikh was still stabbed or deposed, he was generally replaced by someone from his own family. And those families grew rich – very rich – because of the various concessions and licences that the British afforded them. Pretty well all the current ruling families of the UAE became established in power through these truces, and the regions under their rule became emirates. British influence, in other words, did a great deal to shape this region's current organization and politics.

After the Second World War Britain went into decline. Its empire shrank and eventually the British were obliged to withdraw from everywhere east of Aden. The Trucial States were east of Aden. With that withdrawal in the offing, the various sheikhdoms, most of them smaller than English counties, began to sniff the chilly wind of isolation. And although they had often fought with each other, and although there remained unresolved enmities between them, they wisely began to consider the possibility of confederation. And in 1971, when I was still wearing shorts in the third form at Brighton Grammar School, the UAE was formed and recognized as an independent nation by the UN. It's a very young country.

The Emirate of Sharjah, like the Emirate of Dubai, is essentially just a coastal town built on a creek. Throughout the early days of the Trucial States and indeed up until the Second World War, of all the emirates Sharjah had the closest ties with Britain. It had the only airstrip in the region and more ships docked at its port than at any other. So foreign nationals who came to the region came first to Sharjah and they gradually established a sizeable ex-pat community. But Sharjah was not well led. Sharjah screwed up.

The problem was dredging. Sharjah's creek grew shallow and became impassable to shipping for several months of the year. The ruling sheikh did next to nothing about it and the problem got worse. At roughly the same time, Dubai's creek also silted up. But Sheikh Rashid of Dubai immediately understood the urgency of the problem, borrowed money and got the thing dredged. In consequence much of what had been Sharjah's shipping was soon coming to Dubai and a lot of Sharjah's merchants followed it.

Sharjah remained, however, the hub of such tourism as happened in the Emirates simply because of its airport. Then, in the early Eighties, following a coup or two within the ruling family, the State got into financial strife and Abu Dhabi, the oil-rich sugar daddy of the UAE, had to bail it out. More financial strife, and Abu Dhabi bailed it out again. Then the Sharjah government defaulted on some juicy international loans and this time Abu Dhabi did not come to the rescue. Saudi Arabia did.

A Saudi consortium paid off the debts, but it charged for the service. Its price was influence, and that influence was of a heavily Islamic nature. Sharjah found itself obliged to pass a series of laws enforcing Islamic propriety. The most significant of these banned alcohol, not only in hotels but also in private houses. (The only place in Sharjah where you can still get a drink is the Wanderers, the local rugby club, founded by and for ex-pats and granted a liquor licence by sheikhly decree. Sheikhly decree can be revoked only by sheikhly decree.)

Dubai couldn't believe its luck. 'Oi,' it shouted to the thirsty western tourists, 'over here. The bar's open.' And thus an industry was born.

Sharjah has since striven to rebrand itself as the cultural capital of UAE, but with a bootful of contraband grog we don't stop to assess the merits of that claim. We keep to the outskirts of the city, which are little more than a dormitory for its prosperous neighbour Dubai and quite without charm. They resemble the formless edges of one of China's new-built cities, with blocks of flats rising unadorned and unloved out of rubble-strewn spaces. The air is granular. The shops look wretched. Stephen's car, a sleek beast, with a video screen on the dashboard that serves as navigation device, mobile phone and rear-view mirror, struggles, for all its sophistication, to cope with the potholes. But we reach home with contraband intact.

I spend the evening at Arabian Ranches researching on the internet the Islamic prohibition on alcohol. It is founded, as all Islamic law is founded, on the Koran, the word of Allah as recounted by Mohammed fourteen hundred years ago, as written down by his followers, and as then interpreted by generations of scholars, all of which takes it a long way away from the modern international brewing industry.

Mohammed's stance on drinking apparently hardened as the years went by. His earliest pronouncement was merely that a man shouldn't pray when intoxicated. He also said that habitual drunkards would never make it to paradise. Only later did he issue a prohibition on booze, or rather on *khamr*.

Khamr derives from an Arabic word for fermentation and is

41

generally interpreted as meaning wine, which was presumably all they had in the seventh-century pubs. By interpretative extension *khamr* has now been taken to mean everything from Advocaat to Zambucca. Muslims may not drink.

Nor may they take drugs. Scholarly interpretation has extended the meaning of *khamr* to embrace all intoxicants, arguing that Mohammed only failed to mention crack cocaine by name because it wasn't around at the time. That's a reasonable argument but a dangerous precedent. Dangerous because it gives almost unlimited power to the scholars.

Of course, if you accept that the Koran contains everything human beings need to know and that the answers to all questions on earth are held within its pages, then the pronouncements of scholars are law. But if you don't accept that, then the system seems set up for those in power to retain that power and abuse it in any way they wish. Which seems to me to be how every organized religion in history has always operated and continues to operate.

5

Dancing in Sand

I wake on 31 December to discover that New Year's Eve has been cancelled. The sheikh has cancelled it. As an ostensible gesture of solidarity with the suffering people of Gaza, there are to be no celebrations in Dubai. The spectacular hotel bashes that normally take place, won't. A reputed one hundred and twenty million dirhams-worth of fireworks will be returned to the manufacturers or put into storage for next year.

I don't know whether the reason given for the ban is the real reason for the ban. Nor do I know how the suffering citizens of Gaza will benefit from this ban. Nor yet why the sheikh doesn't stick a ban on all things American, given that country's unwavering support for Israel. Nevertheless I get a minor thrill from it. This is my first taste of autocracy in action. For someone who has lived always under lumbering consultative democracies it's excitingly decisive.

But one party is still going ahead, the one I've been invited to, a masked dinner and dance in the desert. For to mark the importance of this once-a-year roll of the Gregorian odometer, we are leaving civilization and tar-sealed roads behind and trekking into the barren dunes, accompanied only by booze-laden, air-conditioned 4WDs, for a distance of about four hundred yards. And at ten in the morning, at the point where the tar seal ends, half a dozen 4WDs have already gathered. With all men bar me being at work, the drivers are all women And, just as I would, they are hesitating before driving onto sand. But the several children and dogs who have come along for the ride have not hesitated at all. They're already romping on the dunes.

Enter Lynn, the jovial South African hostess, a born organizer. She is not the hesitant type. Straight onto the sand she goes in her Pathfinder. She drops over a ridge and out of sight and everyone follows. The party site is immediately below the ridge in a shallow depression. All vehicles make it, and with the sense of a tiny adventure having been had, a niggling fear surmounted, people set to work preparing for the party with an air of merriment. They set up tables, roll out mats to form a dance floor, and pitch tents around the periphery, for not only are we going to eat and drink and dance beneath the stars, we're going to sleep there too. Jokes fly, though some of the South African accents are too thick for me to penetrate.

Indian caterers arrive to set up under Lynn's authoritative supervision and I find myself chatting with an Englishwoman who's been in Dubai a couple of years. She tells me she's from Yorkshire, though her accent has already broken that news. I ask her what she thinks of the party ban.

'What party ban?' she says.

I explain.

'Does that mean this one's off too?'

'Doesn't look like it.'

'Oh good,' she says.

She tells me she relishes living in Dubai, but she expresses that relish in the tone of one admitting guilt.

'I'm shallow, me,' she says, 'but it's lovely having a maid, and the weather's good and I just love me bling, you know, the diamonds and that. Yes, I love me bling.' As she speaks she fingers a pendant at her neck.

'That necklace,' I say, 'I think it's lovely.' And I do.

'Oh, you're so nice,' she says, 'thank you,' and she blushes sweetly. At which point a white 4WD lurches over the dune and halts fifty yards away. Everyone stops working to stare.

The man who gets out of the cab is Saddam Hussein's double. He's wearing a uniform of sorts and carrying a clipboard. Is it possible that the sheikh has already mobilized a squad of petty officials to scour the emirate for parties?

'I don't like the look of him,' whispers Mrs Yorkshire. Nor do I. But Lynn is undaunted. She strides across the sand towards him.

'I bet he doesn't like the look of her either,' says Mrs Yorkshire and she giggles.

Lynn and the man engage in earnest colloquy and the rest of us busy ourselves on any pretext we can find, unloading firewood from a truck, trying to assemble tent poles, pushing pegs into sand, though this last activity seems close to pointless. The sand is so fine and dry that the lightest breeze would rip the pegs out and send the tents bowling across the wastes of Arabia like spent hot-air balloons.

When Lynn returns to the gathering, several women cluster round her. I hang back, feeling awkward, an outsider, but the news soon filters down to me. The problem is not the party but the location. It seems that this arbitrary bit of desert belongs to someone and we are trespassing. The someone in question is a conglomerate that plans to build hotels here. Lynn has pointed out that there isn't a hotel here yet and that we're hardly jeopardizing its future construction, but landowners are landowners the world over and if she wants the party to happen she has to supply a list of all the guests and then drive into town to sign some sort of indemnity.

The pre-party zest has gone. Saddam's visitation has cast a slight pall on the mood, as officialdom always does and probably likes to do. When we've done what we can by way of getting everything prepared, the women gather their children and their little dogs, all of them panting, strap them into the 4WDs – the children, that is, the dogs being left to take their chances in a crash – and head away one by one over the single dune and back to town for the last day of the year. Which I spend doing my washing and feeling vaguely guilty.

It was Paul Theroux, I think, who said that travel is only glamorous in retrospect, and I am with him. I have travelled a bit, and I've always considered it a test of self as much as a pleasure. But I like the way travelling puts home into perspective. Home is a nest that we have built to fit us, in the manner of a dog trampling a bean bag before lying down. Our routines are stamped throughout our homes like the paths of a pygmy tribe through the bush. Here's the cutlery and the wardrobe and the shampoo, all of them just so to suit the convenience of our habits. Those habits become a cocoon, a cocoon that only travel can free us from.

I have never been an adventurer. I don't stray far from reasonable coffee and flush toilets. But I still do feel that travel should present me with some discomfort, some minor tribulations, some difficulties to surmount – if only to remind me that I am privileged, that I live a life of ease and luxury that would be the wonder of even my grandparents' generation, and the envy of perhaps ninety per cent of the world's population.

But here in Dubai, while ostensibly travelling, I am staying as a guest in a house far better appointed that my own and I have more or less perpetual access to that most blessed of devices, the washing machine. And as I hang my pants and shirts on a rack within a closed balcony – no unsightly washing lines allowed in Arabian Ranches – in a climate that will dry them within minutes, I feel this somehow isn't right. And I resolve to get out of Dubai at some stage of this trip and see some of the UAE. At the very least it will put the city in context. But not this afternoon, which I spend by the pool with Wilfred Thesiger and San Miguel.

I feel belittled by every page of Thesiger. At the point I've reached in my re-reading, his five-man party is starving and almost out of water in the heart of the Empty Quarter. Then one of the Bedouin catches a hare. They stop to cook it and to feast:

> When it was ready he divided it into five portions. They were very small, for an Arabian hare is no larger than an English rabbit, and this one was not even fully grown. Al Auf named the lots and Makhaut drew them. Each of us took the small pile of meat that had fallen to him. Then bin Kabina said, 'God! I have forgotten to divide the liver,' and the others said, 'Give it to Umbarak.' I protested, saying that they should divide it, but they swore by God that they would not eat it and that I was to have it. Eventually I took it, knowing that I ought not, but too greedy for this extra scrap of meat to care.

At which point I put aside the book and my beer, haul myself up from the reclining poolside chair, and amble to the fridge to fix myself a sandwich.

It isn't hard to imagine what Thesiger would have thought of our dinner and dance in the desert. My contribution to it is two bottles of 'Wine from the Holy Land'. My concession to it is a plastic Phantom of the Opera mask, chosen for me by Stephen's daughters. I don't know if they mean to suggest anything by the choice. The mask is uncomfortable to wear and difficult to see through, but at least it doesn't hinder drinking.

We leave the tar seal, slither the back wheels on the sand, drop over the ridge and descend into a place transformed. Within the loose circle of tents and 4WDs the desert has been lit and set for dinner. Plastic furniture has been draped in dense white napery and laid out with bottles and glasses and wrapped presents and heavy silver cutlery that sparkles in the artificial light. That light comes from the table decorations, elaborate cones of mesh, a metre tall and wound round with fairy lights and tinselly bits. The matting dance floor is lit from a gantry from which there also hangs a hefty mirror ball. Big music is emerging from a small box of electronics. The electricity for all this is supplied by an unseen generator, its existence betrayed by snakes of cable leading up and over the further dune and away into the darkness.

The Indian caterers are cooking on gas burners. Dogs hang around the food or chase infants and each other in sandy circles. Children too old to frolic with dogs sit around on camp chairs looking early-teen moody and sucking on cans of pop, while perhaps twenty masked adults stand and drink their way through the initial awkwardness. The indomitable Lynn takes me by the arm and introduces me cheerfully to a string of masked South Africans. I shake hands with a pirate, a gorilla, a Pierrot, a tragedy, and two other Phantoms of the Opera. Several people have got Venetian masks on sticks that cause terrible problems with introductions. One hand holds the mask and the other a drink so they end up just nodding hello.

Lynn leaves me in the company of an electrical engineer who, from the nose up, is Batman.

'Great party,' says Batman.

'Yes it is.'

'Isn't Lynn a great hostess?'

'She's terrific.'

'Do you know her well?'

'We've only just met. I'm just a friend of a friend. I feel like a bit of a freeloader.'

'Oh.'

And then we stand in silence for a bit, Batman and the Phantom in the desert, and I struggle to suppress a surge of laughter. Only the cooks and the dogs are active. Everyone else just waits for the booze to kick in.

We hear the Jeep before we see it, hear the music pulsing through the darkness. Then it drops over the dune into the lights of the party, a fat-tyred brute of a vehicle, open-topped and ostentatious, and bearing a freight of the boisterous young. They leap out over the doors and are welcomed as saviours. Beefy, grain-fed South African boys and girls, the sons and daughters it seems of these sober adults. They've been drinking. They haven't bothered with masks. They are happy. They head straight for the drinks supply, then to the stereo where they change Gene Pitney to reggae. The lights from the generator seem to brighten and the adults become infected by the infusion of energy.

Suddenly, out here on the sand, there is the unmistakable fizz of a party about to happen.

The male youths are like giant puppies. They wrestle and clown, chasing each other out of the pool of light and onto the dark dunes, then two of them roll back down a dune into visibility, locked in a play-fight to the death. Their parents look on in indulgent delight at the zest they have brought to the world in the form of these hundred-kilogram children.

Batman loosens up. He's been several years in Dubai and when I tell him that rather than being resident I am merely visiting, he proves eager to tell me how things really work here.

'Dubai's an experiment, conducted by Abu Dhabi,' he says.

'Abu Dhabi's got the cash but the ruling family's terribly con-
servative. It doesn't like to be associated with failure, so it uses
Dubai like a test tube, trying things out here, basically experi-
ments in ways of making money. Behind the scenes it supplies
the money to test tourist markets and business markets and
finance markets and all the rest of it to see what works. If the
place crashes, Abu Dhabi will just say tut-tut and wash its hands
of it. But it will milk everything that succeeds and imitate the
best things in its own emirate. Follow the money and it all traces
back to Abu Dhabi.'

Dubai, he insists, is massively in hock to its neighbour,
inescapably so. Abu Dhabi owns majority shareholdings in all
the big contractors and even in Emirates, the hugely successful
airline.

I have no idea how true any of this is. And Batman is so
clearly convinced of it that there is no point in questioning him.
But in my few days here I've already heard more or less the
same conspiracy theory from several people.

'Dindins,' announces Lynn, clapping her hands. 'Dindins.'
The young sit down immediately while the old, though every
bit as keen to get at the nosh, hover and defer in the expectation
of some system of precedence. As the outermost of outsiders I
hover longer and more deferentially than any until Lynn takes
my arm and sits me down at her table.

Masks come off. Some are laid beside plates, but most are
tucked under seats, where it is my guess they'll be forgotten as
the night grows raucous. They've done their lubricant job, and
now the shifting sands will bury them for ever or they will be
eaten on some distant unrecorded morning by camels. Camels
will apparently eat anything carbon-based. Stephen claims to
have seen one devour a wooden cable reel. 'The lot,' said
Stephen. 'It ate the whole bloody thing.'

There's a present at every place setting. Again we adults hesitate. There is something so nakedly selfish and acquisitive in

50

tearing the wrapping from a gift. Kids do it pell-mell, their eyes on fire, but adults shrink from such honesty. The same distinction holds when the present is revealed. A disappointed kid looks disappointed. An adult feigns delight.

'Oh, how sweet,' I exclaim, when I unwrap, at Lynn's urging, a little box containing a chunk of coloured glass shaped vaguely like a horse's head. I've no idea what it is, unless, that is, it's what it seems to be, a chunk of coloured glass shaped vaguely like a horse's head.

A few glances reveal that everyone else has also got a chunk of coloured glass though not all of them are shaped like horses' heads.

'A toast,' says Lynn, 'to the New Year. May it be better than the last one,' and glasses rise towards the night sky. They glint and clink. 'To the New Year.'

'Let's eat,' says Lynn, clapping her hands, but the young have pre-empted her. The beefy boys are already at the buffet: steak, chicken, vegetables, a stew of some sort, all laid out in metal dishes over spirit burners and constantly replenished by the Indian caterers. Quiet of a sort descends on the desert. The sky above and beyond us is glittering ink.

Plates are finally pushed away, rinds of fat slipped to the patient dogs, and the man on my right, who has so far not spoken, touches me on the arm and shows me his chunk of glass.

'Do you know what it is?' he whispers.

I shrug and he falls silent, turning the thing over in his hand and staring at it as if it held a secret.

'Meryl Streep's bought Cambodia,' says a chubby girl across the table.

'It was Angelina Jolie, actually.'

'Are you sure?'

'Yeah, but then she sold it.'

'To Meryl Streep?'

'Dunno. Don't think so.'

They're discussing The World, the set of artificial islands being built to resemble a map of the world, when viewed from a plane. Viewed from sea level it'll look like islands. The World is another of those audacious show-off ideas that Dubai does so well, big but simple ideas that the popular mind latches on to immediately and retains. It's also yet another project that's rumoured to have stalled, with cash running low and the islands plagued with subsidence. But there is great interest around the table in who's bought what, although I have heard it said elsewhere that whole islands have been gifted to celebrities in order to generate exactly this sort of conversation.

Whatever the truth of things, there seems to be a consensus that Ireland's been bought by a couple of Irishmen and that they plan to turn it into, of all things, a miniature Ireland. Whether this means the real thing, with too much rain, or the tourist version with quaint cottages, quainter pubs, colleens, fiddlers and Daniel O'Bloody Donnell, I don't know. Conversation then moves seamlessly from The World to the Palm Jumeirah and the exciting news that David Beckham has given his house there to his mum.

The South African on my left doesn't join in the discussion of celebrity doings. He's a middle-aged businessman wearing a long-nosed mask of elaborate design that he has tilted to perch on the top of his head in order to eat. I think he's forgotten he's wearing it. It tops a face that suggests the holding of severe opinions. He's clearly the father of at least one of the meaty young men.

When I ply him with a few gentle questions about Dubai he responds like a paterfamilias, delivering emphatic judgements from on high. If I knew enough to argue with his statements, I still probably wouldn't.

'Arabs,' he says, 'are greedy, dishonest and short-sighted.'

'All of them?'

'Pretty much. Except for that Sheikh Zayed, the one before the present one. What he did for Abu Dhabi makes him one of the great statesmen of the twentieth century. A visionary. Far-sighted.'

'But there aren't many like him?'

'None that I know. They all love to trumpet success but most of them have got no idea how to do business. They just pay others to do it. Take Emirates. Ever flown Emirates?'

I have. They flew me here. The service impressed me.

'The whole organization's a mess. I fly first class and I fly a lot. They're supposed to send a limo to collect me. One time in three my limo doesn't turn up. Hopeless. And they hire cretins.'

As he speaks, the nose on his mask jiggles at the night sky.

'Look, they've got a great wine list on board and the girl says to me, 'Red or white, sir?' I say I'd like the chardonnay. 'Certainly, sir, red or white?' I mean, I ask you. What they don't seem to understand here is if you pay shit you get shit. Cheap labour is expensive. Look at the Filipinos. You'll find them every-where in Dubai. They're dirt cheap because the Philippines is a shit hole that they're all gagging to get out of. They smile nicely but they're all stupid. They must be the most stupid people on earth.'

I'd guess this man is roughly my age. He is clearly intelligent and successful. Is it the legacy of apartheid that causes him to judge the world in terms only of race?

Gradually, as the level in the wine bottles sinks, a mist settles into the little depression. It's surprisingly thick, surprisingly cold. It dampens everything except the spirits. With food and drink now taken, the middle-aged resume control of the music. 'Stand by your man,' sings either Tammy Wynette or Dolly Parton through the desert mist, and women with waistlines bulging beneath their finery and no hope of being young again, kick off their shoes and hang around the necks of their men and lay their heads against chests and do their best to dream, or to remember, or just to pretend. It's sweet.

The fire's been lit, a huge thing. I make it my business to feed it. Find me the man or woman who doesn't enjoy staring into the heart of a bonfire, and I'll show you a corpse. I love the sense of danger harnessed. I love the pulsing orange-pink intensity of its primal heart, its rapacity, the way it feasts upon itself. Since our species lost its fur the words hearth and home have been synonyms. An electric fan heater just doesn't cut it. I hunch forward, letting the invisible heat toast my face and front while my back is turned to the dark and limitless hostility of the world beyond. I like it so much my prose could easily get a little overblown.

Beyond the light, party-goers make discreet sorties up the face of the nearest dune to disappear briefly into the mist. Their footmarks show black in the sand.

'Uugh,' says Lynn, coming over to the fire, and she pronounces uugh exactly as spelt, 'isn't this mist just horrid?' She has put on a fur coat.

'Danish mink,' she says. 'I bought it in the scariest place I've ever been. It looked like an abattoir. I only get to wear it about twice a year now, but when I lived in Beijing it was minus ten for half the year and I used to wear it just to go out and buy vegetables. I didn't care. Did you know fur has to be kept refrigerated?

'No. What were you doing in China?'

'Pearls,' she says, 'cultured pearls. They're my business. Look.' And she unhooks the neck of her mink and fingers a massive necklace that she's presumably been wearing all evening but that, entirely typically, I haven't noticed. It consists of sizeable golden pearls interspersed with sizeable actual pearls.

'Solid gold, each of them. My own design. I tried casting them as cardamom seeds, as chilli peppers, then I thought why not just make gold pearls. I think they're rather lovely.'

A teenage girl, drawn to the fire, lowers herself onto a canvas chair then screams as if bitten. I jump up, thinking scorpions.

'Oh,' she screams, like one who has seen the end of the world, 'it's like soaking.'

'Stay there, dear,' says Lynn, 'I'll fetch you a towel.'

I keep the fire fed, building the pyramid, watching the flames eat through the struts, anticipating the collapse and drinking my Wine from the Holy Land. Few people come to talk to me and I don't mind. The party begins to seem a long way away. It's just me and the fire.

As midnight nears the party migrates to the ridge above the campsite, the men helping the women up the dune, the women carrying their shoes and slithering. The mood is joyous. With a beaker of holy wine I slip away in the opposite direction. These are decent people but I am not intimate with them and the moment of the year's turning seems intimate to me.

A fox terrier follows me. I do nothing to discourage him. A couple of hundred yards away I stop and sit on damp sand and the dog noses around for a bit then settles at my side. My watch says almost midnight. I trawl my mind for distinctive memories of the year just ending and come up with nothing.

It was not so at twenty. Then the peaks on the graph soared and the troughs sank low. At fifty-one the graph has flat-lined. Each successive year seems less volatile, less distinguishable from its predecessor.

Cheers reach me faintly on the breeze. The moment, it seems, has come and gone. We are made new. I raise in the mist my glass of wine and pledge it, as I do every year if I'm sober enough, to the few people I've loved. It doesn't matter. I pat the dog.

Faint noise from the far ridge. Are they singing 'Auld Lang Syne'? Here in the Arabian desert? I hope so. A gathering of Africans of Dutch descent singing a Scottish archaism in the Arabian desert would be another trinket for my collection of relishable oddities.

Half an hour later I'm curled in a sleeping bag in a tent. The terrier has joined me, scrabbling down inside the bag and plugging itself against my belly. Its warm, taut, furry presence is a pleasure. Beneath the groundsheet the sand makes a moulding mattress. The oldies have clearly regained control of the music system. 'All you need is love' sings the dead John Lennon. Or perhaps it's the living Sir Paul, who has married and divorced a one-legged woman and who looks every year, as someone recently pointed out, more and more like Angela Lansbury. Mulling over such vital matters I fall asleep.

The sun wakes me. It has turned the little borrowed tent into a sagging greenhouse, the light somehow submarine. The terrier's gone. I crawl out onto sand like something evolving. The mist has burned off but my shoes are still damp. I shake them carefully for scorpions. I am the only person stirring. I amble over the dune and piss, turning the sand black. A few hundred yards away a pair of camels sway across the desert with their steady, loping, patient gait. That'll do me to kickstart a year.

The remains of parties are more telling than the parties themselves. The dance floor matting is ruched and furrowed and about a third of it has been swallowed by the sand. The mirror ball hangs, inane and defunct, catching flashes of the low sun. Beads of moisture have collected like silvered button mushrooms on the sleek black top of the sound system. Shoes litter the place, and half-buried wine glasses.

The zip of a house-sized tent opens and one of the meaty young men emerges in t-shirt and boxer shorts. He staggers round the side of the tent, hunches over a little bush of spinifex, retches, and then vomits. He sinks to his knees, his whole frame drained by the gagging reflex. A pause, then the second rush of vomit, accompanied by bestial groans. He stays there a while, recovering a part of his strength, then lumbers back to his tent to collapse. Happy New Year.

As I step gently past another tent, acutely aware of guy ropes, I catch ragged sleeper mumbles and a bout of snoring. It's good to have the scene to myself. On the knot of dining tables the stiff white napery has been drenched to silver. Heel ends of wine in beaded bottles: Groenekloof, Edelrood, Niederberg, and an Oyster Bay sauvignon blanc. And here's my second bottle of Domaine Jordan Valley, opened but almost untouched. I sniff it. What seemed fine last night repels me now.

My shoe scrunches on a broken glass. Plates are piled on the trestle tables awaiting the return of hired labour to make things good again. Only about thirty of us were here last night but how much mess we've generated. The sordid detritus of pleasure.

A tiny digital camera lies on a wet table, its sleek metal case keeping the moisture from its delicate innards and the snaps of booze-fuelled bonhomie. Surrounded by tentsful of sleeping party-goers, I feel that everything is charged with poignancy, that now, here, are images more deserving of being photographed than any of the planned revelry of last night. There's an underbelly honesty to the scene, the flipside of human order. Puddles have formed in the sagging canvas chairs around the fire. The fire smoulders, blackened at the edge but still emitting heat. Stumps of great logs lie around it like spokes, their unburnt ends pointing away to the desert, their near ends charred like casualties of war. The terrier emerges from whatever tent he forsook mine for, shows little interest in me and noses round the tables for sandy scraps. From time to time he rises like a meerkat on his back legs and thrusts his nose towards a table top that he's too short to reach.

I find a half-full bottle of Vichy water and take it up the dune to drink. The sun has burned off every hint of mist but for a sullied fringe of stuff on the horizon above the city. The sky has deepened to a rich pure blue. Several hundred yards away a yellow 4WD lumbers silently over the dunes heading I can't guess where. I sit a while. A tiny fly, buzzless and quick, lands repeatedly on my ankle. Each time it returns I know it from the tiny tickle of the hair it perches on. I feel abnormally alive and pleased to be here.

Down below, the electrical engineer emerges from his tent. He is no longer Batman. Inside the tent he has put on ironed jeans and a t-shirt. He stretches in the sun, looks around but doesn't see me on the dune top, goes back into the tent and comes out again with a big black professional-looking camera. I don't remember him using it last night. He photographs with care and in detail the wreckage of the party, meticulous close-ups of the strewn and sodden tables, the tipsy bottles, the discarded shoes. Good man.

6

Let's Go Shopping

It's a pyramid. The top floor is occupied by the owner, a minor sheikh. The rest of the pyramid is the Raffles Hotel. What Raffles has to do with a pyramid is anyone's guess. What either a pyramid or Raffles has to do with Dubai is also anybody's guess. And the correct guess is nothing. But if you are seeking cultural coherence, don't come to Dubai. It has all the consistency and profundity of Las Vegas. Indeed it has many similarities with Las Vegas. Like Vegas, Dubai sprouted in a desert, and grew fast from effectively nothing. Like Vegas it was free to create its own identity, and like Vegas it has become fixed in the popular mind as the epitome of something. Vegas is gambling. Dubai is shopping. In Dubai, the phrase 'born to shop' carries no freight of irony. Dubai even hosts a massive annual Festival of Shopping, and no one dares call it an oxymoron. Perhaps no one even thinks it.

There is irony, however, in the Vegas comparison. Dubai has no casinos because Islam forbids gambling, but there is money to be made from casinos and Dubai is fond of money. So Dubai World, a conglomerate owned by the Dubai government, has bought ten per cent of MGM Mirage, the world's largest casino operator. It cost them five billion dollars. Dubai World has also gone halves with MGM on a project to build a nine billion-dollar hotel and casino on the Las Vegas Strip that will be every bit as tacky as you'd expect. But at the time of writing the gamble of this investment looks like succumbing to the recession. Currently Dubai World is suing MGM. Which, as the prophet would no doubt point out, is what can happen when you gamble.

The pyramid has a mall attached, of course. Dubai's got malls like measles, but they make sense here. For half the year the local climate is uncomfortably hot. For a third of the year it's intolerably hot. So most of what happens in Dubai happens indoors in conditioned air. And that's especially true of shopping. You can't expect tourists to dedicate themselves to the task of spending more than they can afford if they're larded in sweat.

Malls are easy to despise, but they are merely covered markets and markets are as old as agriculture. But what a mall offers is far more than agricultural surplus. It offers the ideal fantasy world as seen on television and in magazines. And nothing is permitted to disrupt the fantasy: no weather, no thugs, no traffic, no dirt, no distress. There are security guards, piped music, and cooled synthetic air. Malls are the apex of the consumer society that Dubai has come to represent. And of all societies in history the consumer society is the least social. It emerges from Fortress Home only to make raids on stuff, to take that stuff home in a sealed car, haul up the drawbridge, drop the portcullis and then watch television in order to learn what to get next.

It is so easy to forget how constantly we in the West are bombarded with a single lie. It is the notion that the things we buy – the cheese spread, the duvet inner, the all-in-one barbecue tool – will make us happier than we were before we bought them. The lie is bellowed from the radio, the television, the newsprint, the roadside billboards. Experience tells us that the lie is a lie. Yet some instinct continues to respond to its siren call, and the balloon of hope keeps re-inflating.

In our world the call of advertising is as constant as the call of the muezzin. Commerce and religion use identical marketing strategies. The mall is effectively our mosque and, like a mosque, it is built to impress. Like a mosque it is a focal point, the place where people gather to do a culturally important thing. Like a mosque it confirms a belief and gratifies a need. And if Dubai had to choose between mosques and malls, it would choose malls. Indeed, though it would never admit it, it already has. Just as we have chosen them over cathedrals.

I have come to this mall, Wafi Mall, because with its Egyptian theming it is aimed at the locals, the Emiratis of whom I've managed to see little so far. In addition to the pyramid, there's a colossal frieze that is immediately recognizable as a mummy of the Tutankhamun variety. The stylized face, the mermaidish body, are done very nicely in concrete. Beside it are hieroglyphs whose authenticity – an exquisite word in the context – has been vouched for by a top professor from Cairo flown in expressly to do the vouching.

The parking spaces closest to the door are reserved for the best spenders. Here are Lexuses, Rollers and Porsches, all with far lower numbers on the registration plates than on their price tags. Each has a driver lounging while his employer shops. The doors that grant entrance to the mall are inevitably automatic, the sort that see you coming and politely slide back. I remember seeing such doors on *Star Trek* forty years ago and being impressed by them. Now if a glass door doesn't open automatically I walk into it.

Pass through the deferential doors, enter the main atrium, and you are confronted with, well, what would you expect in this 'Egyptian' mall just after the start of Islamic New Year? Exactly, a Christmas tree. An enormous bloody Christmas tree, a real living conifer flown in from Allah knows where and stretching from floor to distant ceiling, its branches draped with kilometres of tinsel and weighed down by three dimensional golden stars, each looking heavy enough, if it fell, to kill a shopper.

Christmas is the world's premier retail experience situation, when the West does a third of its annual shopping, so Dubai can't afford to ignore it. Up the escalator beyond the Christmas tree there are signs to a branch of Marks and Spencer, the famous Jewish names writ large on the wall in both English and Arabic.

A window nearby displays astonishing jewellery. The gems are chunky, their settings chunkier. The price tags water the eyes. They're a sort of financial porn. And just round the corner is a shop the like of which I've never seen. It sells interior decorations, beginning with a brace of stuffed peacocks by the door. The peacocks have no price tag. Nor has the reproduction oil painting of an Elizabethan woman in a ruff.

A shop assistant is attending to a man in a dishdash. In the concealed pocket at his hip I can make out the bulge of his wallet and cell phone. His wife and two daughters accompany him, all in long black robes but without veils. The two daughters are sloe-eyed and beautiful. The family is studying a chandelier.

This chandelier has the standard glass elements but with additions that include dripping plastic candles, a couple of snarling bats on wire and some foot-long dangles of taffeta in the form of shuttlecocks or perhaps jellyfish. It's frankly hideous. The man asks the price, in English.

'Twenty-two thousand dirhams,' whispers the shop assistant.

That's about four thousand pounds.

Deeper inside this underlit warren of a shop the walls are hung with reproduction Dutch still lifes, mock Gainsborough portraits, medieval pastoral scenes with castles bigger than the hills they stand on, and a framed sepia photograph of an Edwardian grandfather. He is bearded like Abraham Lincoln. As you pass he suddenly grins at you, his hologrammed lips furling back to reveal a vampire's smile. Another pace and he reverts to his stiff forefather look. On the chair below him, a plaster skull wears a monk's cowl.

Here's a swivelling wall, one side all heavy Victorian wallpaper, the other a set of bookshelves holding voodoo fetishes, more skulls, a whip, a pair of riding boots and several volumes of Dickens (*Bleak House*, *Martin Chuzzlewit*) made from plaster. Another alcove holds a hologram of a bat on the wing, with the same vampire teeth as Abe Lincoln. It's flapping above a porcelain urn, vast in size, neo-classical in design, royal purple in colour and brocaded with gold. And everywhere there are chandeliers, each more kitsch or macabre than the last. It's Bram Stoker meets Miss Havisham meets *Antiques Roadshow*, all in reproduction, a mish-mash of cultural references severed from any attachment to meaning

At every corner stands a shop assistant, hands behind back, attentive, and dressed in a parody of formal nineteenth-century European costume – a frock coat that brushes the floor, a pinstriped morning suit, a heavyweight dress that a princess might have been crammed and strapped into for an Edwardian state banquet. These assistants are mostly young Filipinos, good-looking, English-speaking and cheap.

And all in all, I just don't get it. But then again, perhaps there's nothing to get. This is Dubai. This is what the locals like. And *de gustibus*, as the wise man said, *non est disputandum*.

Upstairs is a modern simulacrum of a souk, a maze of individual shops, most of them devoted to clothing. Here you can buy abayas, the black cloaks that women traditionally wear in public. Some have subtle decorations that defy tradition. Also on sale is the ornamental gear the women wear in private.

I don't think there's any mistaking that I'm white, but several shop assistants urge me to buy Arab dress. One Chinese girl, pale as porcelain and with wrists like twigs, is especially insistent. She holds a dishdash against me, fetches an embroidered pillbox that she nestles on my skull, folds a head cloth, wraps it around the pillbox, secures the arrangement with a plaited leather thong (which derives, she tells me, though it takes a few attempts to get the information across, from a camel halter) and leads me to a mirror. Whoa, there's T.E. Lawrence, enigmatic, heroic, strider through deserts and foe of the Turks. I love it. I'm sold.

'How much,' I say, 'the lot?'

She does a little calculation and shows me the five digit answer and I thank her very much and tell her it's been such fun and I leave in the clothes I arrived in to try another mall: the only mall in the world where you can ski on snow.

'Bill Gates is the antichrist,' says Matthew the taxi driver. 'He is killing the languages. If there is a supernatural virus in the computer system, how the people will be communicating?'

'How indeed?' I say.

'I am coming from Kerala. Kerala is my mother. I shall return. Every man wants to sit in the lap of his mother. Do you know that Doubting Thomas is visiting Kerala? I meet people from one hundred and thirty-eight countries. I am keeping a list, you see.'

Matthew is infectiously exuberant. Indeed he transmits that exuberance to the wheel, which renders a trip along Sheikh Zayed Road even more fraught with visions of imminent death than usual.

He considers the ban on New Year celebrations to have been silly, and the Palestinians even sillier. They would be wise, he suggests, to stop niggling the Israelis. 'Why tickle with a feather the ear of a sleeping lion?'

I ask if he minds if I write that down.

'You are very welcome,' he says, 'but I am already writing it down. I am writing a book. It is about my experiences. I am calling it The Gospel According to St Matthew.'

'I'd like to read it,' I say, and I half would. Like most taxi drivers, Matthew has no doubt rehearsed these lines a thousand times, but they're a lot more fun than a London cabbie's views on matters moral and political, which can normally be boiled down to shooting the whole ~~fucking~~ lot of 'em.

'So you're a saint.'

'Oh no no no no,' says Matthew, bubbling over with laughter and patting me on the arm to relieve the pressure. 'Oh goodness me no. I am a taxi driver.'

We move somehow on to India and Pakistan. I ask if there will be war.

Again that torrent of delighted laughter.

'My friend, India is very big. If all the men of India are standing on the border and urinating, Pakistan will be sweeping away in the torrent. In the inundation. Sweeping away, are you hearing me?'

'I am,' I say. 'Loud and clear.'

He sees his work as a mission.

'God and the devil are Korchnoi and Kasparov. We are the pawns. I am giving lifts to many prostitutes. There is Gigi. She is making the money so she can go home to Ethiopia to be married. I am blessing her. I say, Gigi, in my head you are still a virgin. And she is kissing me.'

The laugh roars out again through the dense beard. When he drops me at the Mall of the Emirates I have decided that he is both borderline psychotic and a thoroughly good guy. 'God's people,' he tells me in parting, 'are the people with the positive thinkings. You have the positive thinkings, Joe.'

'It's been lovely to meet you,' I say.

'In the name of the Father, Son and Holy Ghost I bless you.'

*

You can see the ski slope from a mile away. Its enclosed form protrudes from the roof of the mall at forty-five degrees like a giant spectacle-case.

The mall itself is unremarkable, with uniform temperature and vast domed concourses and Debenhams and Carrefour. There's Pumpkin Patch for dressing your toddler fashionably, and Christian Dior for dressing yourself to compete with your toddler. There are women with pushchairs and girls with cell phones and boys in hoodies, though with no sense of threat about them. Poor people swab and polish floors, their faces minimum-wage lugubrious – not that there's a legal minimum wage in Dubai.

But it's the skiing that lures the punters. Skiing is decadent. Technology takes you uphill in a chair. Then gravity takes you down grinning. But to do this indoors within fifty metres of coffee bars and clothes shops seems even more self-indulgent, even more spendthrift than usual. And to do it indoors in Dubai, where the desert can swell a man's tongue and turn it black in a week, feels like the weird apotheosis of capitalism's quest for fun. Wheee and whoosh, and all on a credit card.

And yet, on reflection, a ski slope in Dubai is no more bizarre, no more artificial than, say, a lion enclosure at London Zoo or an ice-rink in Sydney. It's just a bit more show-off expensive.

One side of the main atrium is flanked with a glass wall that rises for ever and on the other side of the glass is the frozen north. It looks like the inside of a paperweight. This is a 'winter wonderland' although that single pair of inverted commas seems inadequate. The place deserves inverted comma confetti.

At ground floor level it's got big fake rocks which, for all I know, may be big real rocks, arranged to form a snowy grotto for clambering through. And there's a grove of little Christmas trees. The nearest one to me is sponsored by Virgin Megastore.

And there are people inside this paperweight disporting themselves. Children predominate, of course, all togged up in blue and red quilted boiler suits. Most of the children are of Indian origins and they seem happy as kids in snow anywhere, romping and squealing inaudibly behind the glass. A smattering of parents in the same blue and red boiler suits are more inhibited.

A single portly Emirati dad is shuffling through the snow holding hands with his little son. Son is boiler-suited but dad has been given a quilted anorak. The hem of his dishdash brushes the snow in a manner that whoever invented the dishdash would never have conceived. Son breaks free from his father and runs behind a rock, gathers some snow and biffs it weakly. The snow ball collapses into disappointing powder, but is unmistakably an invitation to war, and dad proves truly male. With obvious effort because of his portliness he bends and gathers a snowball. The action reveals a pair of furry UGG boots. His ball is better compacted than his son's but worse aimed. Through the glass I can see the son's mouth open in a hoot of silent delight.

Above the heads of the frolickers runs a chairlift, hoisting fully kitted skiers through the roof of the building and round the corner into the giant spectacle-case. And out of that spectacle-case and back into sight comes a steady stream of skiers. Some are rank beginners, frozen in snow-plough posture, terror on their faces and arses aloft, as if awaiting an old-fashioned schoolmaster. But waltzing and winding past and through them come the arrogant majority, deft with skills learned on holiday in the Alps, carving their turns and relishing the liberation of speed without effort, the best of them with upper bodies seemingly unmoving. Their hips swivel like alternators and their knees flex like springs. I feel an urge to rent skis and join them. It is years since I skied. Though I live only two hours from good mountain skiing, those two hours are always enough to put me off. Here you can do it while grocery-shopping. It may be absurd but if you've got the money it is also indulgently wonderful.

At the foot of the slope the beginners come gradually to a halt and unfurl themselves with relief from their posture of terror. The more skilled do look-at-me finishes, flicking the skis parallel, digging the edges in, throwing up their own little boastful flurry of snow. And in the fifteen minutes that I stand with my face to the glass enjoying the whole business, every skier I see is white.

There are so many indistinguishable malls in Dubai that each has to bellow its distinction. Each has to fix in the cerebral cortex of the crowd a USP, a Unique Selling Point, an image that must pop up automatically whenever the place is mentioned. For the Mall of the Emirates that means skiing. For the Dubai Mall the USP is fish. Dubai Mall's got more fish than you can shake a trawler at.

When completed, Dubai Mall will be the biggest of the lot. It will be the anchor of the most ambitious and arrogant of all the city's ambitious and arrogant constructions. For it sits at the foot of the Burj Dubai*, the tallest building in the world. When finished, the Burj Dubai will spike almost a kilometre into the sky. It will be Dubai's landmark, its signature.

When I first saw it I took a while to realize what it reminded me of. But then it became obvious. The thing is a steeple. It tapers like any of the great cathedral spires of England, like Salisbury, say, that took a century to build. It spikes the sky and narrows to nothingness then vanishes at the very feet of God.

The mall at its base has more stores than anyone could need and an ice rink and a synthetic Christmas tree that rises though three storeys and changes colour completely every minute or so, but it's the fish that I've come to see. The fish are bait, devised to lure the shoppers and open their mouths wide with gawping wonder and then to hook them through the wallet. And effective bait they are too. A huge crowd is standing in the concourse

*Renamed the Burj Khalifa in January 2010.

and staring at a glass wall the size of a couple of houses. Behind the glass are fish in prodigious numbers. It's the Arabian Gulf in a tank.

Dull fish, flashy fish, flat fish. Fish like lugubrious old men. Fish with faces like tragedy masks. Fish as pale as ghosts. Fish that are halfway between skate and shark. A scutter of little yellow striped fish that cluster like paparazzi round a monstrous groper. The groper moves as slowly as the moon. Fish with bulbous foreheads, like the cockpits on fighter planes, fish with tails like trenching spades. A school of rays that flap like slow birds. The ripple that passes along their wings resembles a mathematical function made flesh. Here are all the blind permutations of evolution that happened to work. They have all passed the only test, which is to survive long enough in order to reproduce. And they are our ancestors. We came from the sea.

It is tempting to imagine that it is the ghost of this knowledge that keeps me, and perhaps a thousand other human beings, entranced. We stand and we stare, with some tiny portion of the amygdylla perhaps fizzing with ancestral memory. We swam among these creatures. We were and partially are of these creatures. It's deliciously sobering, like examining ourselves through the wrong end of a telescope. It gives perspective, a belittling sense of futility. To stand and stare at the fish is to sense that the whole business of being alive is cosmically comic, an excellent joke told to an empty theatre.

The crowd is enjoying the fish a lot. Indeed, many want more and are queuing to get right in among the fish, to pay a few dirhams to walk though a glass tunnel with fish above, below and on all sides of them. Is there a coelacanth in here? The coelacanth's fleshy fins are thought to have been the first prototypes of terrestrial limbs. It's the fish, in other words, that led to us.

The fishes, as far as I can tell, feel neither joy nor gloom, intent only on the neutral business of going on going on, swimming in wide and pointless swoops, touring the tank until they die. The spectators make up for that neutrality with anthropoidal gibbering and chattering.

The children are particularly ape-like, clambering onto parents to get a better view of the aquatic monsters, running up to the glass and banging it, then recoiling with delighted fear from a shark ten times their size, its snout a few inches from their own. As always, the adults are more restrained, contenting themselves with taking photos with cell phones held arbitrarily, hopefully above the heads of the crowd.

I don't understand why the big fish, and the sharks in particular, don't eat the little fish. But then comes feeding time. Two men drop in through the roof of the pool. I say men, but they are effectively throwbacks. They have regained the bits we lost when we adjusted to living on land. Their oxygen cylinders are clumsy temporary gills. They've acquired a skin to fend the cold off, and webbed propulsive feet. And they bring with them chunks of fish flesh. The big fish have learned about these strange amphibious men and weave around them in a menacing dance of hunger, as if spinning a web. The men haul the flesh from their baskets and hand it into the sharks' forbidding mouths and the sharks dive instantly to a corner to feast, like my dog when given a bone.

The little fish hang around to snap at floating morsels. None of the food that the divers bring goes to waste: it all forms more fish flesh. The whole process is beautifully complete, blindly established and inevitable and cyclical and neither good nor bad, just sleek and greedy and clean. In short, the fish make a cracking USP. Three or four times I make up my mind to move on, but my feet don't shift. In the end I have to wrench them into motion, ripping against the glue of fascination that fixes them to the synthetic floor. It's hunger that does it.

It takes a while to find food in Dubai Mall. I cover perhaps half a mile of galleries and escalators in search of the food court.

This building's as big as a village. I suppose that as malls expand to cover ever greater acreages and embrace ever more diverse activities, mini-malls will sprout within mega-malls. Indeed the process has already begun. In the Dubai Mall there's a distinct region they call the gold souk. It consists of perhaps twenty identical jewellers. The effect goes beyond dazzling. It exhausts the eyes.

When I do find food I find a globesworth of it: tacos, hamburgers, kebabs, sushi, a Chinese smorgasbord, muffins, sundaes, a trillion flavours of ice-cream, hot dogs, cold smoothies, roast meats – nothing from Arabia and nothing I haven't seen before. It's the universal menu and it's wordless. You choose by looking at pictures and to order you have only to point.

From the glistening photos that surmount every kiosk I select a plate of kebabs. The meal takes ten minutes to arrive, is delivered without a smile and resembles fried sadness. In contrast with the bright lit world of its own advertisement, it sits on the plate limp and beaten, a dispiriting incarnation of a platonic ideal. I lug it to the table least littered with the remains of other meals. How many paper tissues are scrunched and discarded worldwide each day? How many sachets of tomato sauce half-squeezed?

Across the way from me an Emirati family is finishing its paper-wrapped meal of burgers and hot dogs. Dad's in a faultlessly laundered dishdash and headgear, mum in a black abaya but no veil. The kids are in junior versions of the same outfits, except for the toddler who wears a light-blue romper suit. The Filipina maid, sitting ignored two chairs away, is in jeans and t-shirt and training shoes. She doesn't seem to have been given food. Discreetly she oversees the children's eating, unwrapping stuff for them and cleaning their fingers with a tissue. She looks down-trodden. She looks defeated.

The mother turns to her for the first time since I've been spying and says a few words, then she and her husband up and leave, taking the eldest girl with them, and leaving the other three kids in the Filipina's care. She is perhaps twenty years old. From what I know of Filipino society there's a good chance she has children of her own, even at that age. An aunt or grand-mother will be looking after them while their mother looks after other people's kids here in Dubai and strives to save money to send home.

The South African party-goer called Filipinos the stupidest people on earth. I'd call them the unluckiest. In the last four hundred years they've been done over by the Spanish, the Catholic Church, the Americans, the Japanese and their own presidents, every one of whom has been as corrupt as Mugabe. In short, Filipinos have been beaten with the shitty end of the stick for so long that they barely know that a shitless end exists. The ambition of most young Filipinos is to go overseas to earn money in menial jobs and remit as much home as they can. The government of the Philippines has a department dedicated to such remittances.

You can see history in the face of this maid. She has dark Spanish eyes. She has a hint of the asiatic features of her indige-nous island-dwelling forebears. She wears a little silver crucifix. She speaks reasonable American English. And she's treated like a household appliance. By geographical accident of birth she finds herself at the bottom of the heap. It's hard not to think of the sharks in the tank downstairs.

When her employers disappear, quite possibly to fritter more money on their daughter than they pay the maid for a month of drudgery, she sags. She visibly lets exhaustion and dispirited-ness get the better of her. Her two older charges, aged perhaps six and eight, start a raucous chasing game around the tables. She does nothing. The toddler starts to cry, I can't work out why. She tries to comfort the child. It wails. The wail's like a saw on metal, a noise designed to grate on adult brains, to cause them to act.

People at other tables are staring. The Filipina desperately tries to pacify the child. She calls to the two roistering kids. You can sense from her shy voice that they hold the whip hand over her, have been encouraged to do so perhaps, or have simply learned it from their parents by osmosis. It seems that she wants to take the toddler to the washroom, but the older kids play up. The little one keeps wailing. The maid looks close to breaking point. I can't take it. I get up and go over to her, ask if I can help.

She looks up from the infant and her face is stretched with horror.

'No, sir, thank you, sir,' she says, and looks desperately around as she speaks.

I offer just to keep an eye on the two kids while she tends to the wailing one. To be frank I'd like to bang their heads together.

'No, sir, no, sir.'

People are looking. She is consumed by distress. I have only added to it. To leave the kids with me would be a sackable offence, or even, from what I've read, a reason for a beating.

I've done a stupid thing. I retreat to my table, and feign interest in an advertising brochure.

Eventually the maid manages to corral the other two kids and leads all three to the washroom, carrying the still wailing toddler, its noise receding as she rounds a corner.

I go. A few people stare at me as I go. I stare back at them venomously, though they have done nothing wrong.

It takes a while to find an exit into the real world. At the door I ignore the monstrous snake of taxis. I feel the need to walk. A few hundred yards, and I turn to take in the steepling eminence of the world's tallest building. Perhaps half of it is clad in mirror glass. The vast remainder stands open to the air like a honeycomb. The arms of construction cranes swing from its side, hundreds of metres into the air. Apparently in the event of a fire the crane drivers are supposed to clamber to the tips of their cranes and await rescue by helicopter.

I try to feel a fitting sense of awe at the scale of the thing. Whether it pleases you or not it's an impressive endeavour. But I just find myself wondering how many people have died in its construction. Poor people, unlucky people, people like the maid who came here with hope.

7

How it Happened

It's the sort of desk that a boss might sit at in a cartoon. Its polished acreage holds a blotter, a gold pen, a telephone and nothing else. All it lacks is a sales graph behind it with an arrow heading through floor or ceiling, plus an intercom into which the boss leans occasionally to bark amusing instructions to Miss Fish.

Thirty years ago this was just about the highest-flying desk in Dubai. For it sits in an office near the top of the World Trade Centre, Dubai's first skyscraper, officially opened by Her Majesty Queen Elizabeth II in 1979.

It's a monolith of windows in a lattice of stark white concrete. It lacks the smooth-honed elegance of the modern skyscraper, but when it went up it was both a wonder and an act of bravado. It rose from the sand like a single inexplicable tooth with nothing to chew. Its main use to begin with was to serve as Dubai's unmistakable landmark. You could see it from everywhere, towering over a mean huddle of next to nothing.

Had any disaffected dingbat thought of flying a plane into *this* World Trade Centre he couldn't have missed. Today he'd have to be a stunt pilot. He'd have to weave through a forest of skyscrapers: show-off, gleaming, my-dick-is-bigger-than-yours buildings with flanks of glass and steel. There are buildings shaped like giant Bic lighters, or like pencils. One resembles a tuning fork.

I'm holding a photo that was taken from the window of this office in 1979. And nothing I have seen has so brought home the suddenness of Dubai, the speed at which it has risen. From here I overlook Sheikh Zayed Road, a mighty eight-lane highway, a roaring river of vehicles. In the thirty-year-old photo it's just a track through sand, unsealed and all but deserted. A couple of blurry dots on it I take for dune buggies. Beside it stands a pair of unadorned four-storey buildings, like accommodation blocks for Soviet workers. These formed the only hotel in these parts at that time. In the background I can make out the coastline and the Gulf beyond, and a sparse scatter of huts and chalets set back from the beach in what is now Jumeirah. And everything else between the window and the horizon is sand.

Today every inch of that sand is built on.

Time after time my eyes go down to the photo then back to the view from the window. In 1979 I was just leaving university. While I have wandered my way through adulthood, working too much, not laughing enough, watching a few puppies grow into dogs, this city, this latter-day Babylon, has come into being in the desert, has been built from nothing. In those thirty years I've built one single-storey, though pleasingly sturdy, goat shed.

The boss who owns the big empty desk and the photograph I am marvelling at and the office in which I am standing and the gold-rimmed coffee cup from which I am drinking, does not want to be identified. I got his name from someone I met at a party and rang him cold and he invited me to his office, but when I explain that I make a living by writing he becomes a little nervous. 'I don't want publicity and I don't need it,' he says.

But most of what he says is uncontentious. It is largely a paean to Sheikh Rashid. 'Rashid', says the boss, 'had vision.'

Rashid, the father of Sheikh Mohammed, succeeded his own father in 1958 and is universally acknowledged as the man who set Dubai on the path to what it's become. He's the reason you've heard of the place. But he didn't have it easy to start with. There were rumblings in his sheikhdom. The pearl industry that had been the economic mainstay of Dubai had collapsed; the emirate was pinched with poverty. And in the wake of the Suez crisis, there were moves throughout the Arab world for independence. This made the Al Maktoums vulnerable because, ultimately, they ruled Dubai because they had the backing of British authority.

And the British recognized their vulnerability. When Rashid took power they sent a warship and gave him a five-gun salute whose booming echoes reminded any would-be rebels that the Brits were in behind the Al Maktoums, as per trucial agreement. All the same, privately, Whitehall had doubts that Rashid would survive.

But Rashid had fended off the threat of insurrection before. In doing so he'd proved himself both clever and ruthless. In 1939, when he was only a young man, a rebel group of Emiratis had sought to rein in the power of the Al Maktoums. They resented the way the ruling family was enriching itself from monopoly concessions granted by the Brits. They wanted to establish a *majlis*, or consultative council, which was how tribal affairs had traditionally been run, with the ruler having to consult with his elders. They wanted the new *majlis* to take control of the money that was presently going straight into the sheikhly pockets. They wanted to distribute it more evenly. It sounded dangerously like democracy.

At the time Rashid was about to marry a daughter of Abu Dhabi's ruling family, a union founded purely on love. As a gesture to the rebels he offered to hold the marriage ceremony near the rebels' stronghold in Deira. They could all come to the beano, he said. It was a popular move, because everyone loves a beano. It also seemed a conciliatory move, perhaps paving the way to some financial concessions.

On the day of the wedding everyone piled into Deira, including a lot of Bedouin supporters of Rashid. But instead of heading straight for the beano and hoeing into the date juice, these men snuck onto rooftops with sandbags and rifles. At a prearranged time they opened fire on the rebels and killed a fair swag of them. A couple of hours later Rashid turned up smiling, announced that Dubai was united once more and got married.

Officially, the British stayed out of the whole dispute. Unofficially they backed the Al Maktoums. The last thing they wanted in one of their protectorates was any form of democracy.

When he finally came to power nineteen years later, Rashid immediately demonstrated the deft political nous that was to serve him well during his long reign. He established a *majlis*. The only difference between this *majlis* and the one proposed in 1939 was that the new one had no authority. Its every decision had to be ratified by the ruler. In other words the Al Maktoums were prepared to compromise on anything except their own supreme power.

Rashid's accession coincided with Dubai's oil coming on stream. Without that oil he might have been dog tucker. With it he was able to appease the dissenters. He gave the most lucrative concessions to his biggest enemies. Within a year or two everyone had by and large forgotten about politics and was busy making money.

But in sharp contrast to most of the other oil sheikhs round the Middle East Rashid saw beyond oil. He realized that Dubai's reserves were modest and finite. So he used the revenues to build the infrastructure that Dubai needed in order to thrive in other ways. When the oil money was insufficient, he borrowed. People cautioned him against it. He forged ahead. He created a city that could trade.

His first mission was to build a deep-water port. Many thought there was no need for one. Planners advised him to build no more than four berths. Rashid insisted on sixteen. Within a couple of years, sixteen proved too few. He built twenty more berths. Then he set about building a new port altogether, Port Jebel Ali, the biggest in the Gulf. It boomed immediately.

Rashid built dry docks too, and roads and bridges. He drilled for fresh water. He told his son to build an airport. When BOAC hesitated to fly there he personally bought all the seats available to ensure it was profitable for them. Rashid made things happen.

Just about everything that has allowed Dubai to boom, from free zones to tourism, was instituted during the rule of Rashid. And the boss in the World Trade Centre watched it all happen. For people like him on the comfortable side of the transformation it must have been an exciting few decades.

When I ask the boss whether the bubble will burst, he laughs. Dubai, he says, is here to stay. It has too many advantages to implode, too much investment has been made. It has location, political stability, climate, tolerance and a head start on everyone else. The sand will never reclaim it. 'Come back in a year and you'll see that I'm right,' he says, and shakes my hand, and I leave him at his empty desk, fiddling with his gold pen, beside the telephone that hasn't rung in the hour I've been there.

Lifts are among the world's most socially awkward places. The people inside have nothing in common except a desire to escape. They are standing unnaturally close to each other. Their most primitive sense is screaming that they should not allow strangers this near. Their sense of social rules is crying out for acknowledgement of each other. In no other circumstances do they stand like this except in crowds at spectacles. And at spectacles there is somewhere to look. In lifts there is nowhere. Most people resolve the problem by staring at the panel above the door that indicates the passage of floors. They silently urge it to hurry up.

When the lift doors open for me on the thirtieth floor of the World Trade Centre they reveal a man on his own. He looks me smack in the eye and smiles.

'How do you do?' he says. He's fortyish, wearing a costly looking suit and a white shirt open at the neck. He has something of Tiger Woods about him, or of Barack Obama, a sleek, tall frame and multi-racial provenance.

'Hello,' I say and step in. He offers his hand.

This could be creepy. It feels the opposite. The man is charming. His unforced courtesy melts my unease. By the time we reach the ground level, which has involved a change of lifts at the nineteenth floor, he knows more about me than anyone else in Dubai does and I know that he works in private equity – which I think means shopping on a grand scale – and that he's off to attend a meeting at the Marina.

'Have you seen the Marina, Joe?'

I haven't.

'Come along if you like, I'm early. We'll have coffee.'

His name, if I heard him correctly, is Varood. The son of an African father and an Indian mother, Varood and his family left Uganda in the early Seventies when Idi Amin expelled all Asians. Because of his father's nationality they could have stayed, but his mother was terrified of the violence that Amin encouraged and exploited. Though Varood was only young he can still recall his mother's fear. The family went to England for a while, then the States.

I tell him I remember Idi Amin being in the news when I was a teenager. He seemed a comic figure.

'Mad and murderous,' says Varood. 'Illiterate too.'

Amin died only a few years ago in the country to which he'd fled when deposed. 'Guess where that was,' says Varood.

I shrug.

'Saudi,' he says, and laughs. 'Saudi bloody Arabia.'

And I am struck once again by the gulf between events and reported events. Every international story titillates for a few days and then subsides. But for those who live through it, it can remain the only story, the cause of distress or poverty that scars a life. Never, in fifty years, has such an event affected me. I have lived a life of ease more or less unparalleled in human history. A part of me retrospectively envies Varood.

'Amin did me a favour,' he says as if reading my mind, and smiles broadly across the back seat of the taxi. 'He got me out of bloody Africa.'

We're on Sheikh Zayed Road, spearing through the tower-block forest. Even if I were to press my nose against the window of the taxi and twist my neck I would be unable to see sky. This is a landscape as unrelievedly urban as Manhattan.

Varood's been in Dubai for several years. The private equity company he works for is one that I will have heard of, he says, but he politely declines to name it. It is based in the States but it has offices in many cities. He enjoys Dubai.

'It's like Singapore,' he says, 'only better. It's exciting. It hasn't had time to get set in its ways. People come here to make things happen. Everyone just gets on with things so there's no real class system. You're judged only on your success.'

'And will it last? Isn't it cracking under the strain?'

'It'll last. There are lots of people who hate Dubai and who want it to fail. They call it a nouveau riche upstart, a brash and shallow thing, because they resent its success. But in reality they're just scared that Dubai's winning and they're losing; that they're being left behind. And isn't that always the way? Dubai's no different really from anywhere else. It exists to make money and it's here to stay. Cities don't disappear, do they? Mind you, even if it does crash and burn, it's been one hell of a ride.' And he laughs with wonderful African teeth.

The Marina is an artificial creek, a huge inlet carved into the land. Apartment blocks are rising all around it. This has been planned as another playground for the wealthy. But at the cafe on the curving concrete boulevard, Varood and I are the only customers. Indeed we are pretty well the only people about.

Impressively, our coffees still take fifteen minutes to arrive. The waiter doesn't apologize.

'That's Internet City over there,' says Varood, pointing at a forest of skyscrapers glistening in winter sun. 'You know about the cities, Joe?'

I do, sort of, but I am happy to hear Varood explain them. They've been integral to the boom of Dubai.

When the UAE was formed it passed a law requiring all companies that traded within its territory to be majority-owned by local Emiratis. The obvious purpose of the law was to ward off the danger of a foreign influx and potential loss of sovereignty. Foreign businesses duly found the law off-putting, as they were supposed to do. But so did Sheikh Rashid of Dubai. It prevented him attracting the sort of businesses he felt he needed to make his city less dependent on oil.

'So he simply ignored the law,' says Varood.

Rashid unilaterally established free zones for international business where the local law didn't apply. He gave these zones names like Media City, Internet City, Healthcare City and so on, but they were essentially just little islands of Dubai that stood apart from the requirements of the rest of the UAE, like the enclaves that European powers established in Shanghai in the early twentieth century.

The move made Dubai understandably unpopular with the

other emirates and just as understandably popular with foreign corporations. Here was an untaxed and largely unregulated place from which to do business. And most importantly it was smack in the middle of the Middle East, a huge market that they had always found hard to tap because of its religious difference and its political instability. In consequence, they flocked to Dubai. And now all the other emirates are trying to do the same thing.

Varood comes close to enshrining the modern face of Dubai. He's an unapologetic capitalist. He's made good from not much. He's ambitious, contemporary, groomed, healthy and effectively stateless. He's a brew of diverse races. He's at home in almost any culture. He is globalization made flesh.

Globalization is the new form of empire. Despite its name it is largely unconcerned with territory. Its unit of organisation is not the nation state but the corporation. It has been enabled by the jet plane and more recently by the internet. It originated in the States but has become a game played by all wealthy nations with the Americans still in the lead, but with countless others at their heels. It's a game of money. For the winners the rewards are absurdly generous. For the losers, for the Filipina maids and Indian labourers, well, they were losing before they began. Nothing much changes for them.

When, with his unfailing good manners, Varood apologizes and leaves to attend his meeting, I take a stroll along the edge of the Marina. A few yachts sit moored and motionless at the feet of apartment blocks, their hulls as white as the breast feathers of gulls. Half the buildings are still under construction. Cranes are bonded to their flanks by some process of engineering that I can only marvel at. They spike so high in the sky that looking up at them makes me sneeze. Their drivers must take half an hour to climb to them each morning. I presume they piss in the cab.

A giant sheet of grey plastic sails down and across the sky like one of those Amazonian gliding squirrels, disappears behind a billboard saying 'Damac. Luxury Delivered', reappears the other side, then, as the breeze near ground level weakens, crumples to the water.

Another billboard announces a forthcoming tower of 'prestige residences'. At present it's just a lattice of steel and concrete. What will become balconies for white-toothed, designer-dressed people to lounge on are just protruding slabs of concrete, like diving boards in the sky. On one of these diving boards, perhaps twenty floors up, a man is standing in blue overalls. There is no barrier between him and the world below. If he fell he would have several seconds to mull things over on his way to a splattered death. The crane swings a load of building materials in towards where he stands. He guides it in by hand leaning nonchalantly out over eternity.

8

Down in Deira

'You have, like, a credit card,' says the girl. She is maybe thirteen years old, dressed like Barbie, and is deep in conversation with another girl at a table over paper cups of Coca-Cola. Both girls have the vowels of an English private school and the intonation of Paris Hilton. Every sentence ends with the rising intonation known to students of linguistics as the imbecilic interrogative.

'And your parents top the card up so you never like run out of money to buy anything.'

'Cool.'

The girls are in the foyer of the Hyatt Hotel. They've been ice-skating. Their skates protrude from bags at their feet. One bag is pink, the other Cambridge blue. The ice rink is inside the foyer, shaped like a kidney and currently being groomed by a machine like a ride-on mower.

'Daddy took us sand boarding.'

'Sand boarding, is that like, like, snow boarding?'

'Yeah.'

'Is it good?'

'Yeah it's cool.'

'Do you go like skiing in France?'

The walls of the foyer are decorated with ads for authentic cuisine of several varieties to be found in the hotel's restaurants and for a clinic that specializes in rhinoplasty. There are before and after pictures of nose jobs.

Down by the sea on the Deira side of the Creek, the Hyatt is a brown and ugly monolith. Most of the thousand windows on its vast flank are sealed shut to retain the conditioned air, but the few that hang open give the building the look of a colossal advent calendar. The Indian car-park attendant has a hut and a uniform and is in charge of the inevitable barrier arm that sieves the right people from the wrong. In their short lives, the skating girls will rarely have found themselves on the wrong side of a barrier arm.

Past the landscaped hummocks with their costly mats of grass, and across the highway and the intervening foreshore, I can see one of Dubai's most ambitious projects. Or I would be able to, were it not blocked by wooden screens the size of houses.

Palm Deira is the third and the largest of the Palms. The first of them, Palm Jumeirah, gained global publicity and sold out. Palm Jebel Ali looked like doing the same. So they launched into Palm Deira. And then the bubble burst. It is common knowledge that work on Palm Deira has stopped. But it is not official knowledge. It has never been publicly admitted.

The developers are an outfit called Nakheel. Like most of the developers in Dubai, Nakheel is a quasi-governmental organization. Which is how, in Dubai, things get messy.

Most of the major Dubai organizations – the developers and contractors, the phone companies, the water companies – are headed by people close to the ruling family. And they operate under rules different to the ones I'm familiar with as a westerner from an ostensibly transparent democracy. The rules here are by and large not written down and the last recourse is not to the law. It is to the ruler, who makes the law. The result is murk. Only the nationals on the inside know what's going on.

It doesn't help that there is no free press to delve into what's going on and report it openly. Many fine things are said about press freedom here but the plain fact is that awkward stuff goes unreported. The reasons are obvious. You don't know how the authorities will react. Journalists fear imprisonment or revocation of the visa that permits them to stay in Dubai. And they want to stay in Dubai, because the going is good.

Few journos are local. Most are expatriates who've exchanged the *Burnley Chronicle* and reporting on council meetings for nice weather, three times the salary, and no income tax. It is not in their interests to stir things up. Nor, more importantly, do they have a stake in the country that might rouse a selfless desire to stir things up. If Dubai implodes it won't matter much to them. They'll just bugger off. They, like almost everyone here, are mercenaries.

The profusion of propaganda and the shortage of hard information leads to further murk, and the murk breeds rumour, and one of the rumours going about at the moment is that Nakheel is in big trouble. The rumour is almost certainly right. No one is working on Palm Deira any more, which is why it's got screens in front of it. But the truth, though universally guessed, must be officially denied because it could damage the image of Dubai. It's not vanity. It's a business imperative.

Dubai has sold itself to business as a politically stable oasis in the least politically stable region of the world, friendly to western ways, and unstoppably prosperous. The tactic has worked better than anyone could have hoped, but the same problem arises with business as with the ex-pat journalists. They too are purely mercenary. The corporations have come solely for selfish reasons. They have no stake in the place except their own advantage. They can leave almost as easily as they came. They don't care about the place or its society or its future.

As a result, anything that threatens to puncture belief in Dubai, such as the cessation of a major project and the possible bankruptcy of a huge quasi-governmental developer, must be screened from view with house-sized sheets of plywood and nothing on the business pages. Because if belief deflates, businesses may leave. If one leaves, dozens could follow. If dozens, hundreds.

I cross the road and find, to my surprise and delight, cricket. Lots of cricket, taking place on perhaps an acre of waste ground strewn with gravel and chunks of industrial rubble. It's very bad cricket, but very intense cricket and very happy cricket, being played by Indians and Pakistanis and Sri Lankans, the labourers of Dubai. Today is their day off, Friday, the Muslim Sabbath, and they have come to town by bus from the camps they live in to play and to be. They are poor and young and they play cricket with a passion that makes me smile.

At least a dozen games are going on. The stumps are breeze blocks or scraps of timber propped up with rocks. Each game has only one bat and a hairless tennis ball that makes a meaty high-pitched thwack when walloped. And how it is walloped. No one plays defensively. The block is unheard of. The only shot played is an enormous heave to the leg side, the cricketing equivalent of a haymaker, a bid to send the ball miles over mid-wicket. Because the pitches are so crammed together, you only know which fielders belong to which game when a batsman connects. The ball flies into the outfield and its presence ignites just one of the many available fielders, like a chemical signal prompting a particular synapse. The fielder scurries after the ball and biffs it back while his team-mates shout at him and the batting side shouts at the batsmen, and the batsmen scamper between the makeshift wickets wearing flip-flops or skimpy leather sandals or no shoes at all.

Every run is fiercely cheered. Every umpiring decision is fiercely disputed. Arguments flare like bushfires. Whole teams rush in to shout at each other with unrestrained ferocity. It looks as if fists may swing into faces. Ten seconds later they're playing and grinning and cheering again.

I amble with feigned casualness to the point on the perimeter where it seems to me most likely that a shot might pierce the field and threaten to run onto the highway. I intend to shimmy along the kerb, swoop on the ball like Jonty Rhodes and casually biff it back over the stumps, whereupon the captains of at least three of the teams will recognize a gifted member of the international brotherhood of cricket and invite me to field for them, there being, as far as I can tell, no limit to the number of players in a team. And having fielded it is only fair that I should be given a chance to bowl. And then, *insh'allah*, to bat. I'd just love to bat.

I have to wait only a couple of minutes. A hoick clears midwicket on the full and deep midwicket on the bounce and is bound for death by traffic. I rise, jog a few paces to my left across the perilous terrain and do my Jonty Rhodes swoop. The ball takes a cruel bounce but I am locked onto it like one of those missiles with nosecam that the Americans just love to biff at enemy bridges. The ball obliges me by taking a second little hop straight into the palm of my left hand, I transfer it to my right, swivel and biff it in to the wicketkeeper with little power because of a rotator cuff damaged years ago by throwing, but with an accuracy that I do my best not to look surprised by. The keeper is wearing sandals, brown trousers rolled to the knee and a yellow t-shirt that says Billabong. He catches the ball and knocks down the planking wicket. It is, all told, and without false modesty, a defter piece of fielding than any I have observed on this wasteland in the last fifteen minutes. And the result? A row. An apocalyptic row.

Though I cannot understand a word of it I fully understand the issue. Can a batsman be run out by a spectator? In an ordinary game, of course not. But in a game as arbitrary as this without boundaries or agreed team numbers or anything approaching formality, who is to say? The answer is that everybody is to say. And say it they do, with ferocious relish, for the best part of a minute, a minute that ends with a tug of war over the bat between the man I've run out and what I take to be the captain of the fielding side. The captain is by far the biggest man on either side. The batsman, who has the advantage of holding the handle, wrenches the bat from his grasp but only so as to fling it to the ground in a gesture of theatrical disgust.

'Very good throwing.'

An Indian youth with matchstick arms and a lot of teeth has come alongside me smiling.

'Thank you,' I say, and his smile ratchets up another hundred watts. And I feel as if I've just run out Ponting on 99 with a direct hit at a single stump from the boundary on the first day of the Lord's test.

The game resumes. I wait for a captain to come sidling over and to issue the hoped-for invitation. I wait until it becomes clear it is not going to happen. Then I go. But my day has been brightened by my own admittedly fluky piece of fielding. The value of even trivial athletic success is underestimated. I used to teach PE. The pleasure of seeing a fat or ill-coordinated child learning to perform, say, a forward roll, or a basketball lay-up, never wore off. You could just see them swell with joy.

And as I wander away, I find myself suffused with memories. The mind often works like that, I find, like a filing cabinet. It sits there fat with stuff that goes for years untouched and seemingly forgotten. But something pulls on a tab in that cabinet and up comes a great wad of material, various and arbitrarily preserved, the events that have somehow stuck when millions of similar ones have dissolved to nothing.

Of course my memories of fielding are by and large the ones where I've done something good. I recall one particular booming throw from the shadow of the oak trees in Adastra Park, Hassocks. And then with full sensory detail a catch swims into my head. The memory must be thirty-five years old but is as fresh as a rosebud. I was fielding at a suicidally close short leg on the old county ground at Hastings. Seagulls wheeled and screamed in a breezy summer sky and from the open window of a tenement that overlooked the ground came the sound of Acker Bilk's 'Stranger on the Shore'. And I found myself swaying to its slow evocative melancholy, inhabited by the music in a way that never happens now. I was awake to everything that was happening around me, to the cricket and the gulls and the sky, but my mind was simultaneously swamped by the song.

The batsman clipped a ball off his pads. He middled it. It was a good shot. Without anything approaching a conscious decision I moved with the shot, was part of the shot, and my hands went to the flight of the ball, which had travelled perhaps ten feet at a speed that would take it to the boundary and everyone looked to the boundary but the ball wasn't there. I had it. It was snug in my palms. And for a moment I stayed crouched and everyone including the batsman was seeking the ball with their eyes, like television cameras swinging. And then, as one, they realized. They came running to congratulate me and the batsman left and the air was still rich with 'Stranger on the Shore'. The bowler's name, I've just remembered, was Geoff Cocksworth and he was a lovely gentle guy. I wonder what happened to him.

And here now, deep in Arabia, as the traffic rumbles beside me on the Muslim sabbath and the whoops and yells of a couple of hundred Indian cricketers fade to distance, I wander along with a head full of 1973 to a fish market.

At its entrance an old man sits scrunched and folded in a plastic chair. His knees are drawn up to his chest and his arms are wrapped around those knees like a child's corpse in an ancient grave. His feet are bare, his toes seemingly prehensile, his skin sallow. His sandals lie at the base of the chair. He wears a stained grey smock and he looks Levantine, or perhaps Iranian, his face the drooping face of a basset hound. And I remark on him only because I realize now that I have seen so few old people here. The population of Dubai is of working age. People come here to work and when they stop work their visa expires and they go somewhere else to get old, which further skews the demographics of this place. Dubai's population is not just preponderantly male, it is also preponderantly young.

Thousands of fish have died to create this market. Many are dying in front of my eyes, sucking hopelessly at inimical air. And what fish they are. Here's the mall aquarium on a slab: huge kingfish, a heap of small shark, snapper, mullet, John Dory, sole, numerous species I've never seen, and pile after pile of the local cod, a sluggish-looking yellowy brown beast called hamour. I ate hamour the other night. It was creamy, meaty, good.

My white skin gets me a 'Hello, how are you, sir, where you from, sir?' at every stall and a soft and fishy handshake that feigns affection then doesn't let go. Instead it tries to draw me and my fat wallet in to admire the fish, to touch the fish, to buy the fish. Prawns, crabs, shellfish. One especially animated vendor presses crab claws on me and illustrates by gesture that brings smiles from all around that they are startlingly aphrodisiac.

The stallholders are all men, and none of them Arabs. The shoppers are almost all men, only a few of them Arabs. And those few are short women in black, each with a face mask that sits on the nose like a visor on a medieval jouster. These women look like black, beaked shuttlecocks.

You buy your fish whole and take it to a white-tiled area like an industrial lavatory, where knife-wielding geniuses gut, descale and fillet it in seconds, biffing the good bits into one bag and the rest into another. You get both bags if you want them.

Beyond the fish a small fruit and vegetable market offers spuds, bananas, tomatoes, an infinite variety of dates, and Gala apples from New Zealand, each single fruit cradled on a little polystyrene frill. And beyond that there's a hall of meat, mainly sheep and goat, where great cleavers hack though bone as clean and white as coconut flesh. The muscles of meat are a dull engorged purple and the encircling fat is the colour of old butter. I can stare at meat markets long and long, and I do. What I cannot describe is their vaguely iron-like smell, a smell of murder and honesty. It's a smell not allowed in a mall.

Huge hooks of tripe hang from rails like used cleaning rags. And here's a bin of sheep's heads, the skulls peeled of their skin and wool but the eyes still wildly staring and looking bright enough to have been seeing this morning. Their last sight would have been the Halal slaughterman who impassively seized them, turned them towards Mecca, invoked his god, and slit their throats in the manner prescribed by Mohammed thirteen hundred years ago.

The main road has an overpass made necessary by the ceaseless traffic. Dubai has grown so fast that its infrastructure is always at the point of bursting. Any new structure – a bridge, a road, a sewage system – is choked to capacity the day it opens.

Coming off the steps on the far side of the overpass I step effectively into downtown Delhi. Hundreds of young Indians throng a scrap of waste ground. They've got nothing to do and no money to do it with. They squat and smoke and chat. They touch each other a lot, standing with fingers thoughtlessly inter-laced, or with an arm thrown over a mate's shoulders. They carry chunky outmoded cell phones and they chatter in lan-guages I do not know.

I would like to know them. I would like to talk with these men, to listen to them, to have them tell me a little of their lives. Their lives have been infinitely harder than mine due simply to the accidents of our births. But my good mornings get no reply and I am shy to press myself upon them. I generally find it easy to make contact with strangers, but with these men I am afflicted by a sense of being patronizing. I want a glimpse of their hardship but I don't plan to do anything about it. The thought holds me back. Instead, I just loiter, smoking, and try to look affable, approachable.

The men flow and mill around me as if I were indistinguishable from the lamp post I'm leaning against. They see me, of course, but they assess me by instant reflex as an inverse untouchable. I am the victim of discrimination because of the colour of my skin. Or so it seems to me. If for one second one of these men makes accidental eye contact, I smile as best I can, but his eyes dart away immediately with a frisson of discomfort, a sense of a rule having been broken. It would be different if we were all four years old. But the world has stamped us.

These are the men who build; who built the Hyatt Hotel, the rhinoplasty clinic, the villa I'm staying in, the hotels where the tourists drink, the offices where the money men work. Critics of Dubai, and there are many of them, like to focus on the plight of these men. They see these men as little better than slaves. They have a point.

On my only previous visit to Dubai, when I stopped over for a few days a decade or so ago, I saw construction workers being shifted around the city in cattle trucks. They travelled standing up, prevented from falling over merely by being crammed in. It was high summer, intolerably hot, forty something degrees. I remember thinking at the time what it must be like to be in the middle of that press of people on that truck bed in that heat. I remember flinching at the thought.

It seems that others flinched too. The trucks were offensive to western eyes, less because of the men's suffering than because of the visibility of that suffering. It brought an unpleasant fact out from under its rock, reminding the comfortable how their comfort depended on the discomfort of others.

So voices were raised. And Dubai is always keen to quieten raised voices, lest its image be blackened. The ruler banned the cattle trucks. They have since been replaced by cheap metal buses from India, the only non-air-conditioned vehicles in the city. In high summer they must be like ovens. But now that the construction workers are seated on board, they resemble more privileged human beings and their plight is less visually offensive.

Like everyone else, these men have been lured to Dubai by money. Agents come to their villages in Bangladesh or Kerala or anywhere on the Indian subcontinent and promise them better money than they can make at home. They often have to pay a bond up front, a sum of money equivalent to up to six months of wages. More often than not they have to borrow that money from wherever they can, which immediately puts them in thrall to their family or a money-lender or an agent. The money-lender and the agent are sometimes the same person.

When workers arrive many have their passports taken from them by their employers. It is supposed not to happen but it does, and the men are powerless to complain. Sometimes they find they are not paid as much as they'd been promised. Again they are powerless to complain. They are accommodated on the fringe of the city in compounds away from the western eye. Conditions can be appalling, with a dozen men to a tiny room and the lanes between the compounds running with sewage.

Recently the ruler decreed that during the hot months construction workers may not be forced to work during the middle of the day when the heat is a threat to life. The law is often ignored and some still die of heatstroke. They die in accidents too. Figures are hard to obtain but you can be confident that the construction of any mall or hotel whose air-conditioned corridors you tread in pampered ease cost somebody his life. And there are suicides in the compounds. Again the figures are hard to obtain. The dead man's family inherits any outstanding debt.

I have heard and read such things. I have no doubt they are true. But I do doubt that they are true for all these men. If they were, surely the word would spread even among the terminally poor of India and the supply of labour would shrivel. These men generally earn about twenty-five American dollars a day, which is enough for them to send money home. A stint of a few years can set them up, if not for life, at least for marriage and a start back home. Which is why they come.

The story in the end is the oldest one in the world. Wealth exploits poverty. It always has. It probably always will. All that differs is the degree to which it does so. In every war in human history it's the rich that have waged the war and the poor who've been shot. In the good old days of Merrie England, that we are so fond of romanticizing, every lice-ridden peasant was inescapably in thrall to the lord of the manor. In the heyday of the British Empire colossal wealth was generated from the actual or effective slavery of countless indigenous peoples, and almost as many British subjects – the coal hewers and the loom workers, the Dickensian victims. And still it goes on, everywhere, and seemingly inevitably. The shoes you are wearing now, the underwear, the t-shirt, the jeans, were made by people far poorer than you, working for far less than you would dream of accepting.

And yet, for many of those clothing workers in China, as for many of these construction workers or maids or janitors or car-park attendants in Dubai, their job is the best they can hope for, given the misfortune of their birth, and the way the world is. And that job is a thing they wouldn't want to lose. It represents a step onto the ladder.

Here among these idling Indians, I'm in the heart of the original Dubai, the little township that Thesiger described before the gaseous expansion of the late twentieth century. It is divided by the Creek. The west side of the Creek is known as Bur Dubai, the east side as Deira. I plunge into Deira.

The place is built without apparent plan. No buildings exist to impress. They exist to house people and businesses. At the same time they shade the narrow alleyways and funnel whatever breeze there might be to cool them. The architecture acknowledges the climate, rather than simply defying it, like a mall. And unlike the vast and daunting show-off bits of Dubai, this is a place for people to go on foot. I wander at random. The writhing intersecting alleyways baffle my sense of direction. And from time to time I come across a you-are-here street map that baffles it further. But I enjoy the energy of the place.

Faces from the Indian subcontinent predominate but there are numerous people I take to be Iranian, plus Africans of all sorts, some in clothing that wouldn't seem out of place in *National Geographic* magazine. I see few white people and almost no Arabs.

Porters squat cross-legged on their trolleys, smoking, drinking tea, killing the day. The buildings rise three, four, five storeys. At their base an enterprise – a barber's shop, an electrical goods store, a bakery, none looking especially prosperous, but all alive. Men do deals on the street, or argue with a benign ferocity that you don't see on the streets of Great Britain or New Zealand. Men in jeans, men in pyjamas, men in grey one-piece shrouds. Men.

Above the shopfronts, balconies are festooned with washing, ranks of it: cheap cotton working clothes that tell the story of the cramped rented apartments behind those balconies, the apartments that disgorge these people onto these streets. It all feels local, compressed, urban, soiled. I take a seat on a low wall by a scrap of sloping land on which a few youths have contrived a game of cricket. 'Hello, how are you, where you from,' says one of the players. I suspect him of wanting to sell me something, probably a fake Rolex. I've been offered a dozen in the last half hour. A recent sweep in the city caught two hundred and sixty-two vendors of fake watches and DVDs. It also netted thirty beggars, sixty-nine car washers and fifty-eight unlicensed butchers and fish cleaners. They will all be deported.

'New Zealand,' I say.

'Stephen Fleming, very good batter, very good captain.' He grins.

I tell him that Stephen Fleming has actually just retired. He already knows. And he knows that Daniel Vettori has taken over the captaincy.

The young man's name, if I have made out his accent correctly, is Ibrahim. He's from Peshawar. His native tongue is Pushtu. I ask him to speak to me in Pushtu.

'What am I saying?' he asks.

'Tell me about life in Peshawar.' It transpires that he feels very strongly about life in Peshawar but the noise he makes doesn't even seem to divide into syllables.

'Thank you,' I say and he offers me chewing gum.

Ibrahim's twenty, though his passport says twenty-six. 'I come Dubai five years.'

'You came five years ago?'

'I come five years ago. I work my uncle.'

His uncle seems to run some sort of textile business, but Ibrahim is both hard to understand even in English and reluctant to say too much. I don't know why. It seems to me a mixture of politeness and discomfort. What had begun as a daring and jocular welcome to this wandering white man has become more intimate than he expected and perhaps wanted. His fresh face is transparent in the mix of emotions. He is pleased to be talking to me, or perhaps to be seen to be talking to me, but he is nervous at the same time. A naturally ebullient character, he repeatedly bursts into a smile that is then just as rapidly extinguished by self-consciousness.

He doesn't work for his uncle any more, but he won't tell me what he does. 'The life is hard here, sir,' he says. 'I sleep one room thirteen people. I save money and return Pakistan. I marry.'

'You'll get married in Pakistan?'

But it's his turn to bat and he leaps off the wall with relief. His first huge slog ricochets off an overflowing dumpster and disappears down an alleyway. He turns to me and grins massively. When he's out two balls later he does not return to the wall.

I lunch at Modern Dish Cafeteria, Home Essentials for the Family. My place mat is sticky from other people's meals. It shows a photo of the Eiffel Tower at night. For eighteen dirhams I have a can of mango juice and two kebabs, one chicken, one unspecified. Both are shorn from rotating pillars of compressed meat by a perspiring man in a glass sentry box. The man weighs about as much as my dog. His arms are just bone within skin. His face is effectively a skull. I cannot guess at his nationality. He is just a tiny exemplum of *Homo sapiens*, a specimen. As I eat I try to imagine the story of his life and I come up with nothing.

I cross the Creek by *abra*, a pretty little put-put water taxi with a bare wooden bench, and after a bit of getting lost in Bur Dubai and not in the least minding, I find the museum and a myth. It's a pervasive myth, deliberately fostered by the heritage industry that has developed to please tourists, but it suits the ruling Arabs too. The myth is that before its recent transformation Dubai was nothing but a somnolent coastal Arab settlement. It wasn't. It was somnolent, coastal and a settlement, for sure, but it was by no means exclusively Arab. Because it's a port that owes its existence to trade, Dubai has always been to some degree cosmopolitan. Indeed you could argue that the difference between the Dubai of a hundred years ago and today's thrumming metropolis is a difference only of scale.

The museum has lots of worthy and, as far as I can tell, accurate displays of traditional Arab life. There's informative stuff on oases and date growing and palm frond shelters and camels and falconry and tough nomadic existence, most of which is being photographed with remarkable dedication by a party of Dutch tourists who step unhesitatingly over rope barriers to shove their lenses deep into a display of daggers.

There is also plentiful material on the pearling industry, which was Dubai's first and most major business. The gulf produced the best and biggest pearls in the world, which sustained the city from the mid-nineteenth century until the 1930s when the Japanese worked out how to grow cultured pearls that were bigger and better and cheaper. Dubai's pearling fleet was effectively scuppered.

What is clear, however, from a few ancient photographs is that the pearl divers were rarely Arab. Some were Indian. Most were African slaves. And once those divers had erupted back to the surface with their screaming lungs they handed their booty over not to Arabs but to Persian or Indian traders and middle men. Dubai was a port of many peoples. It is far from being a shameful truth but it is a truth that the museum makes no effort to highlight.

By 1880 Dubai was not the biggest town on the Gulf coast but it was the leading commercial port, a position it cemented a few years later when the sheikh of the time, an Al Maktoum of course, made it the Gulf's first free port. He abolished all tariffs and taxes and customs duties. It was a smart move, which attracted ships and merchants from all around the Gulf. And of course, it was also a small-scale version of the free zone policy that Varood explained to me. Today is just yesterday written in skyscrapers.

By establishing a free port the sheikh encouraged the trade

that I saw happening on my first morning at the dhow whar-fage. It is the re-export trade, the distribution business. Stuff comes to Dubai and then is despatched to all parts of the region. And once again this trade foreshadows what has followed: the vast incursion of corporate businesses that has transformed Dubai.

In the late nineteenth century there was a sizeable influx of Persian traders. Their presence was resented by some local Arabs but the sheikh welcomed them. He gave them land by the Creek and encouraged them to build and stay and, unlike today's ex-pats, they were allowed to become citizens. I have read that of Dubai's current population of approximately eighty thousand Emirati nationals roughly half are of Persian origin, but you won't see any reference to that in the press. Nor do I find any in the museum. Any Arab claim to racial purity is as false as any other claim to racial purity. Everyone everywhere's a mongrel.

Indians have been coming to Dubai for a long time too. By 1900 there were already fifty or so resident Indian families. By 1950 there were hundreds more. When India became independent in 1948 Nehru imposed import and export restrictions. They were a boon to Dubai, which became the centre of a lucrative smuggling business. Particularly vital was gold. Indians love gold and Dubai was only too keen to get it to them, taking a very nice cut for itself on the way. The people who did this trading were Indian and Dubai was happy to welcome them.

In sum then, Dubai wasn't a little Arab village that simply found oil and bloomed into a megalopolis overnight. It certainly bloomed, and oil gave that bloom its first impetus, but the seeds of the blooming had been planted a long time before.

Once the Dutch tourists have left to hoover the rest of Dubai into their cameras, I spend an agreeable couple of hours in the museum then emerge into the late afternoon and the thronged streets of Bur Dubai. Like Deira it is primarily Indian, though no doubt there are distinctions between the various Indian nation-alities that elude me. But here are the same narrow lanes and little markets and myriad enterprises and ad hoc games of cricket, that sense of a lived and busy city, that you don't find in the ex-pat estates or the gleaming malls. If I moved here, this is where I'd live.

And these non-Arab people who fill the streets are not con-struction workers. They are long-term residents. Much of Dubai may be Arab-owned but almost none of it is Arab.

Near dusk I cross the creek again, find myself back near the fish market and am drawn by an excited, amplified noise like a com-mentary on a particularly close football match. Any traveller is drawn by animation. I follow the noise to its source. It's Friday prayers.

Outside a mosque near the waterfront hundreds of pairs of sandals are piled and latecomers are still streaming in, removing shoes, heading to a washroom and then into the mosque proper. The men are Pakistani or African but not Emirati. And the sermon that I would love to go in and see being delivered is being amplified across the Deira littoral by a loudspeaker. The preacher is getting himself into quite a tizz. It sounds, frankly, like a declaration of war. No vicar ever sounded like this. I'd love to know what he's going on about, but it's unlikely to be especially contentious. The authorities here quietly keep an eye on the local preachers. They don't want anything too radical said to upset the sources of wealth.

9

Come Fly With Me

'Cosmopolitan,' says a huge sign in the headquarters of Emirates Airline. 'Empathetic, Progressive, Visionary, Ambitious.' The biggest print size, and it's very big indeed, is reserved for the word 'ambitious'.

The headquarters is just as one imagines a corporate head-quarters. It feels like the architectural equivalent of Samsonite luggage, the hygienic home of *homo executivus*. Everything in the reception area is sleek and magazinish: automatic doors and polished floors and glass walls and silent escalators and men on escalators in suits and women in clothes that aren't suits but that were bought to be worn in places like this. The floor is studded with islands of padded low-slung chairs for informal business chat. In the middle of it all the receptionists sit, exposed to the world, each with a phone and a computer screen and a work surface improbably free of clutter.

The receptionist, whose nationality I simply cannot guess at and am too daunted to ask, pages the man I've come to meet and then invites me to take an ergonomic seat. I feel obtrusive in my casual cotton clothes. Men in suits size me up with a single subconscious glance, and because of my clothes dismiss me.

A man storms into the building, shouting at his PA. He sounds American. I can't make out what has enraged him but from half a pace behind him the PA dances attendance, upset by his upsettedness, her trouser suit black and shimmering, her high heels clacking across the synthetic floor. The pair of them disappear up an escalator. She stands one step below him.

I follow shortly. My contact, Sam, a friend of a friend, can spare me half an hour. English, pudgy, charming, but with a suggestion of steel behind the pudgy charm, he leads me past Security, along the ice-clean corridors of a corporate world and instals us in a booth of a company coffee lounge.

From here we overlook the huge new air terminal, another bit of architectural show-offery, looking a little like a half-buried Zeppelin and rather more like a giant silver maggot. Plane after plane soars beyond the skirt of urban haze then swings onto its flight path, heading for almost anywhere on earth and glinting in the sun. The con-trails form slowly dissolving grids across the sky.

Sam points at the terminal. 'What does that look like to you?'

'Well, it's a bit like the top half of a Zeppelin.'

'The silver turd, we call it. Right, I gather you'd like to know a bit about Emirates.'

The crisp history he outlines is effectively a microcosm of Dubai's own recent history. It began, inevitably, with Sheikh Rashid. Seeking to do with air travel what he'd done with shipping, he ordered his third son, Sheikh Mohammed, the current ruler, to build the biggest airport in the region. And just as he had declared Dubai a free port, with equal access to all, so he declared the skies over Dubai to be open skies. Any airline could fly to Dubai. And any airline did. By the mid-Eighties over forty were doing so.

When the airport's biggest customer, Gulf Air, financed by Dubai's dear friends in Abu Dhabi, threatened to boycott Dubai unless they got preferential treatment, Sheikh Mohammed told them politely to stuff it. He then ordered the creation of Emirates. He provided the money for a couple of westerners to set it up, and he put his uncle in charge. In other words it was the proven Dubai mix of local money, commercial courage, foreign know-how and ruling family nepotism.

The new airline got no preferential treatment. Dubai stood for competition so Emirates must compete. In 1985, its first year of operation, it made a profit. And it has made a profit every year since. In 1992 it owned six aircraft. At the time of writing it owns a hundred and twenty-three. It flies over a hundred routes. It flies non-stop over the North Pole to San Francisco.

Sam offers me facts faster than I can write them down – the amount of laundry generated daily, the number of meals served, the effect of Emirates on the economy of anywhere it chooses to fly to. Emirates has always flown the best and newest planes. No Emirates passenger has ever died. Collectively the facts amount to one fact: Emirates has been a triumph, and a triumph that has played a massive part in the booming of Dubai. It has enabled trade. It has enabled tourism. It has flown the image-making flag. It has gained renown. It has made a lot of money.

Emirates' female cabin crew wear distinctive headgear, a hat with a tail of gauze that wraps under the chin. It's a nod to the Muslim veil, but only a nod. Few of those cabin crew are Muslim, even fewer Emirati. But the hat creates a distinctive, exotic and mildly Islamic image. Emirates, in other words, is Dubai on the wing.

Like all self-promoting businesses, Emirates aims for maximum exposure, to lodge its name and favourable associations in every consumer's skull. To this end it has sponsored Arsenal Football Club. No one seems to question why a London football club should play in a stadium named after an Arabian airline. Emirates' sponsorship of cricket umpires is more understandable. They will have noted of course that the television camera zooms in on the umpire at the moments of greatest dramatic tension, when the viewer is at his most vulnerable, but I have no doubt they will have also noted the symbolic fit. For just as umpires stand between two teams, so Dubai stands between two worlds, the Islamic and the Christian, and it cannot afford to upset either of them. Thus, by aligning itself with the impassive arbiters of a global sport, Emirates implies by subliminal association its own wise neutrality. If there's one thing Dubai is good at, it's marketing.

'Emirates has a head start,' says Sam, 'because people here travel. They do a dozen segments or more a year. That's huge. Emirates moves the people around who move the bucks around. And we bring the people here who've got the bucks.'

'Are those people still coming?'

He doesn't shy from the question. 'Bookings are softer than they've ever been. Profits for the last quarter are down eighty per cent. We've had people leaving cars in the car park with the keys in the ignition. They've been sacked and they've got a mortgage they can't afford, so they ditch everything and run. You can go to jail here for not paying debts. We towed one car away last week with a message on the windscreen in lipstick, "So long HSBC," it said, "and thanks for the memories."

'People can go as easily as they came,' he says. 'Almost everyone here is a bird of passage. They don't keep their money here because they don't intend to stay for ever. They export cash back to the UK or the States or wherever. Despite the image of stability, they don't quite trust Dubai. Dubai is fluid.'

'Will you stay?'

Sam pauses, then smiles. 'Ever heard of golden handcuffs?'

Sam is well paid. But the true value of his employment lies in the perks. He gets an accommodation allowance. His kids' school fees are paid. His whole family gets comprehensive medical insurance. And his visa is attached to his job. Were he to resign, that visa would be cancelled and he'd have a month to find another employer and another local sponsor or get out. 'Dubai likes to keep us dependent,' he says. 'It's their way of preventing a complete takeover of the city. They keep us dangling from the teat. And the milk supply can be cut off without warning.'

He hasn't bought a house here. He sees the whole real estate market is a speculative hell. 'If the Sheikh can cancel New Year's Eve, what can't he do? And did you know that most of the villas and apartments here weren't bought with mortgages? People paid cash, huge wads of cash; Russian cash, Indian cash, Iraqi cash. A lot of it was hot money that needed laundering. There's a lot of dubious stuff going on here as well as the official stuff, but Dubai's dynamic. I like that. It suits me.'

'Will you die here?'

'I have no plans to die,' he says, and smiles again. 'But in the unlikely event of it occurring, no, I doubt that it will be here.' And on that note, Sam returns to work, the handcuffs glinting.

On Sam's advice I go from Emirates HQ to Money HQ: the DIFC, or Dubai International Finance Centre. 'It'll give you some idea of Dubai's ambitions,' said Sam. The taxi I hail is drawing up when another veers across three lanes of traffic and pulls up at my feet to a fanfare of furious car horns. The driver leans across, opens the passenger door and beckons me with desperate urgency, as if summoning a doctor to attend his dying child. I get in. We pull back into the traffic in a manoeuvre that is if anything slightly more perilous than its predecessor. The driver turns out to be Afghani. I guess if you're brought up in Afghanistan, driving in a suicidal manner through the reckless traffic of Dubai seems like a quiet life.

The driver is transparently delighted to have stolen me from a rival. He is also rather less transparently loquacious in a language that I may as well call English. When I ask him whether he has ever had a crash, he takes thirty seconds or so to grasp the question. He spends those thirty seconds paying rapt attention to the movements of my lips, and none to the road. At the moment he cottons on to what I am asking he erupts with joy. He has a story to tell and nothing in the world could give him greater pleasure. Words prove inadequate to do this story justice. He throws in spectacular sound effects and frequent expansive double-handed gestures, during which the steering wheel is left to choose our route. I learn more from these paralinguistic features than from what he actually says.

As far as I can tell, he once hit a truck at high speed. His car flew like a bird (one of his few verbal successes), rolled end over end (he is very insistent with his gestures on this), came to rest on its roof (which he illustrates by ducking his head under the dashboard for several seconds, during which time he doesn't stop laughing) and then it caught fire. Or the truck did. Or both vehicles did.

When the police arrived he was standing uninjured on the road. They did not believe he had been driving the vehicle. 'Me very God bless man,' he says time and time again, clutching my forearm as he does so. 'Me very God bless man.' And he drives as though he means to prove the truth of the assertion.

I have rarely met anyone so unstoppably happy. Infectiously happy even. Nor anyone who trusts so utterly in his God. *Insh'allah* sums it up. The phrase translates more or less as 'what happens happens'. The man gives the impression of being a practising fatalist, as if he's renounced all responsibility for his fate, and by extension mine, because these things are decided above and we are powerless to interfere. Bernard Levin claimed never to have met a fatalist who didn't look twice before crossing the road. This man would have interested him.

'Me very God bless man,' he says for the umpteenth time as we pull up outside the DIFC, and then he makes a blatant attempt to overcharge me. When I point at the meter and hand him just over half what he asked for, 'You good man,' he says.

The DIFC, which is where Varood's private equity outfit does business, is next door to the twin Emirates Towers. They are very tall, very new, and reminiscent of electric toothbrushes with the brushes removed. On the lawn at their feet stand some fetching sculptures of ants.

A giant electronic ticker-tape announces: 'Lord Falconer, former Lord Chancellor of the UK, to give breakfast seminar at DIFC'. Steps on a fascist scale lead up to the Gate. It's a vast rectilinear arch of a building, a triumphal brute of a thing, four-square and imposing. I watch a pigeon repeatedly trying and failing to find a perch on its sheer and gleaming flank.

A very sweet Indian concierge tells me that unfortunately I can't get inside to have a look around but he does give me a glossy brochure. It's got a foreword by the ruler Sheikh Mohammed, who just happens to be the DIFC president.

According to Sheikh Mo, the aim of the DIFC is 'to create a financial marketplace to serve a region which extends across time zones between London and Hong Kong . . . a region encompassing the Middle East, North and East Africa, the Caspian and South Asia . . . with a GDP of 2.15 trillion dollars and a population of 2.2 billion.'

Moreover it plans to be the 'global hub for Islamic finance' and 'to establish global standards for Shari'a compliance'. In other words it means to settle once and for all the pesky business in the Koran about not lending money for profit.

Like the other free zone cities, DIFC isn't really part of Dubai. It has its own independent court system for settling disputes, using law based on international models. This puts its jurisdiction beyond the reach of Dubai's autocracy. If it didn't, the banks would never have come.

And how they've come. Every bank I've heard of seems to be

represented here, though what they actually do I can't tell you. These aren't the sort of banks where you open a cheque account. They are the movers of big money, whose bonuses infuriate the world and whose startling mixture of greed and stupidity almost decapitated capitalism.

The DIFC and its monumental buildings are expensively dotted with sculptures, including a high wire slung between two banks with mannequins balancing on it. It seems a tad more symbolic right now than was perhaps intended. The art's presence is explained by a nice paragraph in the brochure: 'DIFC', it says, 'supports a strong role for art in the community based on the belief that art can stimulate new ideas and perspectives in business.' This is accompanied by a photo of a chic young businessman sucking the earpiece of his spectacles while staring at a piece of abstract art and presumably arriving at a new perspective in business. But, then again, he could be wondering why anyone bothers to paint things when there is so much easy money to be made in banking. Or even that he ought to buy the painting to appease a little whisper of guilt.

DIFC is surrounded by restaurants for celebrating bonuses and pretentious clothes stores – what the brochure calls 'high-end retailing' – with their windows of sleek suits, artfully folded sweaters and prices that seem like a joke.

As dusk settles I amble a couple of streets away from high finance and find a little restaurant that supplies me with a whole fried hamour and more side dishes than the table can cope with for about half the price of an hors d'oeuvre at DIFC.

I'm outside afterwards, smoking and wondering how I might spend the evening, when a dumpy little man asks me for a light. He initiates a conversation, which makes a pleasant change. He wants to know who I am, where I'm from, what I'm doing here. His name is Andrew. He's a Catholic Pakistani, working for one of the large American investment banks.

'Is your office here in DIFC?'

'I'll show you. Come on.'

I follow him through alleys between tall buildings, then into the lobby of what seems to be an apartment block. He collects mail from the concierge. We enter a lift. It's clanky, dark.

'This is where you work?'

He smiles and says nothing.

It isn't where he works. It's where he lives. The apartment is tiny. He gestures me to sit on a two-seater sofa of soft blue leather. It's the only seat in the room.

'I'll fix you a drink,' he says. The walls of the living room-cum-kitchen are decorated with pictures of Ferraris, rural France and the Virgin Mary. He hands me a tumbler of what turns out to be vodka and orange juice with the normal proportions inverted.

'It's nice to relax,' he says, and sits down beside me. He's little more than five feet tall and his thighs are so plump that when he crosses his legs the top one sticks straight out. He takes off his glasses and lays them aside with prissy delicacy. He tells me he shares this flat with an English banker who has decided to become a clergyman. But he's away at theological college in England.

'I am lonely,' he says. Then, after a pause, 'Relax,' and he looks straight at me with brown, poorly focussed eyes.

In answer to my deliberately diversionary questions he tells me that it isn't easy being a Catholic in Pakistan. They are subject to prejudice, and there is much violence in the cities. But he doesn't think much of Dubai, either. He wants to go to Canada or London but he's been turned down for visas. He sighs.

A few seconds of this then he levers himself up with a small grunt of exertion and disappears into what would seem to be the only bedroom. He emerges moments later in a short blue satin dressing gown. He sits back down beside me and runs a finger gently along my forearm. 'Your hairs are golden,' he says.

'Look, Andrew, I'm sorry but . . .'

'Would you like a massage?'

He keeps me on the sofa by gripping my arm, presses me to have another drink, insists that his friend really is away at theological college. His dressing gown has opened above the waist sash. His belly juts like a hairy medicine ball. But he is soft and weak and peaceable, and when I finally detach his arm and stand, he gives up. He watches me go from the sofa.

'I'm sorry, Andrew,' I say, and I am. I close the door behind me and press the button for the lift. The apartment door stays shut. I can hear no noise from inside.

Back on the main road, where the ceaseless traffic gives no thought to lonely men, it doesn't take long to find a bar.

10

You Know It

You know the Burj al Arab hotel. You may not know its name but lodged in your skull is an image of it standing on the coastline of the Gulf, floodlit by night, or framed by day against a sky of the bluest blue. Its structure is for some reason memorable, as is, say, the giant pylon that's the Eiffel Tower, or the coxcomb roofline of the Sydney Opera House. Just like those two buildings, the Burj has become the best-known symbol of the city it stands in.

It is also common knowledge that the Burj al Arab is a seven-star hotel, the only seven-star hotel in the world. Greater luxury simply cannot be had. Less common knowledge, however, is how it came by its seven stars. It awarded them to itself. No hotel inspectors recommended them, no Michelin Guide awarded them, for the very good reason that the international rating system for hotels runs only to five stars. The proprietors of the Burj al Arab, who are effectively the ruling family, simply invented the sixth and seventh stars and then appropriated them for their own exclusive use. It was pure chutzpah. It was marketing as audacious as Napoleon's march on Moscow. But unlike Napoleon's march on Moscow, it's worked a treat. The fib has become fact.

The masterstroke, I suspect, was the choice of seven. Not only is seven a famously propitious number, with warm associations of luck and prosperity in almost every society, but it also isn't six. Granting themselves a mere six stars would have seemed like sticking a nervous nose into the air to see if it got bitten. Whereas going for seven was to leap from the burrow shouting, 'Hey, look at me.' If you're going to tell a lie, tell a whopper.

And the beast looks good, especially now, mid-morning, with the sun shining. The stretched frontispiece of the hotel does vaguely resemble what it is meant to resemble which is the filled sail of a dhow, an impression only slightly marred by the helipad sticking out from the top of the mast like half an oyster shell. I see no choppers buzzing around it, and I somehow doubt that it gets used all that much, but that doesn't matter. What matters is that it is there and obvious to all. It enshrines a notion, the notion of impossibly rich people, of Trumps and Tigers avoiding the foot-bound hordes of nonentities and coming in to roost here like birds. The sky is theirs and the Burj al Arab a tree for their exclusive nesting.

They advertised the completion of the helipad by having Federer and Agassi play tennis on it. I imagine they played circumspectly. I don't know who won the game and neither do I know whether they hit any balls over the edge. If they did they might have killed someone. But it wouldn't have mattered. From so far up there Andre and Roger wouldn't have heard the scream, and the body would have been whisked swiftly away and the relatives placated with wads.

The game was yet another instance of Dubai's mastery of marketing. The image of these two men playing against the sky arrested the senses. You could guarantee that no news service would ignore it. And its connotations were faultless. These were the best two players in the world and Dubai could afford them. Moreover tennis fits exactly with Dubai's branding. It's a global game, it's awash with money, its stars drip glamour, and it's constantly televised. The professional tennis circuit visits all the globally significant cities of the world, the rich cities, the cities that Dubai competes with and whose citizens it wishes to impress. And tennis itself has all the right connotations. It suggests opulence and leisure. A tennis court in a garden signifies a posh house, a place with real estate to spare. Moreover tennis is nice, in a way that football, for example, isn't. Football is for the mob, and the mob can get out of hand. Tennis fans don't get out of hand. Tennis is Wimbledon and restraint and umpires in tall chairs. There are no tennis hooligans.

The details of the Burj are predictably eye-widening. They were designed to be. We all love to read of needless indulgence. The Burj's atrium is plastered with gold leaf. A suite at the Burj comes with its own butler and a chauffeured Rolls Royce. The nightly rate for a suite is not published because if you need to know it you can't afford it.

When they switched on the air-conditioning for the first time to make the building habitable – air-conditioning that must continue to run for as long as the building stands – it caused clouds to form inside the atrium and a shower of rain to fall. The Burj has its own weather. Indeed, the Burj has its own everything. It stands on its own little island just off shore and it has its own access road. In short the Burj is both a literal and metaphorical totem of Dubai, a symbol of its identity as a place where money is revered and where it buys you unparalleled exclusivity. As a hotel the Burj apparently runs at a substantial loss, but as a creator of myth it must have made the city uncounted millions.

Because of the Burj's magnetic appeal, its access road, like so many roads in Dubai, is blocked by a barrier arm and a guard-house. The guardhouse is called the Welcome Centre, a phrase which is about as convincing as *arbeit macht frei*. On the poor people's side of the barrier there's a swarm of tourists, most of us white, pointing cameras at the top two thirds of the hotel which is all we can see. On the rich people's side of the barrier there stands a thickset African man in uniform.

I duck under the barrier arm and he stops me with a fat smile. Access to the Burj, he tells me, is by restaurant reservation only. Do I have such a reservation? He knows perfectly well that I don't. People with reservations don't duck under barrier arms.

I have a crack. I tell him that I've come all the way from New Zealand solely to marvel at the Burj al Arab. I tell him that I'm a writer and that what I will write about the Burj will bring it vast publicity and patronage from the Kiwi elite. I hint at the enormous influence of my friends. The African listens to rather more of this than I'd have expected and his smile broadens at every lie. I don't get in. I didn't expect to and I don't much mind. The Burj is less a thing than an idea.

I don't get into the Wild Wadi next door either but only because I choose not to. Wild Wadi's a water-themed fun park, guaranteed, as the brochure has it, 'to delight the young and the young at heart', which rules me out twice. It is also 'the perfect location for . . . special events such as team building, business functions and employee incentive schemes', which does nothing to enhance its charms.

A wadi is a valley in the mountains where they haven't heard of employee incentive schemes. Unlike the theme park, which has an unlimited supply of desalinated water, a wadi gets wet only a couple of times a year. But when it does get wet, when the fierce rains come and have nowhere to go in the harsh land-scape, a wadi becomes a torrent. It sweeps people and camels to a messy death. But not here. Through the wooden walls of Wild Wadi, which bizarrely resemble a stockade in a cowboy film, I

can hear the young at heart and incentivized employees squealing with delight.

All cities are to some degree divorced from the land they inhabit,
but Dubai goes a degree further. It could be on the moon. As
could its bus stops. They're dotted along Jumeirah Road and
I've never seen their like. They're air-conditioned. They stand
like reptile houses at the zoo, glass fronted, fully enclosed, and
trapping their customers, like exhibits, in artificially cooled air.

Jumeirah Road runs parallel to the beach and consists mainly
of clinics. The Sports Medicine Clinic, The Dubai Urology and
Nephrology Clinic, back clinics, cancer clinics, clinics for anything that might go wrong with your eyes, your liver, your
lungs, your anything. And clinics too for bits of you that haven't
gone wrong but that you just don't like very much. Here's the
British Lasik and Cosmetic Surgery Clinic, a hair removal clinic,
several clinics for stuffing or trimming breasts according to
whim, and a nose job shop. All are private, all expensive.

Pretty well all western ex-pats have medical insurance and
Emirati citizens are well looked after by the government. But
these two groups account for less than a third of the city's population. The rest of the people, the labourers and menials, the
bar staff and gardeners, the doormen and the maids, do all they
can not to get sick. The medical services available to them are
sketchy at best. Dubai is no welfare state.

The coastal strip known as Jumeirah was the original ex-pat
territory, and it's where a Dubai stereotype originated. She's
called Jumeirah Jane. The pampered wife of a corporate hubby,
she spends her days disposing of his tax-free dirhams, driving a
little yellow sports car, getting her hair done, accessorizing herself and the house, having a nip here, a tuck there, and perhaps
a silicone implant; and all in all leading a life of sunshine and
self-indulgence, the Sunday-supplement, fashion-mag dream.
She also tends to drink too much.

The Jumeirah Beach Hotel is another chunk of show-off architecture. Its imposing humped outline is supposed to resemble a wave. To me it resembles a hump. And I suspect I'm not alone because the public mind has never latched on to this building as it has the Burj. It is just another posh tourist hotel – and one that I can get into simply by walking through the front door.

The lobby is as plush and brightly lit and marble floored as you would expect, with coffee bars and restaurants and uni-formed servants. I could be anywhere from Houston to Hong Kong. A disregarded pianist plays John Denver's 'Country Roads'. It doesn't pay to take words seriously here.

Through the back of the lobby I emerge onto a terrace where the reasonably wealthy are taking coffee and looking bored. Halfway down a path that heads to the sea, a swarthy young man, the sort of character who might wear a leather jacket and drive a minicab in London, steps firmly in front of me. He wants to know, politely, whether I am a guest. I have no doubt that he already knows that I am not.

I don't bother to lie. He explains that the beach is exclusive to guests and that he's mortified by his inability to allow me access but is delighted to be able to inform me that just along the road there is a simply adorable beach with every possible attraction and amenity, and best of all it is open to riff-raff like me. All of which is communicated in English of course. You can live here twenty years and not learn a word of Arabic. Many ex-pats do precisely that. Does Dubai prefigure the global supremacy of English? I hope not, but in the very long run I expect so. Computers and business will probably see to it.

I'm glad it's not Tuesday. In a typical nod to Islamic propriety, Tuesday is 'ladies only' day at Jumeirah Beach Park. I pay a few dirhams, pass down a set of wooden steps and arrive on the sand to meet a scene that doesn't greatly surprise me. European women are splayed like starfish on towels or loungers. They bask in a way that few men can manage for more than five minutes. The women range in age from sixteen to eighty and their bikinis range from the merest smidgens of cloth, to the sort of reinforced and capacious all-in-one costume that can stand up on its own.

Youths with chest hair play volleyball loudly in order solely to draw the attention of the smaller bikinis. Kids build sand castles in the time-honoured manner, and the sea looks as gentle as a bath, though few people swim – perhaps because of the recent tides of sewage.

Dubai's sewage system has lagged far behind the construction boom. This city is a lady who pays more attention to her appearance than her bowels. Much of the human waste has to be collected from septic tanks and trucked out to a treatment plant in the desert. But the drivers claim that the queues at the plant are too long and that they are too poorly paid to wait. So they've taken to dumping it in the storm water drains, whence it flows unimpeded to the sea.

Regardless of the sewage it was to this beach that thirty-four-year-old Vince Acors, a British businessman, led his paramour, thirty-six-year-old Michelle Palmer, one sultry summer evening last July. They'd only just met but, encouraged perhaps by the day-long drinking binge they'd been on, they felt an irresistible chemistry. On the soft sands and amid the warm air, one thing led to the other, though there is some dispute as to the precise degree of the other. Mr Acors acknowledges intimacy but denies that full blown intercourse took place, perhaps because of the day-long drinking binge. Ms Palmer's version of events has not, as far as I am aware, been publicized. Anyway, they did enough to draw the attention of a passing constable and to upset him with their flagrant breach of Islamic propriety. He arrested them. They were sentenced to three months in jail. The British tabloids loved it. In the end the sex-on-the-beach couple were extradited. Sadly, however, their love did not go on to blossom.

The story is typically Dubai. If every breach of Islamic propriety earned a jail sentence, half the population would be
permanently banged up. That they aren't testifies to the fact
that Dubai is not an Islamic city. It depends for its wealth on
non-Muslims working in non-Muslim ways. And they bring
their way of life with them. But as the city fills with booze
and short skirts and gay bars the ruler still has to keep his
own people happy. And even more importantly he needs to
keep the rest of the UAE and the wider Islamic world happy.
It's a pretty balancing act. Hence the occasional much publi-
cised crackdown, such as the arrest of the sex-on-the-beachers
or a raid on a known gay bar. Hence the sudden surprising
gesture, such as the New Year's Eve party ban in support of
Gaza. Hence the hosting of conferences for Islamic scholars
and the granting of pardons to prisoners who have learned to
recite the Koran. Hence too the vast sums of money given by
Dubai to Lebanon and Palestine, or to earthquake relief in
Iran, or to the reconstruction of Kuwait after the first Gulf
War.

All of it is aimed at maintaining good relations with the
Muslim world as well as with the West. Dubai's livelihood and
its security depend on both. But playing a double game doesn't
come cheap.

There is no one shagging on Jumeirah beach right now. The
only intriguing sight is the Indians. They refuse to undress.
Families sit on picnic blankets as fully clothed as if in a park, and
the Indian boys, as frolicsome as boys of any race, go about in
jeans and t-shirts. And whenever someone brings out a camera
they endearingly try to sneak themselves into the shot.

A woman lies reading in the shade of a leaning palm. The
cover of the book carries the squirly font and the line drawing
that warns men against even opening it. I ask the woman if a
nearby recliner is free.

'Help yourself,' she says. 'Lovely day.' She lays the book

aside. She's from Nottingham, here on holiday with her family. Hubby has taken the kids to Wild Wadi.

I ask whether she has relatives here but no, they just came for a bit of winter sun.

'But why Dubai?' I say.

I'm genuinely curious. I find the place intriguing in a variety of ways, but it still seems to me a strange choice for a holiday.

'But it's perfect,' she exclaims and launches into a gentle paean to the place.

There's things for the kids to do and the weather's dependable and it's beautifully clean and the streets are safe and everyone speaks English and the service is excellent and there aren't any drunken thugs about and though it's got more expensive than it used to be the shopping is just wonderful. None of which I can argue with.

We chat a while on the beach and I warm to this woman. She would unhesitatingly lay down her life for any of her three kids, but they take it out of her, and this is her fortnight off, a rest and recharge for her and a respite from the grey monotony of Nottingham in winter.

'Just the sight of the sun cheers me up,' she says.

I ask if she'd be happy to live here.

She gives the question more thought that I expected. Perhaps the possibility has never occurred to her.

'It'd be a long way from family, wouldn't it?' she says eventually. 'But do you know, I think I would. It's the sun. I just love it.' She pauses. 'But Ken wouldn't dream of it. He'd miss the football.'

I enjoyed two letters in the paper this morning. The first was from a Peregrine Ansel-Wells. He wondered whether there was anyone in Dubai who would care to join him in forming a Morris Dancing Club.

The other was from a South African woman. She boasted that

she'd caught a bus. She described it as an 'adventure'. Unable to find a taxi she had gathered her courage, taken the plunge, and found it very refreshing. There was really nothing to be afraid of on the buses and she urged readers to follow her example, while subtextually also urging them to admire her audacity.

The people now waiting in the air-conditioned bus stop on Jumeirah Road do not look as though they are having an adventure. Predictably non-white, they wait as passively as any bus queue anywhere. The bus when it arrives is clean and cool and half full. The front half-dozen rows of seats are reserved for 'ladies'.

I take the bus as far as the turn-off to Safa Park where, according to a man I met in a bar, it is possible to watch Emirati ladies power-walking. When he told me this, immediately an image seized me, an image of veiled women in black abayas, swinging their arms in a western quest for the body beautiful, their white Adidas training shoes flashing beneath swishing cloth.

At the gate into the park an unsmiling dishdashed local behind a grille sells me an entry ticket for three dirhams. On the back of the ticket it says, 'Our Vision: To create an excellent city that provides the essence of success and comfort of living. Our Mission: Through the appropriate investment in our resources we are working to envision, plan, design, build and manage the municipal infrastructure and other related facilities and services.'

Which proves, if nothing else, that Dubai's got western corporate speak down pat, poor thing.

The park is a park, with kiddies' playground, ornamental lake, people strolling; a mob of Africans, who turn out to be a professional team from Cameroon, playing a pick-up game of football; maids with children; grass to lie on; birds to spy on; a garden for women only, and a general air of pleasant indolence. But the Emirati lady power-walkers, whose image enshrines something exact about this city, are nowhere to be seen.

11

RIP Sheikh

Sheikh Rashid bin Ahmed al Mualla, Supreme UAE Council member and Ruler of Umm al Quwain where the booze is cheap, is dead. He was born in a fort in 1932. He died last night in a London hospital. There are perks to being a ruler and one of them is Harley Street.

I never saw Sheikh Rashid bin Ahmed al Mualla in the flesh but from the official photos in the paper I'm frankly surprised he got to seventy-seven. The photos were presumably taken while he was still alive and were carefully selected to show him in the best possible light, but they depict a man standing hard on the brink of crossing that bourne from which no traveller returns. The sheikh has sallow skin, red-rimmed eyes with bags under them, more bags under the bags, and all up he has the appearance of a particularly gloomy bloodhound. A bloodhound, moreover, that has just woken after a hard night on the sauce, though this last comparison is of course unfair because, despite being the ruler of an Emirate that has made a profitable business out of flogging cheap booze to the rest of the UAE, Sheikh Rashid bin Ahmed al Mualla was a devout Muslim and therefore incorruptibly teetotal.

His official obituary is as revealing as all official obituaries: 'The character of Sheikh Rashid was a reflection of his father, Sheikh Ahmed, who was wise, just, modest and tolerant . . . He steered the affairs of Umm al Quwain with wisdom . . . through the building of several leading projects that contributed to pushing the wheel of life forward to match the development of the UAE.' From the looks of him he may have pushed the wheel of life forward in other more interesting ways, but *de mortuis nihil nisi bonum*. Rest his bones.

He is to be succeeded, to the astonishment of nobody, by his son Sheikh Saud bin Rashid al Mualla, who has ten sons of his own. His daughters, if he has any, and with ten sons it would seem likely, don't get a mention in the paper. Sheikh Saud is an enthusiastic angler.

I won't pretend to be upset by Sheikh Rashid's departure from this earth, but I do resent his timing. There is to be a week of official mourning throughout the UAE. Flags will fly at half mast, government offices and financial markets will be closed until Monday, radio stations are supposed to play dreary music, and I'm worried that the company from whom I've booked a rental car in order to have a pootle round the less well-known bits of the UAE – a trip that will, I hope, put glitzy Dubai into context – will take the opportunity to shut their doors and go on holiday for a bit.

But they haven't. In a forgettable first-floor office in a forgettable building off the unforgettable Sheikh Zayed Road, a tiny Filipina makes me sign the usual wad of papers packed with miniature print that both you and they know you won't bother to read, and that both you and they know absolves them of all legal and financial responsibility and heaps it onto you. She sends me off to find my car in the company of a squat and gloomy man with a clipboard.

I'm nervous. I am not a born driver, and traffic in Dubai is literally murderous. I have been told that, because of the extensiveness of their experience, the hospitals of UAE lead the world in the art of patching up the victims of crashes. I have repeatedly heard the sirens and I have seen the charred or concertina'd remains of numerous accidents. I have also read some remarkable and alarming reports in the papers. Alarming not just because of the frequency and near apocalyptic nature of the accidents, but also because of the way in which they are reported. Try this one for size from a recent paper. The headline alone is enough to arouse suspicion:

National and Pakistani die in road accident

... a collision occurred between two saloon cars and a truck and did not result in any human injuries. However, when the three vehicles stopped in the middle of the main road to examine the damages before reporting the collision to the police, the Pakistani truck driver walked to the collision site without paying attention to the heavy traffic on the road.

I interrupt at this point to ask whether you have any sense yet of who is going to cop the blame for this accident.

Using a phrase that banishes any lingering danger of journalistic neutrality, the report continues:

As a result, he was hit by a car driven by a UAE national, 20, who was surprised to see the victim in the middle of the road and could not avoid running him over. Moreover, because the UAE national was driving at a high speed he lost control of his vehicle and violently rammed into the victim's truck which was parked in the middle of the road.

It's an impressive piece of reportage. Who could fail to admire the stress on the nationality of the victims, the use of the passive 'was hit' to shift responsibility for the accident and, in particular, the journalist's knowledge that the Emirati was surprised? Only a few seconds later the man was dead, which would not, I'd have thought, have allowed him time to be interviewed on his state of mind.

And if by chance the Emirati had survived the accident, what risk do you think he would have run of being prosecuted for the truck driver's death? Precisely.

And these are the roads I'm about to drive on.

I've seen plenty of people driving like the dead man of the story. Indeed, in a taxi on my way here I saw a sports car miss its exit on a six-lane, nose-to-tail arterial highway. Rather than driving on to the next exit, the driver stopped and reversed a hundred metres. I won't deny being impressed at the time, not only by the man's astonishing disregard of everything except his own needs, but also by the skill of the rest of the traffic in avoiding him. But I am not a skilful driver and I'm about to share unfamiliar roads with such drivers in an unfamiliar left-hand drive vehicle.

The man with the clipboard says nothing until I've signed a document acknowledging that the vehicle has been delivered to me free of dents and scratches and that should I return it with any they will amputate my limbs pro rata, whereupon he looks up from his clipboard, hands me the keys and says, with apparent sincerity, 'Good luck.'

'Thanks,' I say, and I turn on the engine, adjust the mirrors, flick the indicator switch and find that it works the windscreen wipers.

It takes me a while to find a way of getting onto Sheikh Zayed Road and when I do I wish I hadn't. It's as if I've been seized by a rip tide. I am obliged to travel faster than I wish and numerous drivers encourage me with their horns to go faster still. I feel tension building in my neck, and the distant hint of an urge to vomit.

Dubai's traffic and its road system have grown exponentially over recent years, and the department that erects road signs has not kept up. I begin by looking for signs to Hatta, a township in the mountains to the east. Then I resolve to follow any sign suggesting an easterly direction. Then I just take the nearest off ramp, taking care to indicate my intention by turning on the windscreen wipers.

The drivers of Dubai are reluctant to stop. The city has accommodated that reluctance by building huge clover-leaf junctions. These are counter-intuitive: in order to get onto a road travelling in a particular direction you invariably have to take a wide swinging exit that appears to head in the opposite direction.

In the hope of heading east I point the nose of my little Nissan towards the mid-morning sun. The road promptly swings me through a hundred and eighty degrees and I find I am heading away from the sun rather than towards it, and towards downtown Dubai rather than away from it. I am heading, it turns out, for Jumeirah. The traffic is unrelenting. I can see no way of turning round, I'm in a middle lane and I'm not happy. Taking the path of least resistance, I just keep driving, waiting to become more familiar with the car, urging myself to come off the boil – which of course keeps me nicely on it – and hoping, hopelessly, that the road will eventually lead to a roundabout. I know where I am with roundabouts.

It doesn't. It takes me to the coast and then straight onto the massive trunk of Palm Jumeirah, reputedly home to Lindsey Lohan, David Beckham's sainted mum, and other Middle Eastern luminaries. Consoling myself with the thought that I'd intended to visit the Palm at some stage, I just keep going.

The base of the trunk is lined with palatial apartment blocks.

A few hundred yards out to sea the fronds start, each one consisting of a single road, inevitably blocked by a barrier arm and a guard in a hut, and flanked by flashy villas. Every villa backs onto its private sliver of beach and what looks like stagnant sea.

Near the top of the tree the multiple-laned highway takes a flip through a tunnel and then right and then, suddenly, framed in the windscreen, there's the fabled wonder of the Atlantis Hotel. It looks like a princess's castle in a Disney cartoon, all turrets and titivation, with a veneer of Arab motifs and an arch through the middle in the form of a keyhole. Kitsch would sum it up nicely. The place has only been operating a few months, having been opened with a famous party to which the great and the good came flocking from all over the world in their private jets. They got a concert by Kylie Minogue, complete with pert bum and cancer recovery story. She got five million bucks.

More recently the place has been in the news for a whale shark. The beast was caught by a local fishing boat, whereupon Atlantis management offered to look after it. Looking after it meant putting it on display in their aquarium. Despite it being an endangered species they've shown no inclination to let it go. Rumours abound that the beast was captured to order. The animal rights people are distinctly unhappy. No one has asked how the whale shark feels about it.

I'd quite like to have a look at it, but having already spent the best part of an hour on the road and succeeded only in plunging deeper into the shallow heart of Dubai, I feel that I'd better keep going. I follow the road in a big circle and return down the trunk of the Palm the way I came, heading more or less, at last and hallelujah, east.

I keep thinking I've escaped Dubai only to come upon more of it. It sprawls haphazardly into the desert, with open highway suddenly shrinking to roadworks and seething Indian crowds. I stop at a supermarket for water and bananas, which cost me half what I'd pay in the city proper, and to rub my aching neck. The air is tangy with exhaust and blown dust and urban rawness. A group of young Indians lounge outside the supermarket smoking. They study me with some interest. This is not white man country. Nor is it Arab country. Nor, emphatically, is it the Dubai of the tourist brochures and the carefully cultivated image.

'Can anyone tell me the way to Hatta?'

It proves a provocative question. The Indians discuss it merrily among themselves and reach a consensus that none of them has heard of Hatta. But they do so with great good humour.

I drive on, navigating by the sun, and suddenly Dubai is behind me. All around me is desert: desert with the sort of dunes I want desert to have, stretching evocatively away to the horizon like frozen ripples in tangerine ice-cream. And here too are camels loping beside the highway, ranging in colour from light straw to the grey of a photographic negative. They sway and plod on colossal feet, their faces set in an impassive sneer as if wearily conscious of their own bizarre construction. And they are simply terrible pedestrians. They lumber along beside the road until suddenly, collectively, they decide that the sand is browner on the other side. Twice I have to stop at short notice to let them pass by the bonnet. They don't even look at me.

I have been told that they like to sleep on the road for the warmth and that should you run into one its owner will appear from the dunes within seconds and let you know that the one you hit was renowned for its beauty, a winner of numerous races and a long-time favourite of the local sheikh, and that you are in debt to the tune of your life savings. Though I suspect that if my little suburban Nissan did run full tilt into a sleeping camel, the camel would be bruised, the Nissan would be bound for the wrecker's and I would have no further need of my life savings.

This is the sort of land that Thesiger crossed and made several books out of, but I have no wish to trudge into it. It is barren and forbidding. To look at it makes you thirsty. But any sense of isolation is destroyed every few miles by an outcrop of garish villas or a sand-buggy park or a parade of shops catering for motorists. I stop at one such where I buy a cup of coffee for very little but still more than its taste deserves. Looking for a drain to tip it into, I tour the half-dozen clothing and souvenir shops, all Indian-run. Against the steps leading up to each shop a little bank of wind-blown sand has gathered. Leave the steps unswept for a week and they would disappear. Leave them unswept for a year and the next person to visit would be an archaeologist.

My arrival galvanizes the shopkeepers. They urge me in, each Indian holding up for my western eyes the agreed symbols of an Arabian heritage. 'Coffee pot, sir? Camel, sir? Look, sir, model of Burj.' One folds a red and white Arab headscarf and, despite my weak protestations, loops and ties it around my baldness, then leads me by the arm to a mirror from which he removes a fake tiger skin the better for me to survey the transformation in my appearance. I see a white man in late middle age wearing an Arab headscarf, at his shoulder an eager Indian shopkeeper. I giggle. The shopkeeper is delighted. 'You like, sir, oh you like very much.' He is so eager, so cheery at the thought of money, in this strange little excrudescence of commerce amid barren sands, that I say yes, I like it very much indeed and I will buy it.

Whoa. Deep into the shop he plunges and hauls out item after item, a dishdash, an ornamental dagger, a camel doll, an authentic camel stick that is hard to distinguish from any other sort of stick, a . . .

'No, no,' I say, 'just the scarf.'

He charges me far too much for it. But I am English and

middle class and therefore congenitally incapable of haggling. It is such an unseemly and honest display of self-interest that I prefer to be ripped off.

'Keep Hatta Green', says a sign by the road. It's a poor choice of verb. There's no green to keep. The township squats amid the Hajar mountains that stand stark and naked of vegetation, tawny-red, and looking from a distance as if they would slice the flesh from your feet. Parking in front of a substantial mosque, I step out into midday silence. I am perhaps fifty miles from non-stop Dubai. It feels a lot more.

For all I know Hatta may have been settled for thousands of years, but the only obvious relic is a crudely circular watch-tower standing high above the township from which an eye could be kept on the pass. The houses are mainly cubes of contemporary concrete block with satellite dishes on the roof. They are almost windowless, with walls of thumping thickness painted white, and white only. They look to have been built to withstand heat. And even now, under a hazy winter sun, the place thrums with warmth, collects it in its valley, holds it.

A baker, a vet, an abattoir, a laundry, dim little shops selling household oddments – all of them closed, deserted and silent. Even the 4WDs are asleep.

The only place to stay seems to be the Fort Hotel. It has the obligatory barrier arm and the first human being I've seen in Hatta. He steps out from his little hut to quiz me, sees my white face, switches on a smile, says 'Good afternoon, sir' and raises the barrier arm. A sign by the driveway offers lessons in archery. And here amid the barren Hajar mountains, the hotel plugs the service with the line, 'Want to be Robin Hood?' This is an occupied land.

The Filipina receptionist tells me that they have an exciting special on rooms. I can spend the night and have breakfast for only twelve hundred dirhams.

'Thank you so much,' I say, and drive on into the mountains in the direction of Fujairah, the one major city in the emirate of, astonishingly, Fujairah.

The sweeping highway scoffs at the hostile landscape and the little Nissan sings along. I have to slow only when I fetch up behind a truckload of camels. There's little traffic and I could easily overtake but I choose to follow the camels for miles, engrossed by the sight of these strange creatures crammed together, their heads and necks showing above the truck sides like the heads and necks of ancient sea monsters, swaying with the truck like seaweed. When I eventually overtake they follow my passage with cud-chewing indifference.

On my right, in nowhere and for no apparent reason, there looms a building advertising cheap insurance. A little further on a whole office block, sprouting all alone in rock-strewn terrain, is also devoted to insurance. Then comes a barrier. I slow down but am waved through by a man in uniform. A few hundred yards after that I reach another barrier at which stands another man in uniform. This one does require me to stop. He is standing beneath a sign saying 'Welcome to Oman'.

'Passport,' says the man.

'I don't want to go to Oman,' I say.

'Passport,' says the man.

I give him my passport. He looks at it and hands it back.

He walks round the back of the Nissan, bangs on the boot and says 'open'.

I open the boot.

I hear him unzip my rucksack and rummage. He moves to the front of the car with the slow and menacing smugness that officials enjoy, and taps the bonnet. I open it. I doubt that he's seriously looking for contraband or bombs. He's just relishing the power that his position and uniform confer. He is indistinguishable in manner from, say, a parking attendant in Walsall. Which comes first, the uniform or the attitude? Is there a type of man who gravitates to jobs like these? Or would most of us turn out like this if we were given the accoutrements of petty power?

'Car,' he says, and holds out his hand, presumably for insurance papers available back up the road.

'I don't want to go to Oman,' I say again. 'I want to go to Fujairah.'

'Paper,' he says.

'It's a rental car.'

'Paper.'

'Rental car, hire car.' He does not understand. Neither does he smile. He is wearing, inevitably, a gun.

'You go,' he says, pointing at an official-looking building over to one side. 'Car here,' and he indicates a parking bay. I drive the car there and sit a minute. I must have missed the turning to Fujairah, probably while engrossed by the camels.

A part of me is tempted to go along with serendipity and pay a quick visit to Oman. I know less than nothing about the place. But I am daunted by the rigmarole of getting the right papers, I don't want to deal with uniformed officialdom, and I'm uncertain whether the conditions of my car rental allow me to cross the border.

The camels have reached the barrier behind me. The petty tyrant is talking to their driver. Will he insist on fossicking among the beasts in the back? If so, I hope they hoof him. Then spit.

A couple of cars come up the road from Oman. The barrier on their side of the road seems permanently raised. I start the Nissan, perform a swift u-turn and swing in behind them, hunching as I do so to avoid the gunshots. None come. In the rear-view mirror I see the border guard standing hands on hips. Wrongly but irresistibly I raise him a couple of fingers of farewell.

A few hundred yards further on I have to stop to re-enter the UAE. The cars ahead of me are swiftly processed and waved on.

'Papers,' says an Indian man in a box. I hand him my pass-port. He riffles through it, then riffles through it again.

'Oman visa?' he says.

'Well now,' I say, doing my best to smile, 'I haven't actually been to Oman. I have come from the UAE.'

The man looks at me in exactly the way I would look at him if the situation were reversed. Then he says exactly what I would say.

'You are coming from Oman.'

'Well, yes, but actually I am coming from the UAE. I turned round, you see, at the border.' I say it without much hope.

The man smiles. In my experience, a smile from a man in uni-form can be a very good thing or a very bad thing but nothing much in between.

'So you are coming from Oman but you are not coming from Oman.'

'You've got it,' I say. He pauses.

'Then welcome to the UAE,' he says, beaming like the sun, and up goes the barrier arm. Quite what such a pleasant and cheerful man is doing in such a job, I can't explain. But it's nice at the age of fifty-one to have one's preconceptions overturned.

The turn off to Fujairah proves to be a few miles back. The road swings up and through narrow valleys of gaunt rock, dotted with shaggy, flop-eared goats. The goats have better road sense than camels.

The afternoon sun lights the rock crimson, purple, or brown as chocolate. It's harsh but lovely. Again in places there sprout inexplicable crops of modern buildings, their purposes unclear. I cross several wadis, all as dry as everything else, but with warning signs of their potential to flood. The road is glistening new and quite deserted. It's good to be moving. I sing. The songs prompt memories. Music's good for that, as evocative of memory as the sense of smell. I wallow in distant times and places and then suddenly I notice that the bonnet of the Nissan is tilting down and I sweep round a long wide bend and there's the coastal plain and I behold the Gulf of Oman with the Indian Ocean beyond it. From this distance it looks not hugely dissimilar to any other stretch of sea, but I feel a mild geographical thrill. What's more, I've crossed an entire country in a day. Indeed, if I hadn't got lost and stopped at an assortment of places to pootle around or tangle with uniforms, I reckon I could have done the whole journey from west coast to east in ninety minutes or less. The United Arab Emirates is not big.

Nor's Fujairah. Indeed after the heaving sprawling edgeless metropolis of Dubai it's agreeably human in scale. So agreeably human in fact, that I find that I've driven right through it in a few minutes and am emerging on the road north. I swing into the Fujairah Beach Motel. On its veranda stand two leather sofas in startling pink. At reception an Indian in an old-fashioned dentist's jacket is shouting fiercely down the phone in what I think is Hindi. His fury is impressive. When he slams the receiver back into its cradle the fury does not abate.

'Yes,' he shouts at me.

I smile to help him off the boil, to bring him down to the standard employee-meets-customer mode. It seems to annoy him further. He rents me a room as if I were a multiple axe-murderer.

For three hundred and thirty dirhams I get a big ugly room with stained tiles on the floor, a puddle in the bathroom lying just to one side of the grille that is supposed to drain it, a synthetic zebra skin blanket, joinery of Stone Age crudity, and high on the wall above the bed a vast and clattering air-conditioning unit, alongside its vaster and presumably even more clattering predecessor which has been left in situ after disconnection by a pair of wire cutters. The snipped wires dangle. And I feel infinitely more at home here than in any five-star swishness. This place sings with the sweet sadness of the gulf between aspiration and achievement. It feels human.

The walk into town takes me past acres of construction sites, not on the scale of those in Dubai but with the same sense of modernizing ambition. Apartment blocks are rising, their crude slab skeletons exposed to inspection. It is good to be on foot once more. You see little from a car. In the Nissan I would not get the delicious sense of dusk that I have now, the sun dropping below the Hajar mountains and silhouetting them like the teeth on a shark, and the sky shifting by imperceptible gradations through pink, violet, grey. The minarets of a half a dozen mosques become visible, lit with the sort of neon blue lights that kill flies in butchers' shops. And the muezzin sounds, a wail of tragic commitment that has been discreetly banned in some parts of Dubai for fear of distressing the ex-pats.

Past a floodlit fort on a mound, and I'm in the higgledy-piggledy heart of Fujairah on a mission to eat something. It is not a hard mission to fulfil. The place abounds in little restaurants. The one I choose is fronted by a Pakistani man of tartarean gloom. He hands me a laminated one-page menu, sticky and stained. I ask if he can serve me a beer. He shakes his head. I choose a dish. He shakes his head. I choose another. He shakes his head. I ask what he recommends. He shrugs. I asks what he's got available. He shouts something to the kitchen out the back. From behind a plastic curtain a voice shouts a couple of syllables.

'Chicken biryani,' he says, and takes my menu. The biryani arrives in seconds, along with a bowl of yoghurt and another bowl of what looks like distressed paint. It is delivered by a man old enough to be the waiter's father.

'My father,' says the waiter.

I tell the father that I am pleased to meet him and he gravely shakes my hand in both of his, says nothing and disappears back behind the curtain. His son picks his teeth and watches me eat.

Chicken biryani consists of coloured rice and the bits that remain after a chicken has been eaten. The yoghurt's nice but I can't bring myself to dip into the paint. When I've reduced the food to more or less what it started as minus rice, the waiter asks me where I'm from.

'New Zealand.'

'You have passport?'

'I have passport,' and I extract it from the knee pocket of my trousers. He is magnetically drawn to it. He puts out a hand. I give him the passport. He handles it as one might a religious relic. He looks carefully through the pages, studies my various visas, looks from the identification photo to me and then back to the photo.

'How I get job in New Zealand? You get me visa?'

I explain that it isn't quite as simple as that.

'Business bad here. Very bad,' and he goes on to tell me, as rather a lot of people seem to do, the story of his life. I don't mind.

He runs this restaurant with his father and brothers. It doesn't make much money. The majority of workers in Fujairah are Bangladeshi and they don't like Pakistani food. Races stay separate here. No Arabs ever dine at his restaurant. And it's too hot in summer. There is much better weather in South Africa.

'You've been to South Africa?'

'I work in cell phone shop. Beautiful weather and much freedom. But too much crime. No can live there with family. Here very safe with family. No crime. But too strict. And business no good. In South Africa they come into shop with guns.'

'Did that happen to you? Did they come into your shop with guns?'

'My shop next to police station.' And he smiles for the first time. He is a chunky swarthy man, chest hair sprouting densely through the throat of his polo shirt and ceasing only at the arbitrary point where he chooses to start shaving.

The man hands me back my passport as if giving up a child to adoption.

'How much do I owe you?'

'You are very good man,' he says, and indicates that the meal is free, thereby demonstrating once again the old truth that people think you're a nice guy if you let them do the talking.

Central Fujairah is pleasantly peopled, with shops still open at eight in the evening, but I feel drained from the day's driving and hail a taxi. The driver has a beard that could house an aviary.

'Fujairah Beach Motel,' I say.

'You want whisky shop?'

'No no, Fujairah Beach Motel.'

'You want whisky shop?'

Where was it that I read that strange travel suggestions are God's invitation to dance?

'Yes,' I say. 'I want whisky shop.' And I sit back to see where he takes me.

He takes me to the Fujairah Beach Motel. But having driven in through the gates he takes me past the lobby, past the barrack-like building in which I've got a room, round a couple of corners and then stops by a row of rubbish bins.

'Whisky shop,' he says.

'Where?'

He gestures into the darkness beyond the bins. Curiosity very much aroused, I nose down a covered alley and catch a glimpse, before she slams the door, of a woman washing her feet in a laundry sink, her blue dress of cotton hitched around her waist. I pass through a hallway lined with broken furniture, swing to the right and discover that God's dance invitation is a bar.

As I enter everyone turns to assess me. Their heads move like the heads of cattle.

'Good evening,' I say.

'Good evening, sir,' says the cheery Indian barman. None of the other drinkers greets me. They sink back down to their beers. There are six of them, four Emiratis in their blinding dish-dashes, and a couple of what turn out to be Russians.

Without trying, this bar has matured to a closer approxima-tion of what I think of as a pub than any place that does try. Stuff has simply accreted. A mirror advertising Allied Breweries Double Diamond Beer, which I doubt they make any more, has stayed where it was affixed I can't guess how many years ago and been so regularly polished that the lettering is wearing off. The top shelf holds spirits bottles that look untouched in decades: Canadian Club, Ricard, and a bottle of Pimm's with an inch remaining. On what occasion was the rest of this bottle, this English summer drink of Wimbledon and frocks, ordered and drunk, here on the Gulf of Oman? Who last said, and in what accent, 'I think I'll have a Ricard'?

The ceiling's low, as it should be, and kippered by smoke. A little stage has chairs stacked on it and microphone stands with-out mikes. The plastic ashtrays have burn marks on their rims and the bar itself, thick, wooden and darkened with age, is as sticky as one could wish. When I shift my elbows they make a noise like tearing paper.

I order beer, receive beer and peanuts, and wait to meld into the place, to become a part of the accepted gathering. The Emiratis drink Scotch and grumble in Arabic. The Russians sound bitter. It is partly the language, all spits and gutturals, conjuring images for me of grim apartment blocks and dirty snow and short fat babushkas in headscarves cooking cabbage. At school, unthinkably long ago, I studied Russian for long enough to hold a reasonable conversation. Now I can make out only odd words, including several times, to my great surprise, the Russian for bicycle. In the last few weeks I've hardly seen one.

No one invites me to join them, but I don't much mind. I like it here. I like the sense of absurdity, sitting in an Indian-run bar alongside Scotch-drinking Muslims and wondering what induced these gloomy Russians to come to this place of all the places in the world. I may have left Dubai but it seems I have not left the world of immigrant hope.

I chat briefly with the barman, who is so deferential that he repeatedly echoes whatever I say. No amount of prompting can get him to say anything remotely interesting, but he does name, in batting order, the entire current New Zealand cricket eleven.

12

Where's the Dugong?

I've never seen a dugong. I'd like to see a dugong. Which is why I've driven south from Fujairah to this shallow lagoon. Dugongs are supposed to frolic here.

The dugong is as odd as its name. With the tail of a dolphin, the flippers of a seal, and a snout designed to graze on sea grass, it looks committee-designed, the marine equivalent of the camel.

According to a desperately thin list of local attractions I picked up at the motel, this playground for the dugong is also the most northerly mangrove swamp on the planet. A few loose camels are chewing at its northernmost edge, fractionally reducing its geographical significance. But though I sit by the muddy water a while and marvel at the quite prodigious quantity of litter floating in it, I see no dugongs.

Back up the coast a few miles I stop at a little fishing wharf where not a lot is happening. A few men are mending nets. A couple of old wooden dhows have been hauled onto the beach, but the fishing vessels are made of sleeker modern materials, little more than enlarged canoes piled high with nets and fish traps. Pick-up trucks that, unlike in Dubai, look as though they do actually pick things up, are parked haphazardly on the gravel, and the men who drive them have gathered at the Al Tizkar Restaurant across the road.

'O Allah,' says a fading poster in English on the wall of the restaurant, 'I repent before you of my sins and I shall never return to them.' Beneath it another poster advertises crumbed fish fillets.

The restaurant is thick with flies, the small silent flies that seem ubiquitous in these parts. They are impressively unswattable. A tiny tickle of irritation tells you that one has perched on a hair of your forearm, but the fly is telepathic and takes off not when you make to swat it but at the instant you *think* of making to swat it. The restaurant offers cakes for sale, shielded from the flies by plastic bags, and cans of Mountain Dew and toothbrushes and bars of soap, but like every other patron I buy only a cup of sweet tea and, like every other patron, I take it outside to drink under a straggly tree that seethes with noisy sparrows. They sound like warring mice. My table is crusted with sparrow shit.

A knot of Arab men at an adjacent table discuss the matters of the day with a ferocity that is alarming to my English sensibilities. One man in a grey robe repeatedly removes a sandal and bangs it against his chair for rhetorical effect. He sounds as though he wants to start a blood-soaked revolution. No one seems remotely alarmed. And seconds later he is smiling.

When anyone joins or leaves the group there's a muttered, unconsidered exchange – *salaam aleekum aleekum salaam* – and for the first time in the weeks that I've been in this country I feel that I am in Arabia. Few of the men are wearing the white dishdashes of Dubai. Their robes range from grey to olive. Some go bareheaded. But why are none of them doing any work?

Perhaps that's all being done by women. There are no women here. Not one.

When I get up to leave, the sandal-banger eyes me and mutters *Salaam aleekum* as if by reflex. '*Aleekum salaam*,' I reply and get a general nod of acknowledgement, which is frankly about as far as I have managed to pierce Arab culture to date.

Hidden around the corner at a palpably inferior table a bunch of Indian youths are playing dominoes with quiet chatter. When I stop to watch them they smile nervously up at me with huge teeth in tiny heads. And they fall silent. I smile. They continue to smile. I move on. They start chattering again.

The township of Kalba, though next door to Fujairah, does not belong to the emirate of Fujairah. It is part of Sharjah, the emirate on the other side of the mountains. In consequence Kalba is dry, but it is only mid-morning so I try not to let that bother me.

The reason Kalba belongs to Sharjah illustrates nicely the British influence in these parts. Kalba had been taken over by the Sharjah branch of the Qawasim, the tribe that dominated the west coast. But by the early twentieth century the rulers of Kalba felt separate from Sharjah and repeatedly asked the British Resident to acknowledge Kalba as an independent sheikhdom. The British Resident said no and no again. But then, in the 1930s, the British decided they needed an air base on the east coast, so they offered Kalba the independent status it craved. Kalba's rulers accepted cheerfully and signed a truce similar to the ones signed by other regional sheikhs. Such an agreement would, as usual, keep them in power because of the backing of the Brits, and provide them with new ways to get rich.

After the Second World War, however, things changed again. The British were feeling the financial pinch and could no longer afford to look after so many client states. Moreover, planes had acquired greater fuel capacity and range which meant there was no longer any need for an air base on the east coast. So in 1951, when there was a coup in Kalba and a new ruler took control, the Brits simply declared him an outlaw, had him exiled to Saudi Arabia, welched on the trucial agreement, and gave Kalba back to Sharjah in whose possession it reluctantly remains. Albion, in other words, at its most splendidly perfidious.

Kalba consists of an unprepossessing coastal strip dotted with thumping great mosques. Their minarets resemble elaborately carved pencils. The main drag is lined with all the standard little Indian-run businesses, including an inordinate number of barbers and perfume shops. I guess that grooming is one way to pass a drinkless evening.

Kalba seems an unlikely place to find a restaurant called Rehab Cafeteria. But there it is and in I go for breakfast. And I'm an immediate hit with the other customers, namely Saeed, Ali and Mohammed, all of whom are about eight years old, two of whom are chubby little Arab boys, and the last of whom, Mohammed, a clown with eyes as brown as a dog's eyes and the size of ping-pong balls, is a skinny Pakistani. When I come through the door the three of them stare at me as I might have stared at a dugong earlier this morning, though I would not have said to the dugong in a single breathless unpunctuated sentence, 'Hello how are you what his name?' and then burst into giggles. Or at least not without giving the dugong the chance to answer. But they prove to be lively funny kids, who are fascinated by the New Zealand money that I show them from my wallet and by my New Zealand passport and by the freckles on my forearm. It's always good to be a novelty item and I am in a fine mood as I head back up the road to Fujairah, my belly fuelled by Rehab cakes and tea.

Fujairah specializes in roundabouts. As you approach one a speed bump obliges you to slow. Generally there's a road sign to alert you to the presence of the speed bump, but sometimes, just for the fun of it, there isn't. These speed bumps are serious things. Take one at thirty kilometres an hour and you think the underside of the car has been wrecked. Take it at fifty and it probably has.

But the agreeable consequence of the speed bumps is that they give you time to enjoy the roundabouts. For these are no mere traffic devices. They are cultural installations. One features a colossal coffee pot of the traditional toucan-bill design surrounded by cups. Another depicts a giant hand like the one that rose from the lake to seize Excalibur, only this hand is emerging from some ornamental shrubs to grasp a perfume bottle. A third depicts an eagle landing, its wings vertical, its talons spread and the look in its eye suggesting that it's just caught its rump on barbed wire. All of which is an attempt to brand and theme, and is neither more nor less risible than the efforts of other places that hope to gorge on the tourist dollar. In Ohakune in New Zealand we've got a giant fibreglass carrot.

Fujairah has a fine old fort. And on this particular day the number of tourists flocking to it amount to one, me. The original fort was built in the seventeenth century by the local sheikh. For a couple of hundred years it was the only stone building in these parts and a very potent asset it must have been. For, like the whole of the region back then, this was tribal land and feuds were not so much common as a way of life. Power was generally gained by a coup and lost the same way. Few rulers died quietly in their beds.

The fort stood more or less intact until 1925 when the Royal Navy shelled it into submission. The reason was political. Because the main shipping routes were on the other side of the mountains, the British did not consider Fujairah to be of great importance. Indeed Britain had more or less arbitrarily decreed that Fujairah, like Kalba, was part of Sharjah. Just as with Kalba this rankled. And just as with Kalba, the sheikh of Fujairah, one Sheikh Abdullah, repeatedly petitioned for independent status. And just as with Kalba, the British Resident said no. And there the matter rested until 1925 when it suddenly turned nasty.

A woman in Sharjah complained that her daughter had been abducted and sold to Sheikh Abdullah. The British Resident upheld the complaint and told the Sheikh of Sharjah to tell Abdullah to return the girl. The Sheikh of Sharjah obeyed the British but Abdullah didn't obey the Sheikh of Sharjah. So the British sent a gunboat round the tip of the rhino's horn to make the point more emphatically. On the morning of April 20th, the British bombarded the fort for ninety minutes, destroying three quarters of it. Sheikh Abdullah gave the girl back and paid a fine.

In 1952, however, Fujairah did get its longed-for independence from Sharjah. The reason was oil. One of the conditions of all truces signed with the British was that matters concerning oil exploration had to go through the British Resident, which inevitably led to contracts with British oil companies. In the early Fifties, however, the American oil companies came sniffing and, because Fujairah had no truce with the Brits, it welcomed the Americans.

'Hold on a minute,' said the British Resident to the leaders of Fujairah, 'how about we offer you one of our lovely trucial arrangements that have made your fellow sheikhs in other regions terribly rich? Can't imagine how we didn't get round to it before.'

'Oh thank you very much,' said Sheikh Muhammad of Fujairah, and so it came to pass that Fujairah gained the independence from Sharjah that it craved. Sadly, no significant quantities of oil were found.

And now Fujairah's rebuilding its fort, not to repel foreign invaders but to attract them. It looks as a fort should. Brown and squat, it stands on a little rocky eminence with great slappable walls a metre thick. It has slits for windows and its battlements are cut like crude square teeth. It looks exactly like the castles kids build on the beach.

I try the handle of the huge and ancient wooden door.

Locked. Pigeons coo and broop in the window slits. A pair of green parakeets chase each other round the walls, swooping and squabbling, then settle on a parapet side by side like love-birds.

Around the fort stand the crumbled remains of mud-built houses. The few bits of wall look like melting ice-cream. Nearby, new mud bricks lie drying in the winter sun alongside piles of reddish fibrous planks cut, I presume, from date palms. These are to rebuild the original village and enhance further Fujairah's appeal to the tourist. And it's clearly working because a plush white coach pulls up amid the building site and disgorges about thirty German tourists and about a hundred cameras. One after another the Germans try the door of the fort, just as I did, then resign themselves to photographing its exterior from whatever cute angles they can find. They'll be fine photos. The clear air, the blue sky, the bright light and the backdrop of the Hajar mountains will bring oohs and ahs from the living rooms of Düsseldorf. The Germans are done with the place in fifteen minutes. Back onto the bus they pile for the next raid.

I pass through a gate set in a crude old wall and enter a court-yard of sorts, in which I find a pair of elderly cannon, a few distressed banana trees, a formidable quantity of wind-blown litter, a massive plastic storage drum and, in the far corner, barely signposted, the entrance to the Fujairah Museum. From inside I can hear unmuseumish giggling. When I open the door the giggling stops. Inside the ticket office sit five Emirati women in black abayas and headscarves. Four look down demurely at their laps. The fifth gets up and silently accepts my admission money. I step into the first of the two exhibition halls, the door swings shut behind me and the giggling restarts.

In a glass case on the wall there's a goatskin water bag. I'm delighted to see it because Thesiger wrote of them constantly. They kept him alive in the desert, but he said they made the water taste of goat. It's now obvious why. A goatskin water bag differs only minimally from a goat. The instructions for making one would not be hard to reconstruct: take one goat. Lop off head. Haul out guts. Sew arse shut. Tie front and back legs together to make a handle. Fill goat through neck. Tie neck shut with string. Attach to camel. Set off into desert and good luck.

The problem with creating a museum here is that although the place has been inhabited by human beings for several thousand years, they left little behind. They left little behind because they had little. And they had little because there was little to have. This was a harsh and empty land.

The men who lived nomadically could carry everything they owned on a camel and a wife or two. Those who lived a more settled life were hardly more encumbered. Most dwellings were either the mud huts being rebuilt outside here, huts that would eventually melt back into the land from which they were built, or else flimsy constructions made of *baraisti*, which is just a mesh of palm fronds woven onto a frame of sticks. Most of the time in this climate *baraisti* was all the shelter needed, providing shade from the sun and protection of sorts from wind-blown sand. If it rained you got wet and delighted in it.

They've reconstructed a *baraisti* hut in the museum. The only items inside are some rolls of carpet, a baby's hammock, and a few cooking utensils, all of which adds up to bad news for museum curators. Most of the history these people carried with them over several thousand years was held in their heads. As it was handed from generation to generation it became both embellished and simplified until it hardened eventually, as it does with human beings the world over, into myth.

But the Bedouin did cherish their weapons. Theirs was a life that valued fighting, because it was a life where little else mattered. They owned no land. They sought nothing but good camels and the glory of war. When Thesiger crossed the Empty Quarter to the south-west of here in 1948, he was just in time to record it all. After him came oil and the internal combustion engine and all the material trappings of the West. His book makes a better museum than this museum.

Before the Europeans arrived the locals had had to make do with daggers and there are several of these on display, each with an exquisitely decorated hilt and a blade like a stretched new moon for rootling amid an enemy's short ribs. But then the Europeans brought rifles. The rifle was a dagger you could stab someone with from a very long way away and the Bedouin took to it immediately. They became experts with rifles, maintaining them with the sort of care that some people expend on their cars or their looks. Thesiger recounts how his companions would make a journey of hundreds of miles across cruel nothing for the gift of a good rifle.

At the far end of the room, beyond the cabinets of weaponry, a video with a musical soundtrack loops in perpetual replay. It stars pretty young white people who charge across dunes in a Japanese 4WD, grinning like gibbons as they do so, then stop the vehicle beside a wadi that runs with sparkling fresh water. In their bright cotton clothing, the happy holidaymakers pile out of the vehicle and wade into the water, splashing each other with squeals of delirious joy. Thesiger, I imagine, would throw up.

Archaeology has only just begun to plunge its trowel into the local sands but already it has found several ancient tombs, here reconstructed in polystyrene. The evidence suggests that the tombs were looted and re-used at intervals of roughly a thousand years.

A display of coins includes a Maria Theresa thaler. Maria Theresa was a remarkable Empress of Austria and her thaler was a remarkable coin. First minted in 1741 it gradually became the most accepted currency of international trade, popular throughout Africa, Arabia, and India. It was also one of the first coins used in America which may have contributed to the Yanks calling their eventual currency the dollar. And though Maria Theresa died a couple of hundred years ago, they have continued to mint her thaler, with every coin being dated 1780, the year of her death.

Until 1971 when the UAE adopted the dirham there was no official currency in these parts. Most people traded in the rupee, thus underlining once again the massive and generally unacknowledged influence of India on the trade of this region. But in the Sixties Fujairah minted a few coins of its own and there are several on display here. The currency it adopted was the Saudi riyal. The twenty-five-riyal piece features some suitably Arabic decorations on one side and on the other the hamster-like cheeks of dear old President Nixon. Another coin shows Armstrong and Aldrin on the moon. Fujairah, it seems, in the period of uncertainty when the British were withdrawing from the Gulf and no one was quite sure what would happen next, was keen to suck up to the Americans.

I wander out, leaving the museum deserted once again. The five robed women once again fall silent as I pass them. I emerge into sunshine that smarts the eyes. A kingfisher of startling vividness swoops over the wall and into a forest of dusty palm trees. I follow through a gate into what the dugong-plugging brochure describes as the 'famous date gardens' of Fujairah. The trees lean at debauched angles over kitchen gardens. Dotted here and there are little concrete houses, white-walled, flat-roofed, mud-surrounded, litter-strewn, some with a perimeter wall of concrete secured by an elaborate metal grille. Huge-eyed children silently watch me go by.

I amble a while through town, through a meat-market, past countless little Indian businesses, past the coffee pot roundabout and down to the area of seafront dubbed the Corniche. Efforts have been made to smarten it – concrete seats on the prom in the form of half-open conch shells and grouped table-and-sunshade arrangements on the beach. No one is sitting at either. Perhaps, so far, Fujairah's ambition has exceeded its attraction, but I like the place. Its compactness, its graspability – these qualities are a relief after Dubai.

In a little arcade of Indian shops I finger a pair of trousers, light cotton, cross checked, reddish, the sort of trousers Rupert Bear might have worn in bed.

'Hey, Mr America,' comes a stage whisper from across the arcade. A shopkeeper is beckoning me in a manner both conspiratorial and furtive. He is holding in his arms identical Rupert Bear trousers. I cross the arcade. His shop seems to stock the exact same stuff as the one across the way.

'Forty dirham him,' he says grinning, 'thirty dirham me. What your name?'

'Joe.'

'GI Joe,' he says, still glancing nervously at the shop across the road. I get the sense that the gap between them is stained with bad blood.

'My name Jack.' He shakes my hand softly. 'How many you want?'

I explain that I'd like to try them on. I have already spotted a little changing room at the back of the shop with a curtain on a pole.

'You try here,' he says glancing up and down the almost empty arcade. 'Here good.' I don't mind. I undo my belt and step out of my trousers. Jack inspects my legs and crotch with a directness of gaze to which I am frankly unaccustomed. I pull on the Rupert Bears.

'They fit good? They fit good here?' And so saying he lays a hand firmly on my crotch and squeezes, like a housewife testing fruit for ripeness. 'Good, Joe?' And he looks me in the eye with a nervous appeal that I find simultaneously sad and comic. He is middle-aged, Indian, prissily dressed and quite obviously desperate.

I gently remove his hand and tell him that I like the trousers and will buy them. He is delighted and seems not in the least abashed. 'Forty dirham,' he says.

'You said thirty dirhams.'

'Thirty-five. Thirty dirhams two trouser.'

I like the Rupert Bears a lot. I take a second pair and hand over a hundred dirhams.

'You want shirt?' He gestures at his racks. 'Jacket. Nice jacket.'

'I want my change,' I say. He extracts his wallet from his too-tight trousers, stashes the hundred and counts the change with exaggerated care, licking his fingers as he checks the notes. Then he hands me thirty dirhams.

'Forty dirhams,' I say. 'You owe me forty.'

He smiles, and gives me the other ten as blithely as a man who knows that he's tried his best but this time it just didn't come off.

'Have a nice day, Joe. Thank you.'

And I walk down the deserted arcade chuckling. I have just been sexually propositioned in Arabia by a middle-aged Indian haberdasher, who then tried to rip me off. Add one to the catalogue of absurdities to cherish in a random world.

The Lulu Hypermarket in the town centre is not especially hyper. It specializes in cheap clothes from China and ornaments for the home that would find no home with me. The books section is dominated by a splendid notice saying 'Reading Not Allowed'. I'm not tempted. There are only children's picture books and, in a separate glass cabinet, a stack of Korans. 'Holy Qoran', says a paper taped to the glass. 'Please touch with respect.' Tired from so much walking I go for coffee on a first floor balcony.

'Got any scones, love? I fancy a scone. Sort of settle me stomach.'

The speaker is a dumpy middle-aged woman in a dress that wouldn't look out of place in a family album from the Sixties. Her husband is wearing a Liverpool shirt, stretched over the sloppy tumescence of his fifty-something gut.

The Filipina waitress doesn't understand the word scone.

Don't worry, dear,' says the Englishwoman, patting the wait-ress sweetly on the arm, 'just bring me a cup of coffee, love. White. And tea for his lordship.'

His lordship leans towards me. 'You live here, do you? 'Cos we was just wondering what there is to do. We got the whole day. All seems a bit quiet to us, like.'

They're from a cruise ship. I noticed others of their number half-heartedly nosing round the jewellery and tat stalls in the entrance to Lulu. All were close to retirement age, dressed in leisure gear, a cut-price crowd.

His lordship is not best pleased by this leg of the trip. They docked at Khor Fakkan just up the coast from where they were bussed to Fujairah and dumped in the Lulu car park with a day to kill. 'I mean, is this it? I could get all this at home. And Jesus, we even had to pay for the bus. Should have stayed on the bloody ship.'

'But we're enjoying the weather, aren't we?' says his wife, distressed by the asperity of his tone. In private it just washes over her, but in public, well, there's other people to consider. 'Warm, isn't it,' she says, 'and nice to have a bit of sun in winter.'

She's a full-hearted woman and keen to chat. They flew to Dubai, joined the cruise and steamed round the rhino horn to Muscat. Whereupon the ship turned round and brought them here. Next stop's Dubai again, followed by Abu Dhabi and 'Bay-rain'. Then the plane back to Manchester.

'Muscat was nice enough, sort of old like,' says his lordship, 'but here. I mean what is this place? Is there a marina?'

I suggest that they might enjoy the fort, or perhaps the fish market, but neither idea galvanizes them. The waitress disposes their drinks on the little table. 'Thanks, love,' says the wife, 'very nice. Do we pay you now?'

She turns back to me. 'Dubai's big, isn't it? But our hotel could have been a bit quieter.'

'Right under the flight path, it was,' says her husband who seems intent on dominating any moaning that's going to be done. 'They was roaring till all hours. And then there was this nightclub underneath us. Kept going till three in the morning.'

'We got a taxi down to that palm thing,' his wife chips in. 'You've got to see it, haven't you? But there was so much construction everywhere. We liked the Creek though, didn't we? That was nice. Them *abras* and that. It's the only old bit left. They've knocked the rest down.'

'Well,' I say, 'there wasn't an awful lot there to knock down in the first place.'

This brings no response. Husband looks at his watch. 'The bus don't come back till six. Bloody hell.'

In the end they get a taxi to the museum. Though I'm a little worried that it may have closed.

Mahmoud's from Cairo and dressed like a nightclub predator in a tight cotton sweater and tighter jeans, with chunky gold chains round his neck and wrist. His hair is gelled. He radiates sexual desire, a sense of assured young potency. But where he finds the women to gratify him I don't know. There appears to be a slightly more normal distribution of the sexes here, but I would imagine that Emirati women are off-limits, and he expresses a profound dislike of Indians. 'Too much Indian here,' he says. 'Is big problem. Indian food big shit.'

We're in a cheap Lebanese restaurant in the middle of town. From the next table to mine, Mahmoud rescued me from a menu choice that he assured me I would regret. 'Is big shit,' he said, as I indicated a kebab-like item. 'I choose. You like chicken?'

Mahmoud's come to the UAE to make money but it's been a struggle. 'Egypt no good,' he says, 'I leave Cairo because no money. And because Mubarak. Everybody hate Mubarak. But they choose him. In Dubai everybody love Sheikh Mo. But they no choose him. Is funny. But here very expensive. Is hard here, the life.'

He sees Fujairah as a staging post on his inevitable journey to Dubai where the streets, if not paved with gold, are at least littered with possibility. 'Is much work in Dubai. You do job, you no like, you quit job, you do new job. Is good.'

When I ask him if he has any sense of a decline in Dubai's fortunes, he shrugs. 'Is good, Dubai. Here no good. Too small. Too much Indian.'

He works in one of the two hotels in town that have aspirations to posh. But he's unimpressed by it. Being smack beside the main road and shoddily built it is noisy. 'Every day guests go away for noise. Every day. I don't care. They say me too much noise. I say tell manager. Manager big shit.' Whether the missing verb in that last sentence is 'is' or 'gets' I can't tell you. Either way Mahmoud laughs broadly, exposing more gold in his mouth.

My chicken is unrecognizable as chicken. It comes as a sort of mash, with pickles and a pile of warm flat breads to wrap it in. But unlike the pint of avocado juice that Mahmoud also ordered for me, it's delicious.

'Is good?' asks Mahmoud, who watches me eat and occasionally discreetly adjusts his crotch.

'Is good.'

'You have woman?'

'No, I no have woman.' How easy I find it to lapse into pidgin. And how readily the uninflected English language lends itself to it.

'Is OK,' says Mahmoud generously, and I leave him picking his teeth. He has eaten and drunk nothing while I've been there.

Seven in the evening and out of curiosity I drop into Mahmoud's hotel. The bar is empty. I have a beer. The bar remains empty. I leave. At the reception desk a huge African man with a veiled and tiny wife is demanding to see the manager. He wants a refund on their room because of noise.

The other principal hotel in town is set further back from the road. The bar is of the tinkling-piano and waiters-in-waistcoats variety. The bar staff are Filipino and the only customers a couple of Brits. One's from Durham, the other Scotland and they're both cops. They're here on business, consulting to the Fujairah police.

They're both heartily welcoming, whilst retaining the cagey confidence that police acquire from belonging to a paramilitary brotherhood. They exude a sense of power in reserve, of inside knowledge, of a slight condescension towards mere civilians. They know how things really work.

When I press them for scuttlebutt on local policing, all the Scot will vouchsafe is a cryptic 'Things are not as they seem.' A couple more Heinekens, however, and the Durhamite becomes more expansive. The Indians, he says, are by and large law-abiding, and the Emiratis are effectively immune to everyday policing, especially traffic offences. 'I won't say they get away with murder, but pretty well everything short of it. Though actually,' he adds after a pause, 'when you consider how they drive, murder too.'

When I ask if the cops here are corrupt, the Scot smiles. 'Let's say some of them are not incorrupt,' he says, 'but things are getting better. Remember this place has been like the Klondike for the last couple of decades. It took a while to get law and order in the Klondike.'

And that's about all I can get out of them, except for their shared bewilderment that anyone would want to come here on holiday, and a shared wonder at local building practices. Inspector Durham tells me that in his brand-new apartment he had to call in, on successive days, a plumber, a carpenter and an electrician. And all three turned out to be the same Indian who, in his desire to please, somehow managed to both nod and shake his head at the same time. 'This is a weird place,' summarizes Inspector Durham. 'But we're not having a bad time.'

A Filipino lad serves my drinks with polite deference and evident fear of an unseen manager. When I am up at the bar paying I ask him how he enjoys life here. He looks over his shoulder before answering. 'Oh, sir,' he whispers, and his face is pained, oppressed, conflicted, 'it's hard.' His lip puckers. For a moment I think he's going to cry. I give him a hundred dirhams. He gasps.

13

Wadi Filler

Dibba's an hour or so up the coast, and I've been told it's worth a day trip. I decide to hitch. As soon as I've made that decision I feel happy. I have never liked driving and I've always liked hitching. It makes me feel part of a place and its people. It also makes me feel comparatively young again, and it sticks a toe into the waters of chance that age and money generally keep me out of.

The Fujairah Beach Motel may not be ideally situated for anything else, but the highway that heads directly up the coast from its entrance could have been made for hitching. Though I have to admit I haven't yet seen anyone with his thumb out there. Or anywhere else.

I walk half a mile or so, find a patch of roadside gravel for the driver to pull over, and raise a thumb. I still find it astonishing the effect it has on me. I feel a tasty little worm of nervousness at the importunity of it, and awareness of making myself an item to be judged. But with it comes a flood of nostalgia, a welter of associated memories and a sense of being young and excited by the world, by million-petalled possibility.

The weather is as benign as ever, the air warm, the sea breeze a zephyr. Across the way behind the township of Fujairah the toothed crest of the Hajar mountains is lit sandy by the morning sun. Behind me the smooth ocean, and on the horizon a whole fleet of tankers and container ships a mile or two out to sea and, in the manner of distant ships, seemingly immobile.

Traffic is spasmodic and I am reminded of the virtues of standing still. The senses work in repose to etch a place in the mind.

Fifteen minutes, and the ships seem not to have shifted relative to me or relative to each other. I watch them more carefully. It seems they are actually immobile. Why, I don't know. Queuing to enter the port of Khor Fakhan perhaps, or to round the rhino horn and squeeze through the busy Straits of Hormuz before carrying on to dock at Dubai? Or are they just suddenly unemployed because of the recession?

After an hour the only car that has shown any interest has belonged to the police. It slowed, dawdled past me, the two officers staring with the licence of authority. I smiled, convincingly enough it seems to induce them to drive on. They then pulled off the road a hundred yards further on and parked. Acutely conscious of their presence I carry on hitching.

A car slows. It is the right sort of car, a battered Toyota Anonymous, with a single male driver. It stops. I've got my first lift in Arabia. The driver leans across and opens the door for me and urges me to get in quickly. He's wearing the slacks and short-sleeved pastel shirt that is effectively an Indian uniform.

'I'm Joe,' I say and offer him my hand, but he has already turned to look over his shoulder. He says his name but I don't catch it.

He pulls into a gap in the traffic that I would not have

considered a gap, then becomes so engrossed in the act of driving that I am reluctant to initiate conversation. He repeatedly checks his mirrors. He fingers a stalk to ensure the lights are off. He glances at his speedo. Once he even looks down at his feet, as if he distrusts them. He seems oblivious to my presence. Less than a mile further on he turns onto a side road that leads towards a warehouse. He brakes. He stops. He turns to face me for the first time. 'Good bye,' he says, and smiles rather sweetly. The lift is over.

'Thank you very much,' I say, and I close the door and watch him drive away. Not only was it the shortest lift of my life, it was also the only silent one. And I am proud to say that while his car remains in sight and it is possible that he might see me in the mirror, I do not laugh.

Once he's out of sight and I *have* laughed, and stopped, and then laughed again – a laugh that arrives with an involuntary body-bending surge – I return to the highway where I find myself in a considerably worse position for hitching than where I was before. So I walk back to where I was before, hoping as I do so that the driver doesn't come back the other way and see me.

The police have gone. An hour and a half later so has most of the morning and any hope of getting a ride. If I'm going to see Dibba today I'm going to have to drive. Sheepishly I return to the motel and pick up my car.

The mosque at Bidyah, a few miles up the coast, is the oldest in the UAE. According to an information board it was built in 1446AD, and it resembles nothing I've seen anywhere. Painted dazzling white, it's a squarish building perhaps fifteen by fifteen feet and without windows. Its roof consists of what look like four circular meringues each with a little tip, like a nipple.

Although the building has been tarted up for us cultural tourists, there's a tone of aggressive pride in the sign at the entrance: No Entry Except For Prayer it shouts at the cameras and leisure wear and immodest females of the West. I'm pleased to see it. 'Dogs are not allowed' says another sign, accompanied by a cartoon of a snarling dog head. The image smacks of hatred. In Islam dogs are unclean. I think of the retrievers and dalmatians trotting gently round Arabian Ranches. There is no mosque in Arabian Ranches.

Behind this mosque stand a couple of watchtower-forts which have been recently restored. A mud wall is already scored with graffiti. I note down names like Zachariah, Ikshal and Shehil, all of whom were here in 2004 and keen that I should know it. The wall reads like something from the Old Testament.

A fat African in a white robe stops me on the watchtower steps and offers me a soft handshake and Salaam aleekum. 'Aleekum salaam,' I say and move my hand to my heart as I have seen men do, but he doesn't. Rather he holds his hands out with the palms facing down, as if laying them on the heads of invisible children. He closes his eyes and intones what I assume to be a prayer, then opens them again and looks pointedly at me. I'm unsure of the correct response.

'*Shukran*,' I say which I am reasonably confident is Arabic for 'Thanks, mate.'

To which he replies, in the best religious tradition and in nicely accented English, 'Money money.' And in case I don't understand English he backs the words up by rubbing thumb and middle finger together in what I am confident is the most universally understood gesture of our species.

I am timorous. I am unwilling to offend. I'm a soft touch. But this is too flagrant even for me. I walk away. He says something to my back that I am confident is uncharitable.

Up till now the bulky African and I have had the place to ourselves, but now a Bin Majid Safari Tours minibus draws up and exudes half a dozen hefty Scandinavians with tiny cameras and regrettable shorts. They lumber past the sign banning infidel dogs and the one forbidding entry to any but the prayerful, and enter the little old mosque. They'll fill it wall to wall.

The further north I drive on the coastal highway the thinner the traffic. The view barely changes. To my left the stark mountains. To my right the ocean and its hazy armada of parked ships. Occasional beautiful inlets of rock and water have sprouted hotels in colours that are about as sympathetic to the landscape as the Scandinavians were to Islamic sensitivities. Apparently this region is the coming place for tourists who've done Dubai. The coral reefs are said to offer lovely diving.

I turn on the car radio for the first time. I find mournful music, presumably still in deference to the late sheikh of Umm al Qwain, then a magnificently fierce discussion of I've no idea what in Arabic, but the debate sounds certain to end in bloodshed. I flick through a few stations in what may be Hindi and then alight on Coast 103.2 fm, an English language station. The presenter plays a series of American and English pop songs and intersperses them with a discussion of dog shit. It seems that there's at least one ex-pat in Fujairah who neglects to scoop his dog's shit into a non-biodegradable plastic bag. Instead this miscreant lets it lie. And yesterday the presenter of this radio show stepped out of his car and directly into said shit. He is still unhappy.

He doesn't say shit of course. He reaches for the infantile euphemisms of the media. Poop, he says, and doings and doggy dos, every one of which makes me tighten my grip on the steering wheel.

And he begs listeners to ring in and tell him their own horror tales of unscooped poop. None do, thank God. If there is any justice in this world I am the only listener. He then runs a little quiz competition called the Da Vinci Code, named not after the execrable book but after an Italian restaurant that is offering a voucher as a prize. Today's question: 'How many goals did Chelsea score last night?'

There is no justice in the world. Karen is also listening. And Karen knows exactly how many goals Chelsea scored last night.

'Congratulations, Karen, you've just won a voucher for three hundred dirhams to spend at Da Vinci's. You'll just love that, Karen. You'll have a fantastic time. How do you feel?'

I don't listen to how Karen feels. How I feel can be deduced from the fact that when I turn the radio off I all but snap the knob.

Where do I begin with this offensiveness? With the mindless pap of the music, and the recycled vacuity of its lyrics? Or with the expression here in the desert of a suburban European neurosis about dog shit? Or with the commercial fakery and transparent hyperbole of having 'a fantastic time' at Da bloody Vinci's? Or with the name Da Vinci's itself, so redolent of art don't you know, when it's just – I've no doubt – an Italian restaurant, with about as much connection to the long dead Leonardo as I have? Or with the smugness of the disc jockey whose accent sounds as though it comes from a Barratt estate in one of the nicer bits of Leicester?

No. My anger – and it's true anger, bitter, fuming anger like a vent of magma – surges at the importation to this harsh country of the West's worst. This thoughtless transplanting of commercial mendacity, of fake enthusiasm, fake music, fake notions of what matters. Fake everything.

If you really suffer from such poverty of soul that you feel the need to follow Chelsea, you should live in bloody London. If you come to live in Arabia, you should live in bloody Arabia. Such radio is a form of colonialism. It's Brits doing what they complain about immigrants to Britain doing, not trying to fit in, not respecting the place that's welcomed them. When in Rome, do as we did in Leicester.

Back home in the West I merely sneer at this stuff then ignore it. Here I find it viscerally offensive. It is arrogant, pollutant, transgressive, invasive, witless, ignoble and wrong. I feel ashamed to belong to the culture that spawned it. Come on you Arabs, rise up and boot us out. You have nothing to lose but Coast 103.2 fm.

This seems to matter more here than across the mountains in Dubai. Dubai's gone. Or, rather, Dubai has willingly embraced all this stuff, is more or less a western city transplanted. Imported crassness is no worse there than anywhere else. But here, where there may remain some integrity, it would be good to be rid of it. No Indians listen to it, I'd guess, and obviously no Arabs, but it simply offends me that it exists at all here between the sharp rocks and the sea.

As I approach Dibba, the weather turns sour. Clouds are swelling ahead of me like smoke from burning tyres. One final hotel clamped to a cove, with apparent plans for a holiday village and shopping mall, and then I'm in Dibba. Beyond here lies only the tip of Arabia, the Mussulman peninsula, most of which belongs, by the sort of geographical quirk that I am becoming used to, to Oman. I shall be making no further attempt to enter Oman.

Dibba's got some sizeable chunks of recorded history. It's a small place with the agreeable feel of a backwater but it was not always so. Shortly after the death of the prophet Mohammed it rejected Islam. This did not go down well with the caliph of the time. A battle took place here and according to one report over ten thousand rebels were slaughtered in the name of Allah. It has been Muslim ever since.

Another belter of a battle took place here in the ninth century during the conquest of Oman by the caliph of what is now Iraq. Thousands more men fell. In the sixteenth century the Portuguese arrived, attracted by Dibba's natural deep water harbour. They walloped the region into submission and built a fort here before being hoofed out around 1650. Since then Dibba's star has faded, by which I mean it has just peaceably gone on going on, attracting little external attention to itself and raising its children and doing the good things that never make it into the papers.

The town is divided into three bits belonging respectively to Oman, Sharjah and Fujairah, but you can wander between the three without restriction. I'm not sure who controls the bit I park the Nissan in, but am far too hungry to care. So hungry that it seems obvious to me that the nearest restaurant is the right restaurant. Dutiful tourism can wait.

The restaurateur seems to divine my condition and furnishes me wordlessly and within seconds with a plate of pickles and a heap of flat breads. I am not generally given to pickle sandwiches but these taste as though they've been prepared by Allah himself, may his name be a blessing. The goat kebabs that follow aren't bad either.

I have a window seat. As I eat the world darkens. Lights come on. Then the sky simply bursts, as if a great stretched bladder had been pricked from below with a pin. The windows are instantly awash, are sheets of water. The waiters, the diners, even the cook who emerges from his grim little kitchen, stand and watch in silence. Lightning crazes the sky. The thunder is an expression of divine wrath. It seems to threaten the plate glass. The scene would be spectacular anywhere, but here in this land of warm winters and hot summers, of sand and rock, the intensity of this storm feels biblical. I can picture the wadis in the mountains becoming instantaneous torrents. And all of us in the restaurant, an arbitrary collection of people whom I shall never meet again, including a middle-aged Frenchman whom I overheard five minutes ago asking the restaurateur about his carrot juicer, just sit or stand and stare, our faces neutral, but our eyes huge like the eyes of little children.

Dibba cannot cope. Presumably because rain is rare there's been no attempt to help it cope. Such drains as exist are overwhelmed in minutes. The street is a lake for 4WDs to plough through. Their wash slops against the doors of grocery stores and clothes shops.

A grey and battered sedan stutters into the lake and then dies.

The door opens, and some seconds later the Indian driver emerges, his shoes in his hand, his trousers rolled to the knee. He wades, sees a Land Cruiser approaching, tries to run and fails to lift his trailing foot above the water. The effect is of an ankle tap. His weight is going forward but no foot comes through to support that weight. He plants face down in the lake and everyone in the restaurant laughs and none of us go out to help him. He splutters up, his clothes black and clinging, as the wash from the Land Cruiser slaps against him, incapable of doing further mischief. When everyone else has stopped laughing, the Frenchman's shoulders are still heaving, silently.

The eye of the storm passes over towards the mountains behind us, and we are left with mere rain. The lake shrinks a little but not much. I leave. I'm wearing a cotton shirt, cotton trousers and sandals and have no other clothes in the car. By staying on the top side of the street I stay out of water more than an inch or two deep. The air is still warmish. There is almost no one about. I spend an hour in an internet cafe. When I emerge it's still raining. My car is just across the road. I cannot be bothered with sight-seeing. I take off my sandals and tiptoe towards the car then give up and just wade. Inside the car I take off my sodden trousers and drive cautiously out of Dibba and back down the coast road to Fujairah in my underpants. I am keen not to be stopped by the police. I am also grateful in the extreme that hitching failed.

I spend the evening in the kippered bar. Near closing time two Indians arrive. They are giggling and walking-into-walls drunk. The only coherent thing that I can get from either of them is that they are both barbers.

14

On This Beach

Cartoons have a lot to answer for. What, for example, do you picture when you hear the phrase 'tropical island'? For me, automatically, it means a lump of rock supporting a single leaning palm tree. The tree holds a few outsize coconuts, like testicles. Directly beneath the testicles sits the victim of a shipwreck. In the course of the wrecking process both legs of his trousers have been torn off in a jagged fashion just below the knee. His shirt has acquired holes.

It's a similar story with oases. Because of cartoons, an oasis means a grove of palms amid sand dunes. There's a well with a low stone wall and a bucket on a winch, and there may be a camel or two around. The whole lot – palms, well and camels – is contained in a thought bubble emerging from the head of a thirst-wracked traveller. He is approaching these phantasms by the traditional method of locomotion in such circumstances, which is on hands and knees. The traveller has also borrowed his trousers from a shipwrecked sailor.

I do not approach the oasis of Bithna on hands and knees. I approach it by Nissan. The oasis is not surrounded by sand dunes. It sits amid barren mountains. And it doesn't, as far as I can discover, have a well. But it does have date palms, a whole forest of date palms. And peeping over the top of them is a fort, its sandy walls bedecked with scaffolding.

Bithna is only a few miles west of Fujairah on the main highway across the UAE. It sits above the Wadi Ham, a giant natural gulley. And in contrast to the surrounding mountains it is clearly fertile.

Among the palms, there are little plots with raised edges in which maize stands tall, alongside a broad-leafed crop that looks like tobacco. A scarecrow in a tattered dishdash resembles a warning from the Ku Klux Klan. The whole place smells of goats, the little brown goats that live in enclosures knocked up from date palm fronds and date palm timber and corrugated iron. A sign asks you not to leave litter or do anything to desecrate the place because wadis are a gift from Allah. The notice has been emphatically ignored. The wadi is littered to an impressive extent. Indeed it seems that people have gone out of their way to upset Allah, lugging their refuse here from miles around – old washing machines, engine parts, an incinerated car, a hundred yellow fertilizer sacks.

Just up the road from here Swiss archaeologists have unearthed a T-shaped tomb from the second millennium BC. In other words this place predates the Bible. But you wouldn't know. It consists of a warren of low concrete houses, their flat roofs crowned with satellite dishes. Each house has a wall round it set with a grille of ornate metal and a carport housing a dirty Japanese 4WD. The alleyways between the silent houses are unsealed stone and mud, dotted with puddles after yesterday's rain.

'Hello, hello, hello,' shouts a crowd of kids playing football near the mosque. They are sloe-eyed Arab kids in t-shirts. One kicks the ball to me. I side-foot it back. The kids are thrilled. They urge me to join their game.

The goal is a wall, towards which both sides are playing. In accordance with the ancient traditions of kids' football, the fat boy is in goal. I'm not sure which team I'm on but it doesn't matter. There's no teamwork here. Every player wants to dribble the ball, and the person they want to dribble it past is me. They slither like little eels. I lumber like a tractor. But on a couple of occasions the tractor manages to get a tyre in front of the ball and to wild encouragement I dispossess the opponent and then bear down on the same goal as he was heading for, until foot-tripped by a cynical little eel and falling to the gravel like Gulliver in Lilliput. Unlike Gulliver in Lilliput I am then helped to my feet by little Arab hands and even dusted down by them.

I could happily spend the rest of the day amid this infectious, present-tense energy. But I don't. I've got a highway through the mountains to drive to Ras al Khaimah, the most northerly and reputedly the most backward of the seven emirates. I'm looking forward to seeing it.

'Bye bye, mister, how are you, bye bye.'

As I make my way back to the car past another silent mosque, a Land Cruiser draws up outside the tiny Al Shabiya Grocery, an Arab at the wheel. He honks his horn, waits perhaps five seconds, then honks it again with a long, awaken-the-dead, blast. An Indian comes running from the shop, takes the order at the driver's window, runs back inside, runs out again with goods. This is normal practice. I have seen it everywhere I've been. It is always an Arab doing the honking, an Indian the running.

The sweeping highway takes me easily over the arid mountains, through a forgettable town called Daftah, through other settlements that seem to exist solely to sell food and firewood and carpets to people passing through, and then briefly onto a sort of upland plain of scrub and sand where for the first time I see hobbled camels. A front leg has been bent up at the knee and

171

the hoof tied tight to the top of the leg, so the camel becomes effectively three-legged. Thesiger repeatedly speaks of doing this to camels to prevent them straying overnight, though apparently they could still be a mile or more away in the morning.

The approach to Ras al Khaimah takes me through a gravelly nowhere with odd patches of development: warehouses and cement factories seemingly airlifted arbitrarily onto the land-scape. The whole area is in a state of unbeautiful becoming. On the teeming outskirts of town the highway declines to a pot-holed ruin, passing through an landscape of shacks, loose goats, loose children, date palms, despairing shops, mud puddles, dead cars and an ostrich farm. Downtown Dubai feels an age away. It's less than a hundred miles.

And I would imagine Dubai's success must rankle because, a couple of hundred years ago, when Dubai was a tiny nothing of a place squatting on its haunches and eating fish, Ras al Khaimah was busy and thriving and a minor imperial power with the capacity to upset the might of the British.

When I reach the centre of Ras al Khaimah, built like Dubai round a *khor* or creek, I find a gleaming new bridge and mirror-glass office towers standing alongside areas of rubble-strewn, puddle-dotted nothing. I ditch the car on one such makeshift parking lot and tiptoe round a puddle that's effectively a lake and enter a strange little cafe, its walls made of woven palm fronds. For the tourists, I suspect, though there aren't any. I order a coffee.

'Arabian coffee?'

'Yes.'

'You want *shisha*?'

'Yes.'

Shisha is the hubble-bubble, the hookah, the strange and awk-ward smoking device that I associate with Chinese opium dens and mysterious men with drained yellow eyes and time to kill. I've never tried one.

To my surprise the man offers me a variety of flavours. I choose apple. The place holds a dozen or so men, all of whom are either playing chess or nursing a cell phone. One grizzled Indian repeatedly presses a key on his phone to play 'We wish you a merry Christmas' and stares at the phone as it plays.

The waiter arrives with a tiny brass saucepan the contents of which he then tips into a similarly tiny cup. It's more grounds than coffee and flavoured with something that I suspect is cardamom. It's gone in a couple of sips leaving me slightly thirstier than I was before.

The shisha is two-foot tall, like a stretched and decorated hurricane lamp. There's a glass bulb at the base three-quarters filled with water, an ornate central column, and at the top a metal dish with a sort of bulb in it. The bulb is stuffed with flavoured tobacco. The tray around it holds smouldering coals which burn the tobacco to produce smoke. When you suck on the mouthpiece, smoke is drawn into the water then bubbles up through it, cooling and moisturizing it before it reaches the grateful lungs. And it's actually not bad.

I can't taste the apple, perhaps because of the ferocious coffee, but the smoke is pleasant on the mouth. Even more pleasant is the sense of almost obligatory relaxation. By taking on a shisha you've committed yourself to perhaps three quarters of an hour of dedicated indolence, sitting beside your elaborate contraption inhaling at intervals a mild narcotic and mulling over whatever it is that people mull over in smoking dens. You're detached from the hurly-burly. If ever you're going to be meditative, it is now. All I need is a game of chess.

And here's a man in a dishdash catching my eye, then looking down at the chessboard in front of him. I pick up my hookah, transfer to his table, say 'Salaam aleekum' at exactly the same time as he says 'good afternoon', and then say 'good afternoon' at exactly the same time as he says 'Aleekum salaam'. We shake hands and he thrusts out a pawn.

Chess originated in India but was adopted and popularized by the Persians. The phrase checkmate is a corruption of the Persian *shah mat* meaning the king is dead, which I for one find good to know. From Persia chess spread through Arabia, and reached Europe in the eighth century with the Islamic conquest of Spain. With its devious malice and its scheming complexity chess seems a fitting game for this part of the world and its long history of war.

My opponent's fluent 'good afternoon' was like an early attack with a lone queen. It looked promising but there was nothing much to back it up. I'd love to chat with the man but my first few sentences elicit responses that are not only hard to understand but also bear little relevance to the question. Ah well, chess is best played in silence. He sucks on his shisha, I on mine. He orders a Coke, I order another coffee and a glass of water. The game is even. I'm not much good at chess but neither is he, and I'm utterly engrossed and happy as can be. With my cup of Arabic coffee and the regular bubbling hiss of my shisha, the chessboard in front of me, and on the other side of it a man who looks like Osama bin Laden run to fat, I feel I'm getting just a little closer to Arabia. And I win. He takes it well.

The Nakheel Hotel is seedy. The lift hesitates and clanks. There's a pervasive smell of something rotting. In the corridors I repeatedly meet people who seem alarmed to see me, as if they were engaged in something naughty. And my room resembles an under-stocked second-hand shop. Nothing remotely matches anything. The only decoration is a watercolour of an Italian railway station. The tiles on the bathroom floor have been selected for that pre-stained look, the sink has been emphatically post-stained, and the toilet cistern sits at an angle of twenty degrees to the horizontal. I cautiously try to twist it back to a conventional angle, but it is screwed firmly in place.

Most toilets in these parts come with a side-slung hose and

nozzle. Initially I ignored these things in the properly suspicious Anglo-Saxon manner, but I have since experimented and, after a few early mishaps of aim and range into the details of which I shall not go, I've grown accustomed to and indeed fond of these devices. I find the sensation agreeable and the service exemplary. The Nakheel Hotel, however, has a bidet.

I have never used a bidet. I am unsure how to. I presume you sit on it with your back to the wall, but if so, the taps are awkwardly behind you. Out of curiosity I bend and turn on the tap and have to sway back to avoid the jet that leaps three feet into the air. Which is more than enough to confirm my instinctive distrust. Like most English travellers, I shall continue to reserve bidets for the emergency washing of underwear.

A late-afternoon wander through Ras al Khaimah confirms first impressions. It's a bit of a mess, a half-built place. It has ample ambition but too little money.

The khor is effectively a lagoon, with the big new bridge spanning its neck and passing over fishing boats and sleek white sheikh-carrying pleasure cruisers. Just beyond the bridge stands the regulation fort, now restored and turned into the regulation museum. Not far beyond that a warren of shops and little houses, Indian run as always, but catering far more than in Dubai to an indigenous population. Emiratis are a lot more evident here, little gaggles of women in full veils and abayas being deferentially served in clothes shops, perfume shops and shops dedicated to ornaments of great ugliness.

Behind and between the shops run rutted lanes, unsealed and littered, some still impassable for all but 4WDs after the recent rains. I'm intrigued by a little concrete house with an open courtyard and a neatly tended garden of plastic flowers in pots, protected not by the standard concrete wall or metal grille, but by a low and dirty picket fence.

'Christian Baptist Mission' says a sign. 'Pastor Benigno Navarro III, Missionary. Sending church, the Baptist Church of

Bulacan, Philippines. The end of your search for a true church, and the beginning of yours for a true.'

I knock on the half open door. No answer. I stick my head round the door and call. No answer. My search for a true will have to wait a bit. I carry on through lanes and shops then emerge spectacularly into a scene that lifts the heart.

It's the seafront. It's not in a great state of repair. A low wall separates the crumbling pavement from the beach. On the beach fifty kids of all ages are playing football. Behind them, a glassy sea of mauve, like shimmering ink. And on the horizon a sinking sun, a vermilion glory, dropping through clouds. The undersides of the clouds pulse scarlet, orange and pink, like embers.

The kids play in virtual silhouette. The goalposts are pieces of driftwood, repeatedly shifted to lengthen the pitch as more boys hop over the wall to play. It becomes about forty a side. And I sit on the wall and delight in it. I'm not sure why it pleases me so to sit on this wall in a spectacular sunset as the players pound pointlessly up and down the beach like puppies. But it does.

Ras al Khaimah hopes to boom and I hope its hope is fulfilled. But no boom will make it as present-tense happy as kids on a beach playing football.

It was up this beach that seven thousand soldiers ran in 1820, most of them Omani but under the command of British officers. They fought hand to hand with the local Qawasim for several hours, and blood soaked into this sand. Above the fighters flew a rain of cannonballs from the Royal Navy ships anchored a little offshore, cannonballs that thudded into the sandy flanks of the fort, behind me, that is now a museum for tourists. They reduced it to rubble. The Qawasim lost the battle and control of the local trade routes.

The British task force sailed on down the coast, subdued the Qawasim bases in Umm al Qwain, Ajman and Sharjah, then reached Dubai and found the rival Bani Yas people friendly. They made a deal with them, the ramifications of which are still being felt.

Since then Ras al Khaimah has struggled. And it has been the maverick sheikhdom. In 1971 it refused to join the fledgling UAE. Its reason was partly a traditional distrust of Dubai and Abu Dhabi, the Bani Yas emirates down the coast. It feared that with their wealth they would outmuscle Ras al Khaimah in the new federation. Ras al Khaimah also hoped to find oil of its own, and in its bid for independence it quietly hinted to the USA that it had a splendid port that the US Navy might find useful.

No oil was found and the States expressed no interest in an alliance. Within a year Ras al Khaimah had grudgingly joined the UAE. But it wasn't at ease. At the height of the Cold War in the late Seventies it offered the use of its port once more, this time to the Soviet Union. The Russians declined, but Ras al Khaimah still didn't give up. During the interminable Iran–Iraq war in the late Eighties, it sneakily offered the use of its airbases to Saddam Hussein. All it asked in exchange was recognition as an independent state. This offer horrified the other emirates. Iran is only a hop and a skip away across the Gulf. The UAE could become a war zone. The rapidly self-enriching sheikhs of the UAE had no desire to get involved. But to everyone's relief, the plan came to nothing and Ras al Khaimah still writhes under the yoke of the UAE.

Its current rulers are doing all they can to make the place prosperous along the lines established by Dubai. But there is discontent, apparently, among its local population, especially the members of a tribe known as the Shihuh. No one knows quite where the Shihuh derive from. Some contend that they were the original inhabitants of this region, predating the colonization by Arabs; others that they are descendants of a lost biblical tribe. All that is known for sure is that the Shihuh are

largely excluded from power because of their traditional dis-
loyalty to the Qawasim. And they aren't happy. It was a Shihuh
man, Marwan al-Shehhi, who piloted the second plane to hit the
World Trade Center, on September 11th, 2001.

I amble gently back to the Nakheel in a merry mood, past chess
players outside the Nice Palace Restaurant and past two Indian
hairdressers three doors apart, one called Good Evening Saloon
and the other Good Morning Saloon. The muezzins wail.

15

To the Tip of the Tent

The shower in the Nakheel Hotel is predictably dysfunctional. Standing naked in the off-white bathtub, that wasn't off-white when manufactured, I finally work out how to get warm water but the showerhead sways like a dancing cobra. I reach up to tame it, a foot loses its grip on the bath tub, I grab the shower head, feel it detach from its mooring, grab the shower curtain, feel that sheer away, twist to save myself, and both feet lose all traction.

I'm not sure whether I've been knocked out. If I was, it was only for a second or two, but my vision is blurred. Tiny dots of light swim across my eyes like anti-aircraft fire. I have to make a conscious effort to remember where I am, to wit, lying on my back on a bathroom floor in a hotel in Ras al Khaimah, UAE, with my knees hooked over the rim of the bath. The shower curtain is partially wrapped around me like a plastic toga and the pole that supported it is on the far side of the room. Inside the bath I can hear the showerhead still squirting. And the plastic toilet seat is on the floor beside me, broken. My head must have hit it as I fell. I feel weak and cold and I don't want to move.

If I'd left the toilet seat up, my skull would have smacked against the bowl. The thought brings an involuntary wave of nausea. It would have been like a falling apple hitting an anvil. Death by vitreous enamel. But it strikes me at the same time that this would be a magnificently arbitrary way to die and place to do it in; a fittingly bathetic final chapter to a book with no plot. And despite my condition I half chuckle.

I haul myself up and discover a throbbing ache in my neck and left shoulder. I am fragile, mortal, shaken up. I have to lean on things as I make my way to the bed, staggering like a just-born wildebeest on the savannah, unsure of my limbs. I lie down, and feel like a curious spectator as the jigsaw of mental normality reassembles itself piece by piece.

'I've had a little accident.'

The tubby Indian at reception eyes me through balloonish glasses, their left-hand hinge repaired with insulation tape.

'In the bathroom,' I say, smiling to trivialize the incident. 'I fell over.'

He doesn't smile. Nor does he provide the sympathy that I now realize I wouldn't mind a bit of. Nor yet does he even seem surprised.

'Yes,' he says flatly.

'I'm afraid the shower curtain needs fixing and, um, and the shower too, I'm afraid. And the toilet.'

'Room number?' he says.

I can't remember. I have to fish the key out of my pocket.

'OK,' he says, and I walk out into the morning. After the gloom of the lobby the light spears my eyes. I take refuge in a restaurant next door and drink three thick coffees. I'm surprised by the degree to which my fall has shaken me. I feel the need to go somewhere quiet and remote for a few hours, somewhere I

can sit and let my jangled mind recover its customary equilib-
rium. I go to find my car.

As I drive north, without destination, my mind rehearses my
bathroom tumble. And I begin to turn it into a story in my head,
to mythologize it. I name it 'The Fall'. Like the Fall of Troy, or of
the Arabian Empire, or of Man. The battle to be upright, to
stand, to see over the swaying stems of grasses, to glimpse the
horizon, is a battle that must be lost in the end. With the predator leaping on its neck the wildebeest strains every muscle to
remain on its feet. Because to fall is to die.

Falls kill the elderly. Their brittle bones snap and that's that.
To hospital they go, where they are laid out on beds like corpses.
Like the thousands of corpses in the stark dry valleys around
here, the corpses whose tombs the archaeologists fuss over with
trowel and brush. All of them, every one, over the long dispas-
sionate years, eventually and inevitably fell. As will the
archaeologists, every one.

Engaged in such cheerful meditations I see signs warning me
of the approach of Oman, and I turn right up a valley. Beside the
surprisingly well-made road the mountains gradually steepen,
jagged, devoid of vegetation, inimical. The valley's flanks are
dotted with occasional hovels of piled stone, looking too low-
roofed to stand upright in. Most are now derelict but a few have
washing hanging from a line and are surrounded by tiny terraced fields, cut into the hillsides, where crops are growing.
They must be irrigated by some sort of channelling. And there
are pens of camels or goats, held in by walls of dried and woven
palm fronds. Here's an infinitely tough subsistence life in a place
as harsh as they come. In summer this place must hold heat like
an oven.

Another mile or two further up, a dumper truck is adding a
few more tons of sand to a football pitch of sand. The pitch is
surrounded by piled rocks to stop the sand melting away. Half

a dozen kids stand watching. A little further and the valley splits, and here at the junction is the village the kids must have come from: a cluster of square white dwellings, some dirty 4WDs, a dusty little grocery shop. I stop the car and get out. The air is warm, still and silent. The place feels eerie. I had expected to find nothing like this in the UAE.

Three boys emerge from an alley and stop some yards away to stare with big dark eyes. They wear brown robes, like sacking nighties. And they say nothing. There are satellite dishes on many of the houses but the sight of a white man in the flesh must be a rarity here. Two of the kids disappear. The youngest, a kid of perhaps ten with close-cropped hair, follows me up through the village. He hangs a few paces behind me, saying nothing. I see no adults, no movement, only occasional birds, and little brown goats down alleys.

The village ends. The road becomes a gravel track. I walk on. I like the silence. The boy walks on. Either side of us rise sheer walls of grey brown rock, their strata tipped this way and that by forces beyond imagination. If, as I presume, this is a wadi, its depth bespeaks hundreds of thousands of years of serious water flooding off the mountains and raging down the path of least resistance. And yet the place now is as dry as thirst.

The occasional wiry shrub has been fashioned into a toadstool by the browsing goats. They prop their front hooves against the stem and nibble at any foliage they can reach. Even up here the silent local flies abound, finding momentary perches on face and arms. The boy comes alongside, looks up at me with wide-eyed seriousness, and doesn't speak. We walk on.

I worry that he might be missed, that the other kids might tell his mother, that she might emerge to see her son heading into the mountains with a stranger. But I want to keep going and if he wants to come he can come. Then he reaches up and takes my hand. I feel a learned western discomfort. Almost all societies I've seen are more at ease with tactile contact than I am. I don't know why. I stop. He looks up. I smile down at him and sit on a rock. He lets go of my hand and sits at my feet.

Back down the valley his village looks like what it is, a tiny human settlement in a hostile land. For thousands of years kids born in this valley would have died in this valley, but in the last fifty years all that has gone. The cause, I suppose, is the oil they found here and elsewhere to power the engines that have shrunk the world. Anyone can go anywhere and all the old notions of tribal home, of genius of place, of ancient bonds and traditions have dissolved or are about to. The story is not unique to this valley, this country.

This child, surely, will be lured by the bright lights of Ras al Khaimah twenty miles down the road, and then perhaps by the even brighter ones of Dubai. And from Dubai he can catch a plane to anywhere. The isolation of the ages is gone. There is no point in debating whether that is good or bad. It simply is. And it has happened so spectacularly fast. Thousands of years of accretions gone in half a century. This is an age without precedent. And in this tiny, once remote land the effects have been more sudden and startling than in most.

The boy is flicking stones at a rock. I do the same. He aims at a more distant rock. I follow suit. He looks up and laughs. Then a gulping clacking noise erupts below us, and out of the village there emerges a white 4WD, its engine knackered and hammering. It heads up the valley. The boy is watching it. It comes perhaps halfway up the track. I feel threatened, nervous, oddly guilty. I can see now that it's an old-style Range Rover, two heads in the cab.

Then, to my relief, it veers off the road and goes joyriding through the valley. The driver flings his battered mechanical beast round boulders, throwing up dust and diesel smoke and noise that echoes between the valley walls and murders the peace. Young men, no doubt, with nothing to do. They careen in nowhere to no purpose for perhaps ten minutes, then return to the track and down through the village and beyond, and we watch them shrink down the road, the noise shrinking with them, until they round a distant corner and are gone. The silence floods back in.

'Come on,' I say to the boy, and we get up and head back down to the place where he lives and where I bet he will not remain. I'd love to know what happens to him, how his life pans out. His future seems to me uncharted, guideless, fraught with every possibility on earth, and every danger.

The village is as deserted as when we left. The boy stops and stands to watch as I get in the car.

'Goodbye,' I say, and start the engine, and he smiles and I turn the car round and head down the valley and he runs after me, waving, for a hundred metres till I accelerate away and out of his life. Just a brief and random convergence of two lives but I was touched by his trusting company. I also feel a hell of a lot better than I did a few hours ago. And seriously hungry.

In the al Saha restaurant, in an apparently nameless settlement just short of the Omani border, proprietor, cook and clientele alike are transfixed by an ancient television mounted high on the wall. It's showing a kung fu movie. Despite the subtitles the volume is on max. No one speaks, but the little restaurant reverberates with thwacks and grunts while a dozen Indian labourers lift rice and goat meat to their mouths with greasy fingers. When the film is interrupted by an ad for Colgate toothpaste, they look down at their plates.

Quite how the word corniche gained popularity here, I don't know, but Ras al Khaimah's got one too. It's not the seafront where I watched the kids play football, but the road that runs beside the lagoon. And it aspires, of course, to tourist posh. It's got a little theme park of sorts with a replica fort, walkways among irrigated banks of marigolds, water courses built of concrete but fashioned to look like rock, ornate lamp standards, a cafe, and a puzzling free-standing turret with windows of mirror glass. A notice trumpets that this is an example of 'Innovation, Creativity, Tourism, Design, Art, developed by RAK Dream Tours', and that it offers 'a unique tourist experience and exciting amenities'.

'God willing,' says the sign, the place will open for business in October 2008. But October 2008 has been and gone and the place isn't open yet. God was not willing.

It must be tough working for RAK Dream Tours. They've seen Dubai draw visitors by the million and gain an international reputation. Here in Ras they've got the same benign winter weather and similar sandy beaches and warm seas, but they've barely started on the myth-making process, the image creation, the branding.

I can't see this corniche hauling the tourists north. However much RAK Dream Tours may puff it, it's just a bland straight boulevard thick with traffic. Halfway along it, just when I'm thinking of hailing a taxi, I hear amplified chanting. Following my ears, I find a spanking new building. The neon signs that decorate it are all in Arabic, an unprecedented oddity. Even government departments here advertise themselves in both Arabic and English.

Outside the building an open courtyard. Around the courtyard a mass of sofas and armchairs, indoor furniture lugged outside and arranged for an audience that has yet to materialize. Inside the square stand two lines of young Arab men at right angles to each other. The young men are immaculately arrayed in red and white headcloths, snowy white dishdashes and gleaming leather sandals. In the space between them four other young men are leading a chant. They carry microphones and move with a lurching dance step while wailing repetitively into the microphones to a background of recorded music set very loud. The two lines act as choruses, picking up the chant at prescribed places, swaying their heads, and beating time with their camel sticks. They chant and sway with gusto.

The audience begins to emerge from the building behind. All of them Arab, all of them men, most of them older than the chanters. They too have camel sticks, whippy peeled stems a couple of feet long, which they absent-mindedly swing in time with the chanting. The sticks look too clean and new ever to have whacked a camel.

The older men stand around in knots or sit on the sofas to watch the dancing. A television crew arrives by van and rigs up shoulder-toted cameras and walks straight into the midst of things to get close-ups of the action with the licence granted to camera crews everywhere by a world in thrall to television. The cameramen are Indian. Press photographers, who are also Indian, arrive. And servants with refreshments, trays of drinks and sweetmeats. For the first time I see one of those vast toucan-billed coffee pots being put to use.

An imperious sheikhly figure cuts across the square in my direction. I am on the pavement, several yards back from the nearest sofa. He smiles and beckons me inside the square, shakes my hand – his skin is soft as chamois leather – and invites me with a gesture to sit. 'Shukran,' I say. He smiles and sits beside me, then with the subtlest movement summons a servant. A youth comes trotting across and I get a tiny cup of cardamom coffee from the beak of the giant brass pot.

My host is clearly a significant figure. His shift across the square brings others as if by slow magnetic attraction. As each approaches he stands to shake hands. I feel obliged to do the same which disconcerts the new arrivals. I leave the decision whether to acknowledge me to them. Some shake my hand and mutter a greeting before moving on with relief to the man I now think of as the sheikh. Others walk on past. I sit back down. Another approaches. I stand back up.

The chanting, stopped for a while, restarts, with renewed

vigour. The chanters and dancers are evidently enjoying themselves, belting the stuff out with hypnotic intensity. This is no
display of Morris dancing.

A boy of a similar age to my wadi companion wanders out
onto the square and rocks merrily about, imitating the lead
chanter. Everyone smiles at his antics. A servant collects my
coffee cup and pours me a glass of sticky, lemonish tea. I am
now on the edge of but clearly distinct from, indeed alien to, a
group of about thirty Arab men, most of them fifty years old and
more, who chatter and laugh with easy familiarity.

I am increasingly confident that this is the male half of a wedding party. And though I have been invited to be part of it – the
first example I have witnessed of the traditional Arab hospital-
ity that I've read about – I feel like a gatecrasher in my western
clothes and my ignorance of everything. I would like to stay, to
see what happens, but it would be wrong to stay. The sheikh has
played his part by inviting me in; now I must play mine by
leaving. I stash my tea glass discreetly under the seat, hover
near the sheikh until he notices me, and thank him. He smiles
and says, 'You are welcome.' I turn and head off up the darkening corniche of Ras al Khaimah, the music still blaring.

It was an important do, so much is clear. The prominent location, the large numbers in immaculate dress, the numerous
servants, the abundant refreshments, and the attentions of the
media, all suggest that this was a wedding involving a significant local family. But more than that I can only guess. The
chanting and dancing seemed as old as the mountains, and you
could see from the older men's reactions that it came from their
roots. I saw one man who must have been eighty, hollow-eyed
and helped into a chair by a youth. But once sitting, his toes
bounced with the music and he watched the dance intently.
What must he have seen in eighty years? I wonder what he
makes of RAK Dream Tours and its synthetic fort.

*

At the reception desk in the Nakheel the same tubby Indian is on duty with his derelict spectacles. When I collect my key he makes no reference to the damage inflicted on my bathroom. I take the clanking lift with an Aussie. He's here, he tells me, to train pilots. As the lift stops at his floor, I ask him what he thinks of Ras al Khaimah. 'Mate,' he says, 'not much.'

My bathroom's been fixed. They've even managed to find a replacement toilet seat with similar stains to the original. I shower with elaborate caution, gripping a pipe that runs up the wall and soaping myself with one hand. When I step out of the tub I grasp the rim with both hands. In the mirror I catch a glimpse of my naked self, hunched like Montgomery Burns in *The Simpsons*.

There's karaoke advertised in the bar of the Nakheel Hotel this evening. It consists of two Filipina girls running to fat. They wear matching leather bustiers and denim skirts and in the inch-wide gap between skirt and bustier they have matching bulges of flesh. That flesh is the colour of new honey. They jig side by side on a tiny stage, singing along competently but without commitment, to Abba and the Eagles. I recognize every song. The girls smile with parodic rapture, the performance equivalent of a tourist poster. As so often here I find myself speculating on the story of their lives. Born in the teeming squalid barrios of Manila, perhaps, or on one of the fish-eating, fruit-laden outer islands, they have found their way, after only half a dozen years of adulthood, to a low and smoky bar in a mess of a town in a Muslim land, singing to a gathering of the glum who pay them no attention.

The bar manager is a busy little Indian man in a regulation white shirt with a regulation little pumpkin gut pushing at the buttons. He rarely moves far from the till. But the true spirit of the place is enshrined in the two girls behind the bar, sisters by the look of them, tall and blonde and unmistakably Russian. Only from Russia do you get that pallor, that severity, that hard-bitten pugnacity that seems to sing of potato vodka, harsh weather and adversity. Even the women tennis players from Russia retain that look, despite having escaped to the circus of global sport and the swaddling wealth that comes with it.

Neither sister smiles or makes any pretence of caring, and their manner echoes that of the customers. Seated at the semi-circular bar, reading from left to right, are a huge black African in a brown robe topped with a fur vest, a couple of full regalia Emiratis plotting in low voices over vodka, a morose Eastern European with acne scars like the surface of the moon who keeps eyeing me then looking away, two Indian men with a bottle of South African wine and, to my surprise, an Arab woman. She wears the full abaya and headscarf but no facial veil and is alone in looking cheerful as she drinks bottled Heineken with her man. Or at least with *a* man. Completing the merry gathering is an elderly solitary Arab in grey. When the leader of Hamas appears on television, the man leaves his bar stool to turn up the volume. I can't tell you what the Hamas leader has to say, but I can tell you that he's passionate about it. He drowns 'Hotel California'.

The wall behind the bar is pinned with banknotes from the world. An American dollar bill has been autographed in black marker pen. O.B. Laden, it says.

16

Pretty Flamingo

The drive south out of Ras could not be described as prepossessing. It's that halfway world again, where what used to be hasn't quite gone and what will be hasn't quite come. What used to be is a coastline of long sandy beaches backing onto scrubby desert. What will be is a continuous urban world housing wealthy ex-pats and even wealthier Arabs. The future is exemplified by the sudden eruptions of ornate villas with tall walls round them and no road to them, or by the shopping mall where I stop to buy a sandwich.

Inside the Spinneys supermarket the shelves are stocked to overflowing with the bright mendacious packaging of commerce. The aisles are wide, the air is cool, the whole is as clean as an operating theatre, and it's almost empty.

A billboard the size of a house fronts the empty supermarket car park. 'Live Your Dream' it says in massive cursive script, a phrase that is not translated into any other language. Beneath the words is a picture of a white woman in a white dress on a white horse on a beach of white sand. A second picture shows two men snorkelling. But the ads don't seem to be working. The dream isn't pulling them in. The vast warren of villas and apartments between the shops and the private beach seems barely occupied.

A little further along I stop at a beach, a remnant of what was. The warm sea laps like a cat. The beach is long, gently arcing, sandy as any adman could wish, and thick with trash. Plastic bags, plastic bottles, broken flip-flops, shampoo tubes, noodle bowls, used car tyres to fit any make or model, and a prodigious quantity of glass – much of it, I presume, biffed cheerfully from the windows of passing cars to burst into flesh-slicing shards. All of which may explain why I see no one snorkelling. And if you want to get hold of the white woman who galloped her white horse here at dawn, her hair blown by the wind and her white dress billowing behind her, I suggest you ring the equine vet.

A little further south I find a sign to the Al Salama slaughter-house. One side of the sign shows cartoon camels and goats looking vigorous and cheerful. The other side shows them swinging as carcases. But it's Friday and the pens are empty and the place is shut.

Surprisingly soon there looms on my right the familiar shape of a dead Russian freight plane. I'm back in Umm al Quwain, little more than an hour from Dubai. The UAE really is tiny. For old time's sake I drop in on the Barracuda Beach Resort. Mid morning on the Muslim sabbath and the liquor store is thrumming as before, with the car park holding a million bucks' worth of cars. Two of the cars have Saudi numberplates.

On the other side of a chain-link fence, a crowd of Indian families has gathered under an awning to listen to an Indian man in a suit. I stop to eavesdrop a while. The man is animated. He is a motivational speaker. He is explaining in English how to become rich. He is expounding the five golden rules of investment. He is telling them the secret of success. What I don't understand is why he is bothering to do so. What is he doing on his day off shouting into a microphone before a small crowd when he could be lounging on his three hundred-foot yacht in the Caribbean, drinking a cocktail from a golden beaker as he recuperates from a frenzied bout of no-holds-barred sex? Unless, that is, he is just trying to suck people in.

I hang around a while in the hope of seeing the audience snatch the cutlery from the table, advance en masse towards the little podium he's speaking from, and fork him to death. But no such luck. They are either too gullible or too nice.

Umm al Quwain has caught a dose of Symbolic Roundabout Syndrome. As well as the standard issue coffee-pot and bird-of-prey roundabouts it's got a dhow roundabout, a fort roundabout and an especially fetching shark roundabout. I had intended to drive on to Sharjah but decide on a whim to stop here for the night.

At reception in the Flamingo Beach Resort I ask what the nightly rate is.

'Six hundred dirhams,' says the receptionist.

'Thanks,' I say, 'but that's rather more than I am prepared to pay.'

'Three hundred dirhams,' he says.

Either this is the celebrated haggling in operation, in which case I seem to have a gift for it, or the Flamingo Beach Resort is desperate for custom.

It looks quite recently built. It has a central garden with lawns and banks of flowers, and concrete fish ponds spanned by decorative wooden bridges, but it seems to have fallen into the always hungry gulf between aspiration and achievement. It aspires to be a playground for the rich and white. But the only visible guests are a couple of Indian families sitting fully clothed on the little private beach and a single fat Russian male with a face like a punctured rugby ball. He dives repeatedly and heavily into the swimming

193

pool. In traditional Russian style he is wearing a pair of Speedos so tiny they threaten to disappear up the dread crack of his arse.

The outdoor cafeteria is deserted. Hooded crows ransack a wastebin. The Flamingo Beach Resort, it seems, is indeed desperate for custom – or perhaps I've struck a slack period. The promotional brochure in my room paints a markedly different picture of the place.

I dump my bag and head out into the area marked on my map as the old town. Most of the old bits of it are crumbling, uninhabited and uninhabitable. The rest is a warren of concrete hovels. The whole area smells of cooking and drains and bodies. It's the smell of urban poverty that you can find in most places in the world.

The locals are all from the Indian subcontinent. They squat outside the Bangladesh Cultural and Social Centre, or gather in knots in foetid alleyways and stare dispassionately as I pick my way between the puddles. But if I smile at them and say hello, they smile back with shy charm.

The alleys terminate in rows of despairing shops: Al Taweil Water Supply, Ulmar Mohd Bakery, Wall Street Exchange, Star Laundry, Najah Pipe Fitter and Key Maker, Al Nasr Typing Centre, all of them tiny, dusty-windowed, overstocked and under-patronized.

On the edge of this old town I find a restored fort, the place of birth of the sheikh who died so recently in London. Outside it stand a couple of cannon and a tank. It's now, of course, in accordance with best practice, a museum, but in 1929 the fort was still very much the ruler's palace, and it was then that it witnessed – and here I am quoting from the official website – 'the martyrdom of H. H. Sheikh Hamad Bin Ibrahim Al Mualla in 1929, the 8th ruler of Al Mualla family in Umm Al Quwain.'

It's an illustrative story, and according to the website it ran as follows, though I should warn you that the writer is no champion of spelling, punctuation or syntax (and he's also caught a nasty dose of brackets):

One day, while H. H. Sheikh Hamad was taking his supper, (others said he was sick), in the presence of his cousins, as usual in the room adjoining the tower, entered two of his guards- his nephews-; Abdul Rahman and Saeed (Al Abd) to greet him and to take supper with him (some people said that he was fasting). However, Saeed was carrying a gun, suddenly, he shot his uncle. Then they held his body up to inform the people of Umm Al Quwain that Sheikh Hamad was dead and that by tomorrow people of Umm Al Quwain would know their new ruler.

At that time, the people of Umm Al Quwain were furious and upset, so they were alerted and mobilized under the leadership of H.H. Sheikh Ahmed Bin Rashid Al Mulla and supprted by his cousins in order to control the situation, Abdul Rahman and Saeed were seeking shelter inside the fort. As the fort was high, it was easy for them to impose their domination upon the situation outside. After the matter had thoroughly been discussed, it was agreed to destroy the fort completely by a cannon, Saeed and Abdul Raman were able to see a vast area around them, so they saw that some people were towing the cannon towards the fort. Saeed Al Abd shot Hilal (one of those who were towing the cannon) in his leg.

After deep thinking on the matter, the wise and powerful men of Umm Al Quwain made up their mind to dig a moat around the fort. After that they filled the moat of palm leaves and put on fire, as soon as fire was put up, it burnt Abdul Rahman and Saeed, so people of Umm Al Quwain got rid of both of them and suceeded to keep peace and stability in the Emirate. This incident shows how the citizens of Umm Al Quwain were faithful to their leader and to what extent they loved him.

All of which is just far enough back in time to be quaint, exotic and enjoyable for us museum-goers, the hooded crows of history. But the account leaves rather a lot out. And what it leaves out, for reasons that may become clear, is the part played by outsiders behind the scenes, in particular and inevitably, the British.

The martyr of this story, Sheikh Hamad, was no innocent. Indeed he could be said to have got what was coming to him, for he had acquired the throne of Umm al Quwain half a dozen years earlier by assassinating his cousin. In this he was supported by Abu Dhabi, which, in the endless complexities of local politics, was keen to gain more influence in Umm al Quwain.

More crucially, Sheikh Hamad didn't like the British. Whereas the cousin he'd murdered did.

The British bided their time. Then, when the opportunity arose in 1929, they connived with the rulers of Sharjah to engineer the coup described above. Sheikh Ahmed who, as you may recall, mobilized the wise and powerful men of Umm al Quwain to dig a moat and set it on fire, and who subsequently became ruler to universal delight, was an anglophile. He once described the British Agent in the Gulf as being always right and having special gifts from God. Hardly surprising, really, since he owed his position to him.

Ahmed ruled for fifty-two years. In 1981 his son succeeded him. It was this son who recently died in London. Britain may have withdrawn from the Gulf but her legacy lives on.

The fort-museum, at which I am as usual the only visitor, doesn't fascinate me greatly despite such splendid items on display as Umm al Quwain's first driving licence. But I am intrigued by a small storeroom where, and again I am quoting from the king of brackets, 'bags of dates are put aside for a certain time, affected by humidity and high temperature, dates turn to liquid gathering into a designated hole, this liquid is called locally (Dibs and sometimes Sih).' I know what Dibs (or Sih) sounds like to me and it suggests that perhaps the Barracuda isn't practising a trade entirely new to this region.

I cross waste ground beyond the fort where Indian youths play cricket as badly and happily as ever, and arrive, *mirabile dictu*, at a corniche. This one's busier than most I've seen, perhaps because it's Friday. No one swims but there are plenty of families about, most of them Indian, squatting on the sand or on the grassed areas above, just idling in the mild weather.

Further south the beach gives way to a sea wall from which men and boys fish. On a patch of grass a black tent has been pitched behind a Land Cruiser. A mother and daughter in black abayas squat at the door of the tent washing dishes. The son comes running along the sea wall in red shorts and t-shirt, excited. He has only one arm. In his solitary hand he holds a freshly caught flatfish, flapping as it drowns in air. He shouts with joy, hands the fish to his mother, collects a tin of bait and runs perilously back along the wall to dad, his empty sleeve flapping like the fish.

I cut in from the beach past the tall blank walls of a sheikhly palace, walls crowned with security cameras and razor wire. At the giant metal gates there's a sentry box complete with sentry. The new town centre is impersonal and ugly, a grid built for the motor car. On the dead-straight boulevards the locals drive like maniacs between speed bumps, and like nuns over them.

I get a taxi back to the Flamingo and eat there in front of a television showing a programme about an American who's converting a car wash into an automatic wash tunnel for people. The narrator seems excessively excited about it all. I am the only diner in the restaurant and I ask the dispirited and inevitably Filipina waitress if it can be turned off. She promises to ask. She never comes back.

17

A Use for Roundabouts

'Parking for men', says the sign outside the mosque in Sharjah. I park, grinning. I'd like to see more such signs. Any supermarket, for example, that advertised 'Checkouts for men' would get my custom immediately. The queue would move so swiftly. No man would be surprised when asked to pay. Every man would have his bank card already poised above the slot and he'd have the magnetic strip the correct way round. He'd remember his pin number, and he wouldn't try to push the buttons through the back of the machine. He would never pay by cheque. If he paid with cash he wouldn't rootle through his bag for a purse and then rootle through the purse for coins. Nor would he then lay those coins on the scanner so the checkout girl found them hard to pick up. He'd just hand over a wad of notes and then he'd station himself behind the driving bar of the trolley and when the checkout girl handed over the receipt and his change he'd accept them like a relay runner taking the baton. In short, it would be lovely.

And this is the lovely bit of Sharjah. The unrelievedly urban drive from Umm al Quwain offered nothing to please the eye, but this down-town area has been tarted up. Here are more show-off buildings, more grass, fewer potholes, less litter, and more of a sense of civic pride backed up by civic money than anywhere I've seen outside Dubai itself. There's also a lot more evidence of religious commitment. The mosque with the gender-based parking is a vast and glorious beast with a tiled tower that reaches for heaven. I'd like to mooch around inside the building, but I like even more the fact that being an infidel I can't. When religion becomes a spectator sport for tourists it is no longer a religion.

The mosque overlooks the old port and a mass of beautiful battered dhows. A sign says 'Fishing and Getting Closer are Prohibited'. I can't see anyone getting closer, but there are scores of Indians fishing, tossing hand lines into the clear water between the old wooden hulls and following the progress of a shoal of sprats. The sprats shimmy this way and that, all shifting direction simultaneously, an aquatic herd driven by an unread-able collective urge. They dart and nibble at the baited hooks in an ignorant frenzy, competing to die. The Indians haul them up two, three, four at a time, tiny sparkles of fish flesh, their backs as green as moss. Into plastic bags they go to flap, expire and stiffen.

The sprats attract a diving bird, half cormorant, half duck it seems. When it dives the Indians excitedly try to catch it. As it cleaves through the clear water like a motorized bottle, hooks plop in beside it, behind it, right on its beak. To my relief it ignores them. When salmon fishing in Canada once I hooked a guillemot. It took ten minutes to land. The bird had taken the treble-hooked lure so deep down its throat that I had no choice but to kill it by bashing its head against the gunwale.

And once, from a second-floor flat in a grim bit of North London, I watched a shaven-headed child lay a baited hook in a backyard then retire inside. A pigeon descended, took the bait, flew off. The child emerged from indoors with a stout little fishing rod. He let the pigeon fly, then hauled on the rod. The bird fell through the air in a sudden entropic tumble, a chaotic blur of feathers. He loosened the line. The pigeon became a pigeon again. It swooped then rose, then rowed through the air, until whammo, he hauled on the rod again – and again and again. The scene held me like a horror movie. I hated it but couldn't turn away. The kid was whooping with delight. The kid was evil.

Across the road from the dhows and the fishermen is a vast tunnel of a building reminiscent of one of London's Victorian railway stations. But its roof is crowned with a golden dome that announces it emphatically as Islamic. It turns out to be a former shopping mall, built in the Eighties as the first wave of western consumerism swept the UAE. But with a nice twist of irony it has now been converted into the Museum of Islamic Culture, part of Sharjah's bid to become the region's moral and cultural epicentre. And the conversion is splendid. The building has the feel of a temple: spacious, reverential, subtly lit; a place where the clock doesn't tick and where you tread with quiet deference.

It is perhaps unfortunate that the first gallery I step into houses a range of swimwear for Islamic women. The range was designed in Australia and is called MyCozzie. The conflicting demands of modesty and streamlining make it purely comic. But I didn't come in here to laugh, and in the next gallery I don't. I gawp. I gawp at an exhibition on the Hajj, the greatest human pilgrimage on earth. By far.

There are about 1.3 billion Muslims alive today. That's about four times the population of the United States. That's one in five of the world's people. And every one of those 1.3 billion is supposed to do the Hajj to Mecca at least once in their lives.

The Hajj happens every twelve months. With Islamic months

being lunar months, the date of the Hajj moves back a few weeks every year and sometimes takes place in high summer. High summer in Mecca is impossibly hot. How do they cope? The answer is that some don't. Every year hundreds die on the Hajj. Sometimes there's a stampede and the hundreds become thousands. But still the next year there will be millions more undaunted pilgrims.

Last year three million turned up. And here in the museum there's an aerial photograph of most of them at prayer simultaneously. It's prostration for as far as the lens can see. All of them in white. All on their knees. All with their foreheads to the soil and their backs to the sky. It's a field of devotion. It's like wheat flattened by a storm. It's astonishing to stare at. Harness this devotion, this self-abasement to belief, and what could you not achieve? This is Islam made flesh. The word means submission to God.

The mosque that they're kneeling in and around is an open-air amphitheatre. The aerial photo shows only the mosque's top storey. Apparently there are two more storeys below ground. The building can accommodate two million people. That's a church the size of more than twenty Wembleys.

The object of these people's veneration is a black cube on a plinth, the Kaaba. It's the holy of holies, the house of Allah, the literal centre of Islam. In my hotel room in Ras al Khaimah there was an arrow on the wall beside the bed. It pointed towards this building. Five times a day, every day, at sunrise, sunset and three times in between, 1.3 billion people are supposed to kneel in this direction. And a goodly percentage of them do.

Finding the right direction for prayer is straightforward in the Middle East, where most Muslims live, because every mosque is aligned to Mecca. And if you can't find a mosque there's an Islamic pocket compass that will do the job for you. But further afield the business gets trickier because of the curvature of the earth. A Muslim in New York, for example, has two options. One is to pray in the direction that an aeroplane would fly if it were heading to Mecca. That's the great circle route, heading north-east over Baffin Island and the Arctic tundra. It's the shortest route by far but it seems counter-intuitive and perhaps sacrilegious. The alternative is to kneel in an east-south-easterly direction, following a straight line ruled between the Big Apple and Mecca on a Mercator's projection map of the world, as in an atlas. It's a far longer route, but to our literal minds it seems somehow more fitting.

The difference between the two is close to ninety degrees and that right angle has provoked a fierce dispute among American Muslims. There is now a schism between the flat-mappers and the great circlists. It has not yet led to bloodshed, but in the course of human history millions of people have lost their lives over far more trivial theological disputes.

The Kaaba is an ancient place of worship. It predates Islam by thousands of years. Its original function seems to have been as a place of truce, a white flag, as it were, of black stone. The leaders of warring tribes could meet in its peaceable shadow to thrash out their differences without fear of being killed.

Which suggests that, just as Christianity grafted its nativity myth onto the winter solstice and its resurrection myth onto the celebration of spring (what exactly have bunnies and fluffy chicks to do with Jesus?), so Islam grafted itself onto what was already there. Long before Mohammed was even a twinkle in Allah's eye, the Kaaba had been a place of mystical reverence, a place apart. Islam simply purloined it.

With only a couple of days of car rental left I ought to go to Abu Dhabi. It's the paterfamilias of the UAE, and I have been told so many things about it: how its wealth drives development throughout the UAE; how it has resisted Dubai's headlong rush into the brasher qualities of twenty-first century capitalism; how it works quietly offstage while Dubai charges to the front and seizes the microphone; how it is smugly enjoying Dubai's current financial woes with more than a hint of, 'Don't say I didn't warn you'; and how indeed it is quietly stepping in with its petro-dollars to buy Dubai's distressed assets.

Of the seven emirates Abu Dhabi is by far the largest. The city of Abu Dhabi itself sits on the coast but its domains stretch hundreds of miles south and west. Most of those domains are sandy nothing, but underneath them lies the good black stuff that has paid for everything; the stuff that has allowed the ruling Al Nayhan family to snaffle up any trinket that catches their eye: a squadron of American fighter jets, say, or Manchester City Football Club. And there's plenty more oil yet, about seventeen million American dollars' worth, or so I've read, for every citizen of the emirate. Abu Dhabi can afford to be smug.

As you may already have deduced, the United Arab Emirates is not preponderantly Arab. Nor is it very united. The ruling families of Abu Dhabi and Dubai trace their ancestry back to the same tribe, but that has not always made them brothers. When Thesiger arrived on his best camel in 1948, Dubai and Abu Dhabi were engaged in a minor war with each other. To some extent it seems that they still are, though the war these days is economic and rarely acknowledged. There is, for example, a dogfight taking place right now in the airspace above the UAE.

One of Dubai's greatest successes has been Emirates Air. It serves the world. And you can drive to the Emirates terminal from Abu Dhabi in less time than it takes to drive to Heathrow from central London. Yet Abu Dhabi has recently launched and heavily promoted its own airline, Etihad, which competes directly with Emirates. The reason for doing so does not, one suspects, have an awful lot to do with economics.

Abu Dhabi likes to see itself as mature, whereas Dubai is the exuberant headstrong wilful teenager. Abu Dhabi specializes in grand civic buildings, huge bravura pieces of contemporary architecture, done with a less overt obeisance to glamour and commerce. That maturity, however, does not extend to its citizens' driving. Abu Dhabi's drivers manage to kill themselves in even greater number than the drivers of Dubai. Last year almost a thousand people died on Abu Dhabi's comparatively few roads. That's roughly twelve times the rate at which New Zealand drivers die. And I read in the paper yesterday that because of the abundance of vehicles and the shortage of space, people have taken to parking their cars overnight in the middle of those roads. The police say they're going to take this new offence seriously and the culprits will be in hot water, but since those culprits are certain to be Emirati nationals, I doubt that the water will be more than lukewarm.

All of which means that I ought to go to Abu Dhabi to have a look round. But I don't. Instead I point the Nissan towards Al Ain, the second city of that emirate, partly because I have an acquaintance there so I won't have to pay exorbitant hotel rates, and partly because I doubt that in forty-eight hours I'll do anything more than scratch the surface of Abu Dhabi. But mainly because I don't think Abu Dhabi would surprise me.

Al Ain on the other hand, I know next to nothing about. I know only that it is described as an oasis city, and the word oasis still performs its cartoon magic on my mind.

I crawl through traffic jams out of Sharjah, swing round the unappealing backside of Dubai and spear across the increasingly desertish desert on highways that dismiss the landscape as an irrelevance, a mere backdrop to air-conditioned comfort. I get vistas of sand stretching limitless to the edge of the world and I simply keep going. And when I reach Al Ain after a couple of hours, unwracked by thirst, untroubled by anything except a numb foot from keeping the throttle depressed, I take to the place immediately. It seems better tended, better built, and better laid out than anywhere I've been in these parts, probably because it's got more money.

It's got more money because it's part of Abu Dhabi, and it's got even more money because it's the birthplace of the ruler of Abu Dhabi. He looks after it like a shrine. Al Ain's suburbs are suburban, its streets wide, its pavements clean, its poor less obvious, and though it's caught the standard dose of decorative roundaboutitis, it seems immediately a comfortable place to live.

And the first thing I come across, slap bang in the town centre, is what I think may be a graveyard. Nothing odd about that, of course, because they've been dying hereabouts for several thousand years, yet this, if it is a graveyard, is the first I've seen. It's surrounded by a wall of concrete block, one corner of which has been flattened and reveals a patch of what appears to be wasteland dotted with trees and several little hummocks, some of which end in what could be a headstone.

I clamber in over the rubble. The place is about a third of a football pitch in area. No one's about. Litter abounds. The hummocks are of roughly the right size and shape to be graves. A couple of the rough headstones have an Arabic inscription on them though these don't seem to have been done with any care. The place feels unloved, ignored. I climb back out over the rubble, uncertain what I've found.

The main drag is busy with Arab men and women shopping, though the shopkeepers and stallholders are still predominantly Indian, as is the English on the shop signs. It has the usual errors of transcription. I am particularly taken by Hawazen Lungerie.

By a patch of wasteland near the top of town there's a line of Toyota pick-ups. They're all dead. They've sunk to their axles in the sandy ground and their tyres are long gone. Collectively they now form a goat market, with the goats penned on the flat beds of the trucks, bleating, clambering over each other, their long ears dangling like the side curls on a Hasidic Jew. Their owners squat in groups, playing cards or chewing on bread or smoking or snoozing. Most of these men give me only the most cursory of glances and dismiss me as a gawper. One man however is convinced that there's a hole in my life and that hole is exactly the size and shape of a goat. He follows me, speaking in broken English, taking my arm, leading me twice back to his pen of little brown and white goats as skinny as orphans. 'You like goat. You buy goat.' He's half right, as it happens. But I've already got two at home.

Just below the goat market is the oasis proper, the reason for Al Ain's existence. It is a dense mass of date palms, a forest of date palms, encircled by a daunting wall. A gate with a barrier arm permits me entry and I wander a while down roads that wind and threaten my sense of direction. But I find only more date palms and I am prevented from wandering among them by more walls, mile after mile of wall. I emerge with some relief through a different gate, to find myself in a part of town that looks similar to the one I parked in but that no longer seems to contain my Nissan. I solve the problem temporarily by going for lunch.

The restaurant is Arab. My fellow lunchers are Arab. It's a first for me. But these are not the landlord Arabs of Dubai, the spotlessness of whose dishdashes is matched only by the spotlessness of their Porsches. These men, and there are only men of course, wear dun-coloured robes, unironed and lived in.

Before I came here, just about the only thing I knew, or thought I knew, about Islam was that the left hand is unclean. The reason, as I understood it and without wishing to go into detail, is lavatorial. So you greeted people with the right hand and you ate with it, exclusively.

Well, not in Al Ain. Or at least not among these rough-shaven men in this cheap restaurant in Al Ain. In consuming a heap of meat and rice and grease, while devotedly looking up at a screen showing motor racing, they go at their food with both hands. I go at mine with cheap cutlery.

The intermission for lunch solves the problem of my missing car in the same way as taking the dog for a walk often solves the last clue in a crossword. It's as if the subconscious mind chews things over better when the conscious mind isn't telling it to chew, a truth that I suspect applies to far more than crossword clues. I leave the restaurant and find a phone booth. Then another phone booth, then another. There's one on almost every street corner. And the fifth one I find actually works. The others have not been visibly vandalized; they just seem to have died. I dial my only acquaintance in Al Ain.

Jim sounds as pleased to hear my voice as I am to hear his, which I find encouraging because we haven't met. He's the brother-in-law of a friend and he's reputedly fond of a good night out. And by way of showing what good company I shall prove, I hand him the problem of the lost car.

'What a laugh,' he says. 'Where are you?'

'I don't know.'

'Right,' he says. 'Do you know the clock roundabout?'

'I presume that's a roundabout with a clock on it.'

'Beside it,' says Jim. 'Ask anyone. I'll pick you up there in half an hour, then we'll fetch my daughter from ballet and then we'll find your car and then we'll dump both cars at my place and then we'll go out for a bit of a laugh and a carry-on. What do you say?'

I grope for the exact phrase to convey my feelings, and find it. 'Yes,' I say. It sounds as though a problem shared with Jim is a problem solved.

The first person I ask, an Indian youth, knows exactly where the clock roundabout is and insists on leading me there by walking a yard behind me, which is an odd way to go about it and which rather inhibits conversation, but I'm grateful for his kindness. Jim soon swings by in his standard issue Land Cruiser, honks the horn and comes to a halt not before the roundabout, nor after it, but on it. I think he may have been in this country for quite some time. With his shaven head and angular features he reminds me of that gaunt rock singer from Midnight Oil who went on to become the Australian Minister for the Environment.

The ballet school is in some quiet backwater of suburban ex-pat villas. I wait outside as a series of predictably costly cars draw up to disgorge a series of predictably dressed western women, gym-toned and salon-groomed. And it strikes me once again that one of the attractions of living in the UAE, apart from the weather, the wealth and the freedom from taxation, is the absence of an underclass. Or rather of an underclass that sneers at nice ballet girls, that threatens and swaggers and swears in the street during the day and vomits on it at night. There is an underclass here, of course, a vast army of people from poor countries, but they are unobtrusive. They defer. They smile. They lead you kindly to roundabouts. They don't wear track pants or scoff burgers or say 'Who are you ~~fucking~~ looking at?'

Jim finds my car without difficulty, simply by driving me around till I recognize a roundabout. I'm so pleased to have found their purpose at last. Then it's a simple business of retracing my route into town until I behold, as mute and patient as all mechanical devices, my little silver Nissan. A few hours later I'm installed in a palatial spare bedroom in an ex-pat enclave, I've made friends with Jim's daughters by playing games that exhaust me rather quicker than they exhaust them, and I've showered and shaved and am ready to see whatever Al Ain has to offer by way of evening entertainment.

'So what do you want to see?' says Jim.

'The truth,' I say portentously, and Jim, bless him, says 'Follow me.' We take a taxi to a vast hotel. A wedding's going on. Arrows pointing down separate staircases say 'Womens wedding' and 'Mens wedding'. But we go down a third staircase to a bar where Jim is greeted by the barman – always a good start – and half a dozen pool players, all of whom are young Emirati men. Some wear dishdashes, some jeans and t-shirts. All play better pool than I do and all of them drink. But the man who my eyes keep straying back to is in a far corner of the bar, staring up at a television on the wall. He sits at a table, ostensibly with a group of other men, but he doesn't speak. He is Emirati, dressed in all the gear. He fiddles occasionally with what looks like a diamond-encrusted cell phone. On the table in front of him are a packet of Rothmans, an ashtray, a glass and a three-quarters-full bottle of Chivas Regal. And he looks too fat to stand. He's a colossus of fat, a mountain of blubber. His chins have chins. For him a trek to the urinal would be like Thesiger's trek across the Empty Quarter, which is presumably why he sticks to Scotch.

I feel at ease in bars, always have. The pool players stop being Emiratis and become merely men I'm playing pool with. I'd like to ask them questions about unclean left hands, Islamic burial customs and the significance of roundabouts, but it somehow doesn't seem the right time or place, and anyway the softening sway of booze makes such matters matter less. One of drinking's many virtues is to quiet the analytical mind and to stress the importance, the vitality, of the present tense. So I just play pool, lose, drink lager, and take peanuts from bowls with whichever hand comes naturally.

'We're off,' says Jim suddenly, 'let's go,' and I follow like a puppy, delighted to have the decisions made for me, my tail wagging.

Our route takes us through a maze of corridors and into a dark car park. The unconditioned evening air comes as a surprise, a warm slap of reality. Somehow we hook up with a chubby man from Cornwall in a pink polo shirt and a Bostonian in glasses.

'You'll love this,' says Jim as we push through doors into sudden noise. I don't. The noise is an assault. It's noise that makes me want to back straight out again. The place is thronged with men, most of them Emirati and all of them seated at tables. Waitresses scurry among the tables with drinks and shisha pipes and plates of fruit.

All the tables are aligned towards a stage, on one side of which stands a man. He is the embodiment of sleaze. His white trousers cling like a second skin. His embroidered shirt is unbuttoned to the navel. His chest is a cluster of medallions, his hair an oil slick. He is wailing into a hand-held microphone. The noise he makes sounds like the call of the muezzin performed while undergoing surgery without anaesthetic. The amp whistles with feedback.

In the middle of the stage, girls. Perhaps a dozen girls. Dancing. No, not dancing, jigging on the spot. No, not even jigging, shuffling. Girls of half a dozen different races it would seem, or mixed races: Filipina, Chinese, Indian, Thai perhaps, and a single coal-black African. One wears Levi's, another a skimpy parody of a sari, another gauze and sequins. Some chew gum. None feigns the least pleasure in what she's doing. They exhibit all the zest of cattle beasts at auction.

'Great,' shouts the Cornishman and he claps his hands and we sit down. The Bostonian leans in to me, cups his hand over my ear. 'They can't take their clothes off,' he bellows. 'It's against their culture.'

A plate of fruit slices comes to our table and four small bottles of Heineken. The waitress drops a bill on the table for two hundred and forty dirhams. That's several times what we were paying in the pool bar.

The Cornishman's eyes are gleaming. He's rapt. But he's alone in his rapture. The men at the tables just sit in silence amid the assault of noise and look on with a sort of vague blankness, a low-voltage sexual assessing.

In one sense it is obvious what is going on. In another I just don't get it. I particularly don't get Mr Sleazy. What's his role?

The girls take a superfluous breather from their shuffling. They repeatedly glance offstage to where, no doubt, some unseen pimp is orchestrating this parody of a show, this seedy debasement. Mr Sleazy takes his cue to come centre stage and make even more passionate love to his microphone. He wraps himself around it. Only he and the Cornishman seem to be enjoying themselves.

I chug my beer and leave. Not for moral reasons. Not for financial reasons. But for reasons of noise. I have never borne noise well. It physically hurts me. I sit on a wall outside.

I know what I've just seen but I haven't quite grasped it. It was sexual titillation, but how much more than that, I don't know. The women were not Emirati women. They were alien chattels, distanced from motherhood or love or indeed from any form of humanity, just as at any peep show, any strip show, any staged eroticism anywhere in the world. But what was bizarre was their refusal to fake it, to suggest sensuality, lust. Here were no raunchy come-on grins, no coquettish teasing. You would have had to be obtuse not to sense their resentment, or to be utterly put off by it. Theirs was just an honest expression of the dreary injustice of sexual exploitation. They made no effort. They endured.

And the men too. They let rip no raunchy bellows, no yeehas of the blood. Just a grinding apparent impassivity, as though they didn't much want to be there either but that they too were powerless to do anything but endure the call of the loins. Lust would milk them of their money and the women of their dignity. And they were powerless to fight it. No one dared to say boo to it. I have never been anywhere like it.

Erotic dancing is nothing new in Arabia, but this was not erotic. It was a pale and wretched simulacrum of the erotic without the zest of disinhibition. Add the strange overlay of Mr Sleazy's vaguely Arabic wailing, and the whole shebang was as odd as God, and sadder than a wet Sunday afternoon in Luton.

The others emerge quite soon.

'More?' says Jim.

'Different.'

'Come see.'

We follow ramps that wind and take us further below ground level in the same building. We push open swing doors and noise floods out once again, laced thickly with smoke. This bar is lower, smaller, darker, dirtier, cheaper and exclusively Indian. Not an Arab to be seen. The beer comes in pints at exactly half the price of the bottles upstairs. And yet the scenario is replicated. Men from the Indian subcontinent sit at tables. Women from the Indian subcontinent perform on stage. They show a tad more gusto than the women upstairs. The men don't.

Again there's a singer of sorts with a mike. He wails lyrics from a spiral-bound notebook that he holds in his spare hand. The absence of any attempt at theatricality only adds to the grimness of it all.

Stage right there's a line of chairs as if for dignitaries at some civic event. When the dancing girls stop they sit down. On the far right of the line one of the girls picks up a book from under her chair and opens it to read . . .

Thereafter the evening loses shape. Different hotels, more pool, more girls. I lose all sense of time and location. I just follow and trust and grin. Towards the end of the night, as we cross a patch of waste ground, I trip and fall. 'Watch out for snakes,' says Jim. 'There aren't any nice ones.'

18

Quivering Dhabi

When I wake, late, there's a cup of cold tea beside my bed. I lie a while feeling less than loved by life. But the symptoms are familiar, they'll fade, and I've got a mental tape of last night to review and be entertained by. It's a jumpy thing, speeding up in the final reel, becoming disconnected, mere flashes of vivid isolated image – climbing a wall I would never have climbed sober; the warning about snakes; an Emirati playing pool in a red sequinned glove; bending to tie my shoelaces in a bar, falling against the table, giggling, and being helped up by a worried Indian – but eventually the film dissolves into incoherence and then static and I get up. At least, as far as I can tell, there is nothing excruciating, nothing to wince over, nothing to go back to time and again like a tongue seeking out an exposed nerve in a tooth.

The house is empty, the kids at school, the parents at work, a note on the bench telling me to help myself. The coffee percolator is of a design I haven't met before, but I have never yet been defeated by a coffee machine. When it fires into life, spitting, coughing through its narrow pipes then dripping joy into the pot below, I immediately start to feel better. One of the few things I disliked about China when I went there a couple of years ago was the difficulty of finding coffee. How else am I supposed to start the day's engine?

I take the mug outside and sit on a wall in the silent lane. The air is five degrees warmer than inside the house. The place is silent. Perhaps fifty ex-pat windows overlook me. I see no faces at those windows, no twitch of blind or curtain. All at work, I suppose. A ginger cat slides over a wall like a furry Dali clock. Its head appears round the foot of a pillar, utterly immobile, its eyes fixed like lasers, taking me in. Those eyes swing away a fraction of a second before I, too, hear the flop of sandals on concrete, a maid in a light blue apron carrying a green bucket of cleaning stuff. I look back and the cat is gone. Like a thought. Like the swish of a blade.

I smoke, happy to be idle, slowly regaining a toehold on normality, ordering the world after the jangle of the night before. It is an old familiar process. As though the constructed self has taken a thump from the wrecking ball of anarchy and needs to be, if not rebuilt, at least repointed and replastered, smoothed back into its usual form as a bulwark against chaos. I don't know if anyone else goes through this. I've done it all my adult life.

More maids trot by and slip through the front doors of one or other of these silent, terraced, air-conditioned, well-appointed villas. When the owners return the place will have been put to rights, the dishes washed and dried, the clothes ironed, the beds made. What does a maid think as she makes good another's mess, dealing always with the leavings, the detritus? Does she hope? Or does she accept and get on and get by, one day at a time, one hour at a time, one ironed shirt after another. I do not know. And it would be impertinent to ask, wrong, patronizing.

I mull once more over that thunderhole of a go-go bar, where the girls didn't go go and the men just sat. How do the girls feel right now? Or the men? Do they feel they had a good time? Or are they battered by Islamic guilt here in their own country that has changed beyond recognition during their own lifetimes? Their country, which has been showered with dollars, invaded by invitation and severed from what it was. It's won the lottery, this place, Abu Dhabi in particular, and lottery winners are famous for struggling to cope with their luck.

And how's Fatso doing? Fatso the blubber heap, with the bottle of Chivas and the wham bang American movie on the widescreen telly and the gimmick-laden cell phone? What's he up to right now? Has he levered his bulk from the mattress yet, planted his feet on the floor and paused to recover from the exertion? How does he fill his day? I don't know, though I don't think it would be impertinent or patronizing to ask. Indeed, I think late last night that I did ask some of the Emirati pool players what they did during the day. I can't remember them being affronted, but neither can I remember what they said. Given the scenario and the hour, I doubt it's much of a loss.

Back indoors, I look up Islamic burial practices on Jim's computer and discover that the neglected place I found was indeed probably a graveyard. The funeral rites of Islam are simple. They wash the corpse, wrap it in plain cloth, and bury it without a casket and with its head pointing towards the Kaaba in Mecca. As far as I can gather no holy man is required to officiate, perhaps because in a hot country you've got to bury them quick. Like Christianity and Buddhism as originally conceived, Islam is as much a practical social code as a religion.

Women are discouraged from attending burials because they tend to become emotional. The mourners toss soil into the grave while reciting a prayer: 'We created you from it, and return you into it, and from it we will raise you a second time', the similarity of the words to the Christian liturgy affirming

217

that the two great monotheistic faiths sprang from the same source, and continue to have far more in common than they have differences.

Having prayed, the mourners slightly overfill the grave to create a mound, then pat the soil down with their hands, and that is pretty much that. If there's a headstone it should be simple and unadorned, because the Koran discourages ostentation. Though according to Wikipedia, '. . . it is becoming more common for family members to erect grave monuments.' I'm willing to bet that the late Sheikh of Umm al Quwain will get a cracker.

In the centre of Al Ain there's a Lulu hypermarket. Its aisles are narrow because it caters mainly to the immigrant races, few of whom manage to grow fat. I choose a couple of little gifts, go to a checkout and am offered service ahead of a Filipina who was there before me. 'This lady was first,' I say. The Indian checkout girl looks surprised. The Filipina looks flustered. 'Thank you, sir,' she says, and she fumbles with her purse to hasten the transaction and she blushes. It isn't the first time I've been offered preferential treatment. There's something close to implicit apartheid here, or at least an ethnic pecking order, with the local Emiratis at the head of the list, in second place the immigrant professional whites, and then come the rest.

On the top floor a little restaurant serves me more restorative coffee. At the next table a small Indian and a substantial man of Mediterranean complexion are studying a floor plan. They turn out to be partners in an interior design business. The big boy's from Morocco, the Indian from Kerala. He's garrulous, confiding, patriotic and opinionated.

'America, England, is weak culture, sir. India very strong culture.'

'Then why aren't you in India?'

He makes the money sign and grins. 'I am paying no taxes

here. If I have two million dirhams here they are asking me no questions. I have two million dirhams in India they are asking me where they are coming from. I am in Saudi ten years, two years here. My grandfather and father before me. When I am succeeding I am bringing over my son to take the business and I am going back to Kerala.'

'Your wife is still in Kerala.'

'Of course, sir. Wife is wife and ladies is ladies. You understand me?' And he grins conspiratorially. 'Here is everything in UAE, drunk ladies, but it is all covered up. I am finding you everything you want but it is all covered up.

'In America is blue movie business. Oh dear me, but in America everything is fine with blue movies if they are paying tax. If they are not paying tax they are in big trouble. It is very weak culture, very buggered up. I am not offending you, sir?'

'You're not offending me.'

'You are good man, sir. I am finding you everything you want.'

The Moroccan has not once looked up from his floor plans, marking them occasionally with coloured pens, saying nothing, and chain smoking Marlboro directly beneath a sign forbidding him to do so.

In the paper there's a report on the Dubai marathon, run yesterday. It was sponsored by Standard Chartered Bank and held, inevitably, 'under the patronage of HH Sheikh Mohammed bin Rashid Al Maktoum, UAE Vice-President, Prime Minister and Ruler of Dubai.' The winner, almost as inevitably, was the world's best marathon runner, Haile Gebrselassie, who duly took a cheque for a quarter of a million dollars back home to Ethiopia, or wherever it is that he now lives, which I suspect may not be Ethiopia any more. Cheques for a quarter of a million get you out of Ethiopia.

But there, in a simple sports report, is a microcosmic representation of Dubai's daytime face. The ruler's position is constantly bolstered. Western corporate money underlies every-thing. The best of the best is bought in from wherever. And another brushstroke is added to Dubai's image. That image makes no effort to reflect the life led in Dubai. It merely paints a way of life that Dubai wants the world to imagine it leads. It's PR. And it works.

Feeling much recovered, I collect my car and drive out of Al Ain to the suburb of Hili, where there's a fun park that doesn't attract me and an archaeological site that does, or at least mildly. There in the 1960s some Danish archaeologists uncovered a five thousand-year-old tomb. On its lintel there are ancient drawings of a cheetah, an oryx and some people. The cheetah is long since extinct in this region, and the oryx is critically endangered, but people have multiplied exponentially. They're the temporary local evolutionary success story.

Inside the graves the Danes also found vessels of clay and soapstone of a design identical to vessels found in both Iran and Iraq. More interestingly still, they found clear evidence of agriculture. These people grew wheat and sorghum, which undermines the tendency in these parts to suggest that before the discovery of oil the UAE was occupied only by Bedouin, those implacable, hawk-eyed, dagger-bearing, fearless nomads of the desert. It wasn't.

The suburbs of Al Ain have an ordered quality that's missing from Dubai. And amid the neat villas and parks and sports sta-diums and hospitals, there are so many and such reliable road signs that I find without difficulty the Hili archaeological site with its great iron gates. They are locked. I ring Jim. He and his family are going to visit friends, a married couple, the husband very much an Al Ain local. Would I care to join them?

The couple live a little way into the desert. Our route takes us past several camel farms, fenced-off areas of sand where a farmer is retained to live on site and tend to the beasts. Their fodder is brought in. Most camels are kept only for the pride of ownership.

The couple meet us in their front yard where they keep a small menagerie, including a horse and, to my surprise, a couple of dogs. And right by the house, enchantingly, there's a pen of indigenous gazelles. These are the *dhabi* after which Abu Dhabi was named. They are quivering delicate creatures, no more than thigh height, with the huge eyes and electric reactions of all deer. They are half tame, and in response to my coos and clucks come hesitantly to the wire fence, butting against it with horns like miniature plaster moulds of themselves. No one is quite sure how many of these exquisite beasts survive. With the big cats long gone their only predator is Man. But he's an outstanding predator, though, more often than not, an inadvertent one.

The house is a simple, open-plan, single-storey building of plastered concrete. Carpets on the floor, a scattering of traditional artefacts, a model dhow, a brass coffee pot – though we get tea – an ancient Martini rifle, and a tame pigeon that flutters across on invitation and perches on my shoulder. The carpet is speckled with pigeon shit.

Said is a gentle, educated man, bespectacled, affable, slim in his dishdash. And he's worried about the desert. I cannot imagine anyone I saw in the bars last night being worried about the desert. But then neither could I imagine Said in any of the bars I visited last night.

The problem, says Said, is that so many desert animals have been lost. Those animals spread seed. Without them, the desert just keeps getting bigger. He is the first conservationist I've met here, indeed the first person who has expressed any interest in the land beyond the cities. To most people I've met, the desert is an inconvenience, or an adventure playground or just real estate in waiting.

Said is nevertheless proud of the industrialization of his country. Abu Dhabi, he says, is building infrastructure on a magnificent scale. Its vast new ports will lead the world. A huge aluminium smelter is under construction. I have to remember, he says, that the UAE is only thirty-eight years young, a mere baby on the international stage. Things have happened here at a headlong pace and it was inevitable that mistakes would be made. The worst have concerned immigration. There is, says Said, by way of illustration, an island in Abu Dhabi that is populated entirely by Indians.

He says this sadly, not with racial rancour but as someone who feels that something worth keeping has been lost. It is a sentiment I have been waiting to hear expressed. There are simply too many ex-pats here. They have little stake in the place. They don't identify with it. They are birds of passage. In the event of war or economic meltdown, they would simply fly away.

Said is equally unimpressed by the sheikhs of the minor emirates. 'All they want is more money for themselves,' he says. 'But democracy will come.'

'Really?' I had not expected to hear this.

'Oh yes, it will come.'

'When?'

'Soon,' he says, 'quite soon. But you must remember we are young.' And he stresses that the sheikhs of Abu Dhabi and Dubai have been people of vision and courage. And without such strong leaders the UAE could not have come as far as it has, or as fast.

I've no doubt that he's right.

He lets me hold the Martini rifle. It's British army issue, first used in the 1870s and much loved by the Bedouin. It's brick solid. When I raise the thing to my shoulder, point it out of the front door and peer down the barrel at the darkening desert, I struggle to hold it steady. Rifles like this once governed the world. The bullets they spat felled fuzzy wuzzies, Zulus, dervishes, rebel sepoys and no doubt many an astonished delicate gazelle.

*

After dinner in Al Ain, Jim has work to do. He sends me out into the warm night with the names of a couple of places I might enjoy. The Peach Bar, he tells me, is popular with sexually ambiguous Filipinos.

'Get the right night,' he says, 'and it's a riot.'

This is the wrong night. The Peach Bar's dead as meat. A couple of gloomy Indians sit drinking alone and staring at a small and unlit stage where nothing's happening.

In an ex-pat hotel bar nearby I meet a Health and Safety officer from Yorkshire. He's currently tending to the health and safety of a gang of North Koreans building a hospital. 'They don't do health and safety in North Korea,' he says. 'Hadn't got a clue, this lot, not a bloody clue. Had to teach them from the bottom up.' He drops all h's, pronounces up 'oop' and turns the word 'the' into a glottal stop.

'And guess how many accidents we've had, how many injuries?'

'None,' I want to say. I don't, of course. It wouldn't be playing the game. But I'm struggling to take an interest in North Korean health and safety.

A guitarist appears on stage and rescues me by attracting my friend's attention. The guitarist is wearing a young man's shirt and hair the length of a young man's hair, but it is grey.

'Where are you from?' says a woman's voice behind me.

Its owner is tall, Chinese and dressed to sell sex. She looks deep into my eyes, and smiles with a thousand teeth.

'New Zealand.'

'Nooseala?'

'New Zealand.'

'What country?'

'Australia,' I say, because it's always easier.

'I love Australia,' she says, and she forces herself to laugh and brushes her hand against my forearm.

It doesn't take her long to work out that she is wasting her time. And when I ask her a few questions, she drops out of performance mode with what seems like relief. She has been in Al Ain for five years. She is still lonely here. She would love to return to China.

I tell her I've spent a bit of time in China and she tells me where she's from, and by a fluke I have been there, or at least near enough there, and she asks me more detailed questions than I can answer, and she tells me how much she misses everything, and I think for a moment that she's going to cry but she is tougher than that. She offers to buy me a drink and then laughs at the reversal of roles.

Every couple of months she has to leave the UAE to renew her visitor's visa. I ask her why she doesn't just pack up and go home. Money, she says. She is no doubt paying off a debt to a pimp, or to some cartel that trades in dreams and poverty and female flesh, but she will not elaborate. I press her gently but she begins to look worried, and I suspect that she suspects I may be someone in authority after all. I back off.

'I like talk you,' she says as I finish my drink and make to leave. 'You are nice man.'

I'm not. I'm a voyeur. I like to peep into lives, to come alongside them as it were, see in through their cabin windows, get a titillating glimpse of their otherness, and then sail safely on.

And as I steer my little boat of self across the hotel courtyard, I sense that she and the Yorkshireman and the North Korean labourers building a hospital that will never treat them, are of a piece. They are the people who come to boom towns, who migrate to wherever there's a new place growing, a place that promises work and money, that offers an escape from poverty. That offers hope.

The UAE, where all the major cities are only an hour's drive apart, is just one big boom town. All the whores and labourers and the western professionals and the Filipina maids and the Indian middle men have come here in the same way as people once went to the goldfields or west across the States, to prosper or to fall, to take their chances. Each has brought a story with him and adds a chapter to it here. All hope to write a happy ending. Few do. The Chinese girl doesn't look like doing so.

It's midnight. In the two hours since I left it, the Peach Bar has come alive. To get in I have to push past a big black doorman. On the stage inside, now garishly lit, a Filipino transsexual is singing Shirley Bassey. He wears a Dolly Parton wig and a sequinned vest and a denim skirt and the floor at his feet is pulsing with dancers, male dancers and female, brown-skinned and black. And there's happiness here, happiness I didn't find in last night's bars, or in the Chinese whore bar or indeed in any bar I've visited in this Islamic world. It's no-thought-to-tomorrow happiness, don't-give-a-toss happiness, flinging itself around without restraint, like kids playing football on the beach.

'Darlings,' exclaims the singer as he ends a song, 'DARlings,' and the crowd squeals with delight. They're poor people most of them, menial people, a long way from home but right now happy. The air is fierce with smoke. A tubby Indian manager presides over a till on which the cash drawer lolls open stuffed with notes. Happiness is good business.

Crossing waste ground on my way home I stop a fraction of a second before my foot comes down on a black coil. I leap back. My heart rises in my chest. I can hear it beating. The coil doesn't move. 'There are no nice ones,' said Jim. I biff a stone at it. The coil doesn't move. I edge closer. It is irrigation tubing. I boot it. It skitters across the gravel, rolls, tilts and falls to the ground. I laugh and feel happy under the Arabian stars.

I turn off the highway. Ahead of me lie a few days in Dubai then the long flight home to the green of New Zealand. Here's my last chance to get a taste of Thesiger's desert.

The road that spears across it towards a blank horizon is new and smooth and black, but its edges are eroded by little fans of blown sand. After every storm this road must have to be found again, dug out.

On an English language radio station there's a programme about real estate, that middle-class obsession the world over. Worried property owners ring in to ask questions of an expert. You can hear fear in their voices. There is talk of an eight per cent reduction in Dubai's population and of house prices having sunk fifty per cent with no bottom in sight. And the callers are worried about a recent decree from the sheikh. What, they want to know, does it actually mean? The expert can't tell them. A whole edifice of wealth is creaking. I listen to the urgent anxious voices and I look at blank impassive desert and I turn the radio off. Now there's only the sun hot through the glass and the whirr of the engine and the hiss of rubber on tarmac.

Up ahead of me in nowhere the figure of a man takes shape. As I approach he steps into the road, waving with both arms. Not frantic, but insistent. I seem to have no choice but to stop. I stop a yard or two short of him. His robe is off-white cotton. He steps forward, pats the bonnet with both hands, comes round to the passenger side, opens the door and gets in.

I turn to smile at him. He doesn't smile back. Middle-aged, face of leather, three days short of a shave, he barely even glances at me.

'Salaam aleekum,' I say, 'my name's Joe,' and I offer a hand. He mutters, takes my hand briefly, distractedly, as though it's a tedious preliminary to be got out of the way, and then gestures that we drive on. We drive on. He leans forward in the seat, looking eagerly ahead.

'Where we go?' I say, conceding the language.

He says nothing. He smells as I would imagine a medieval peasant to smell, of animals, and sweat, and unwashed clothes.

The road forks. He gestures that we go right. We go right. I've become his chauffeur. This is top-quality hitch-hiking.

We drive through perhaps half a dozen miles of sandy nothing, dotted with the occasional ghaff tree or spindly, leggy shrub, passing a few errant camels loping at the pace of pointlessness. It seems that I'm committed to I don't know what. Another of God's dance invitations, perhaps. I'll just keep driving this silent man into the desert until either the road stops or we get where he wants to go. I check the fuel gauge.

Suddenly he drums on the hood of the glovebox with the palms of both hands, then grasps my arm. I stop the car. He gets out and shuts the door gently but without speaking. Then he sets off across the sand. A few hundred yards away I can see the tops of rough fencing. I watch him disappear over a ridge, reappear on the next one, then sink once more from view. I put the Nissan into gear and drive on. The tarmac shimmers and dances with heat. I reflect on what's just happened and soon decide that there is nothing to reflect on. The man just needed a lift.

A few miles and the road comes to an end in a village with no name and apparently no people. White-walled, flat-roofed bungalows with mirror windows are set around a vast plaza of sand. On the sand a pair of goalposts and a mosque. 4WDs outside the houses. I park and step out into silence. No kids, no pets, no smells, no sounds from the houses. In every yard stand a few date palms. I can feel the warmth of the sand through my flip-flops. A flight of doves whirrs past. The football pitch is marked with the hoof prints of camels. The prints are as long as my foot and twice as broad, and tipped with two prominent toes.

I pass through a gap between houses and emerge into orange desert, fading with distance to a tawny haze. The crinkle of dunes stretches to the horizon. A quarter of a mile away a crude fence of netting and wire and shade cloth encloses a mob of camels. As I near, I can hear them low, grumble and belch. Some are almost white, some close to black, most the colour of the

227

desert. They crowd to the fence to observe me. Alerted by his camels, a man emerges from a hut inside the camp. When he sees me, he freezes like a cat. I wave, shout 'hello'. He just stares.

I veer off over the dunes, go perhaps half a mile into the desert. It is hard walking, my steps up each dune shortened by miniature landslides under each placed foot. On the flatter, seemingly finer-grained down slope, my feet sink and have to be hauled out each time, the grains cascading like table salt. I sit on a dune. The camels, the village are out of sight. This place feels like no place. I take note of where the sun is in the sky.

Halfway between the calm of Al Ain and the frenzy of Dubai, this place feels as remote and indifferent as the surface of the moon. Just sky, sun and sand. I sense how I would shrivel here like a raisin. I don't hear the call that Thesiger heard. I wouldn't want to take this emptiness on, this perpetual, barren present tense.

As I trek back to the village I can feel the clock restarting. I get back into my little silver car, my petrol-powered Japanese camel, and I drive it, smooth and cool, to Dubai, where the hands of the clock hurtle, where more has happened in the last thirty years, more buildings built, more changes wrought, than in the whole of its previous history. The highway spears across the sand and the city comes out to meet it and absorbs me and my car without noticing.

19

Racing with Wayne

Before I went away I tried to find out about camel racing. Every tourist brochure refers to it. In a place without much in the way of quaint local stuff to photograph, or indeed much to distinguish it from any tourist destination, camel racing is a splendid novelty draw card, indigenous, apparently traditional, odd. Though it isn't, as it happens, that traditional. Bedouins raced their camels only at weddings. But in recent times, as the Arab identity of Dubai and the UAE became ever more diluted, the ruling families of Dubai and Abu Dhabi in particular saw the need to foster indigenous activities and pumped a lot of money into it to please their countrymen. But I haven't been able to find it.

I found it with ease on my only previous visit. A taxi driver took me out a little into the desert to see the camels training. It was among the more bizarre sights of my life. In crippling heat a string of camels thundered across sand. They ran with their necks stretched out, as if reaching for tit-bits. They didn't gallop as horses gallop but they reached an impressive speed. And strapped to their humps were little children. They held on with one hand and with the other they whacked the camel.

Behind the camels came a motorcade of owners and trainers in the inevitable 4WDs, throwing up a dust storm that billowed and floated behind them like a terrestrial con trail.

The jockeys were miniature creatures, aged, I was told, as young as five. They were bought from Indian or Pakistani families who had too many kids and too little cash. The kids were brought to the UAE and housed in camp with their camels until the day when they grew too big to be jockeys, though big meant only one step up from starved. At that point they went away and were not seen again.

As Dubai's international profile rose, so did the international outcry against the baby jockeys. Nothing frightens Dubai like a threat to its reputation. The response was typically innovative. They replaced the little children with little robots.

The robots are strapped to the hump in the same way, they are dressed in the racing silks of the owner, and they too whack the camels. They do so with a motorized arm holding a stick. No one's been able to tell me whether the arm automatically whacks throughout the race, which would seem a bit tough on the camel, or whether the trainer carries a remote control to turn the whacking on at critical moments. I suspect the latter, and am very keen to see it in practice, but I haven't been able to find out where to go.

I know that racing takes place in winter, and early in the morning, but though a much vaunted attraction it seems to be one that Dubai now wants to keep to itself. The tourist office claimed not to know, the taxi drivers either hadn't heard of it or told me the race track had been bulldozed and even George Appleton, friend of Stephen's and aficionado of all things racing whom I ring on my return, doesn't know. But he does invite me to join him for this evening's horse racing.

'Yes please,' I say, 'thank you.' And I can't help noticing how spontaneously generous most ex-pats I've met have been, how welcoming. More generous and welcoming, I'm sure, than their compatriots who sneer at the soulless superficiality of Dubai.

'Allah give to all people,' says the taxi driver on the way to the Nad al Sheeba race course. 'If you put a needle – you know a needle? – in the sea and pull out, it has little drop of water on the end and the sea is less. Yes? But Allah no. Allah is never less. Allah give and give and is never less. Allah is very rich, no? You are cat-lick?'

'No, I'm not. And anyway, it's OK.'

'You are good man. I am sorry for talking like this. It is fifty-eight dirhams.'

The car park is close to full. Crowds swarm and the sun is setting like the pink blush on a trout's gills. Gathered in the lee of the grandstand are thirty or more men, most of them black and African. They stand in silence, looking away from the grandstand, then in their own time they squat on their heels, bend forward, put their foreheads to the ground and stay there a while in prayer, before rising, standing a while longer, then ambling off to watch the races.

One tall black man in white robe and pillbox hat comes straight from prayer to me. 'You have copy of Gulf News?' he says. 'I want to check selections.'

I haven't. The man is from the Sudan. He wonders whether perhaps I can get into the clubhouse to fetch him a copy of the form guide. But the clubhouse door is blocked by a young bouncer type in jacket and tie and George Appleton has yet to arrive to bestow privilege upon me. I tell the Sudanese that I am confident his selections are inspired. He laughs, exposing teeth that in the States would cost thousands.

He and everyone else gets into the course for nothing by decree of Sheikh Mohammed who, unsurprisingly, owns the place. Free buses are laid on from town for the immigrant functionaries of Dubai. This is only a minor meeting but thousands have flocked. They enjoy the spectacle but they enjoy even more the remote hope of getting rich.

Islam does not permit betting. When a woman recently found that she couldn't sell her house she tried to raffle it. But the authorities forbade it.

Nevertheless, here at the racing there's an accumulator game that's free to enter and that can win you a few hundred dirhams, and there's a more serious Pick-Six competition that can jackpot over several meetings to a hundred thousand dirhams or more. Quite how that gets round Islamic law I'm not sure, but I've no doubt that it's been ratified by the least corruptible of scholars. Perhaps they were the same scholars who found a way to establish Islamic banks.

When the big race meetings take place later in the year more conventional betting is to be had, serious betting. International bookmakers give odds and all you need to place a bet is a mobile phone. And in Dubai if you've got money to gamble, you've got a mobile phone.

George Appleton is from Middlesbrough. He ran away to join the navy the week Elvis died. He was sixteen years old. His mum, he says, took three weeks to notice he'd gone. George's face testifies to a vigorous life. When he left the navy thirty years later his captain had this to say: 'It has been my pleasure as captain of a serving warship to transport George's golf clubs, cricket bats and penis about the world.' I've read worse testimonials. George is understandably proud of it.

It is immediately apparent with George that what you see is what you get and what you hear is free of linguistic varnish. He sees money as a chance to enjoy himself and joy means sport. He intends to die, broke, at the age of fifty-nine, 'like Emlyn Hughes and Alan Ball'.

The syndicate he belongs to owns a horse called Wayne

Rooney. I ask whether that means it's ugly and bad-tempered, but apparently not. The horse just belonged to one of Sheikh Mo's sons who is a devotee of Manchester United, but he tires of horses quickly and sells them off cheap.

'Wayne's won in Abu Dhabi,' says George, waving an owner's pass at a doorman.

He leads me to a second-floor box overlooking the course. And the course, floodlit at dusk, is simply beautiful. At the heart of it a lake. Around the lake, a golf course. Around the golf course, gleaming white rails. Around the rails a track of turf as green as New Zealand. Around that track, more rails. And around those rails another track, this time of sand.

The saddling enclosure in front of the stands is surrounded by hedges trimmed geometrically square. The crowd mills around it. Stewards in what looks like hunting gear patrol on horseback. But for the racial mix of the crowd and the balmy evening this could be an English race meeting.

The royal box has open air seating for perhaps forty, with chairs of thick red plush. The central seats resemble thrones. The area is scattered with a dozen or so dishdashed scions of royalty and one plump white man in a suit. He cosies up to one dishdash after another and repeatedly flings his head back to laugh toothily.

The most recent of the stands is a sleek and elegant wonder in chrome and glass, lit eerily blue by floodlights. It was built to great fanfare to commemorate the millennium. And a year from now, after a decade of race meetings, it will be rubble. They're pulling it down. They're pulling everything down. And they're putting up something better. A whole new track and stables and stands and hotel complex are already near completion just a few hundred yards away. The new venue is explicitly intended to out-Ascot Ascot. The main stand will be a kilometre long.

The history of this sort of racing in Dubai stretches all the way back to the discovery of oil. Sheikh Rashid's vastly enriched sons travelled to Britain, enjoyed what they saw, bought some horses, won a race or two, got a taste for it, bought more horses, established stables in England, established stables in Dubai, built this track and brought it to the world's attention in 1996 by hosting, in the proven method of modern Dubai, 'the world's richest horse race'. The notion worked as the seven stars of the Burj worked. People loved the flaunting simplicity of the title. And owners loved the prize money. They flocked. More PR for the emirate and a lovely hobby for the ruling family. Though it should be said that Sheikh Mohammed is apparently an outstanding horseman in his own right, and a world champion at endurance riding, whatever that may be.

The horses are beautiful. Preened and delicate, stepping as if on tiptoe and strung like violins, they look smaller than racehorses I've seen elsewhere. 'Arabian thoroughbred stock,' says George, who is addressing himself with equal intensity to the form guide and a bottle of Stella.

The first race is run on sand. Huge electronic screens show the horses in close-up. The broadcast commentary is fruitily English, rising to orgasmic pitch as they near the finish line, hauling the crowd forward to the rails, then subsiding in a post-coital sigh as the horses slow and the crowd falls back and the balloon of arousal deflates.

'Shit,' says George, and he pulls on his beer. There are perhaps a couple of dozen people in our box, several of whom also own a bit of Wayne Rooney. Tractors emerge to rake the sand flat, red tractors polished to a gleam, and I am introduced to Chris from Essex, once a banker now a mortgage broker. He's sanguine about Dubai.

'There will be failures,' he said. 'Projects abandoned half-built, that sort of thing, but Dubai is here to stay.'

'And you?'

'Oh I think I'll hang around,' he says, smiling. 'It's a bit more colourful than Essex, isn't it?'

Food and drink abound, the crowd below our box are entertaining to watch in their diversity, there aren't too many races for me to become bored, and I have a lovely argument about Wall Street with an investment banker that we both enjoy because we both think we win.

When the last race is run and the workers in matching boiler suits scurry onto the grass track to tamp the clods down with mallets, and the poor people file out to the car park and onto buses, we privileged few potter down a corridor and past the entrance to the royal box and out into the arena where a circular bar with a thatched roof is surrounded by women in hats. I don't know where they've been until now. In other boxes I suppose, but there are huge hats, ridiculous hats, tilted hats the size of bicycle wheels, hats like fluffy bowling balls, hats striped like zebras with gloves to match. And five foot six south of the hats, ridiculous shoes. Flimsy things for tottering in, ending in heels that could puncture a lung.

The men accompanying the hats are in Flash Harry suits, and everyone is clamouring for booze. They've been at it for three hours now and the men's voices are getting boomy and the women are starting to shriek.

The bar staff are various shades of brown – Sri Lankan, Indian, Filipino, Somali – and they are little more than boys. They knock up cocktails with swift dexterity, flip the tops off Belgian lagers, ease the corks from champagne and present bills that make me gawp. The suits pay without surprise, hesitation or resentment. Money pours across the bar like water. The till is crammed. The drinkers bray and squeal in the warm night air. Meanwhile the beautiful thoroughbred horses that drew the hats and the suits to this place have been led back to their stables to sleep on straw.

The conversation turns to cricket. George used to play against a mullah.

'You'd have loved him, Joe. Kershid the Mullah from some

mosque in Bur Dubai. Mad bastard he was. Had a red beard. When we tossed before the game he used to kiss me full on the lips. I've got this Thai girlfriend – not married or anything – and he always used to ask after her.

'And boy could he bat. Whacked it everywhere. I loved bowling to him. I always used to try and wind him up. I'd call him a dirty cheating bastard. And he was, too.

'"You can't say that to him, they'd say, he's a mullah."

'Fuck that,' I'd say, 'we're playing cricket.' And he never minded. Always used to come back to the bar for a Coke or something after. "Very good game, my friend, very good game", then off to evening prayers. Proves they're not all mad bastards.'

Too energized to go home I take a taxi down to the Creek. Warm air, abundant people, a fizz on the late night streets and an abundance of seedy hotels. They are the original hotels of Dubai, now superseded by the plush corporate chains – Hyatt, Radisson, Intercontinental – and the one-off, show-off Burj.

The first bar I step into resembles an underground cafeteria segregated by sex. I immediately think of withdrawing but am insistently ushered to a roped-off area where men sit at Formica tables. On each table is a pot of unconvincing plastic flowers. Most of the men are Indian and solitary. They wear polyester suits and no ties. Waiters keep them supplied from the little bar. By the pool table on the far side of the bar the women are gathered. They are a united nations of prostitutes. Gleaming black, honey brown, Russian pale and Chinese sallow, they chat casually among themselves, dressed in cut-off jeans or strappy leather. From time to time they glance casually across at the men, who cradle their drinks and commune with themselves, looking more in need of a laugh than a shag. This is not a happy place.

One girl is extraordinary. Tall, lithe, walking as if she carried a water pot on her head, she wears jeans and a provocative waistcoat. She has the cheekbones of Mongolia, the lips and teeth of perhaps Kenya, the skin of the Middle East and the enterprise to note my staring and to come and sit down at my table. I don't know what the form is. She is wasting her time, but my upbringing, while never having been explicit about the correct way to address the unwanted attentions of Middle Eastern prostitutes, assumes its default mode of polite apparent interest.

'I'm Joe.'

'Joe,' she says as neutrally as it is possible to say Joe.

She accepts my reluctant offer of a drink by flicking her fingers and catching the eye of a barman, an eye that was already aware of her relocation to my table, and in short order a bottle of Budweiser arrives for her and a beer for me to replace the one that I had decided was the only one I was having here.

She takes a straw from a glass on the table, slowly peels the wrapping from it with fingernails as long and crimson as you'd expect, pops it into her beer, sucks on it, puts the bottle down, looks at me, then looks away towards the bar and pops some chewing gum into her mouth. She is young, perhaps nineteen. She's really just a girl. She is strikingly handsome, but she has an understandably hard edge, a bitterness no one her age should be saddled with.

She wants money. She gets money by getting laid. She's not going to get laid by me. The kindest thing I could do for her at this stage is to leave.

'Where are you from?' I say. In my defence, I do actually want to know.

'Uzbekistan.'

Her accent sounds huskily guttural. She glances assessingly at me as she speaks, and I can sense that she assesses me rightly.

'What's the capital of Uzbekistan?' Where that question came from I'm not sure. I don't know the answer, but neither do I want to know it.

'Uh?' she says.

But now I've embarked I feel obliged to take the conversational journey. And it's better, fractionally, than a dismissive silence.

'The capital, you know, the big city in Uzbekistan. England capital London. Russia capital Moscow. Uzbekistan capital . . .?' and here I shrug my shoulders and splay my palms in a hollow-jolly gesture of interrogation.

She sneers. She turns away. She makes eye contact with another girl. I get up, go to the bar, pay my bill and leave.

'Good night, sir,' says the Indian barman. 'And thank you.'

Dubai abounds in prostitutes for obvious reasons. Men vastly outnumber women here. Many of the men are too poor to hire a whore, but clearly there are plenty who aren't and who do. And then there's history. The Gulf has a long tradition of slavery. East African slaves were shipped through here for centuries. It was often slaves who dived for pearls. Every sheikh had slaves. And every sheikh further inland wanted slaves and he got them through ports like Dubai. From the mid-eighteenth century the British did much to minimize the trade, but it was still going on in the 1950s. And in the form of this Uzbekistani girl and the Chinese girl I met the other night it still is. The exploitation is illegal. But too little is done to enforce the law.

In its most recent Report of Human Trafficking the UNHCR had this to say:

> . . . women from Eastern Europe, South East Asia, the Far East, East Africa, Iraq, Iran, and Morocco reportedly are trafficked to the UAE for commercial sexual exploitation. Some foreign women also are reportedly recruited for work as secretaries or hotel workers by third-country recruiters and coerced into prostitution or domestic servitude after arriving in the UAE.

The report acknowledges that the UAE government has made some efforts 'to prosecute and convict sex trafficking offenders during the year and made modest progress to provide protections to female trafficking victims' but the report also makes it quite clear that the government hasn't done much.

The trade carries on partly because of the fundamental nature of Dubai. The place was born of a western belief system, a belief system that took hold in the Seventies and was championed by Reagan, Thatcher and Wall Street. It was the belief in the free market, or if not free, as unfettered as it could be. It got its moral imprimatur from the collapse of the Berlin Wall and the Soviet Union. Since the Communists had so clearly got it wrong, the free marketeers must have got it right.

Dubai was and is a crystallization of that belief. It is the freest of free markets. No taxes, no welfare state, few scruples and the chance to create simply colossal wealth. So in they flocked, the banks and corporations, to a new world hub, and the hub blossomed.

But the same qualities that made Dubai blossom, have also made it shady. The same qualities that have attracted the giant corporations have attracted the racketeers. The parasites and exploiters, the traders in misery, the organized crime syndicates, fell in love with Dubai for all the same reasons and saw all the same possibilities. It was in Dubai, to name just one example, that AQ Khan set up shop. AQ Khan was for years the head of Pakistan's nuclear weapons programme. But he liked to do a little business on the side, selling nuclear materials and know-how to anyone who would pay. Those who paid included Libya, Iran and North Korea. And as a place to conduct trade Khan found Dubai just so convenient.

It's hard to go for a night on the town in any city of the world without meeting, or preferably observing from a distance, a drunk Scot. The one on the steps of this hotel is in the process of being bounced. Three chunky bouncers are restraining him. He wants to fight them. His t-shirt is torn from right armpit to waist and drenched with what I hope is only beer. He is drunk enough to be effectively incomprehensible. The only word I can make out is ████. He says it a lot. He shouts it. His face is contorted with rage at the blind injustice that life has meted out to him. He looks rabid, impossible. I'm impressed by the bouncers' restraint. I want them to thump him. '████████,' he screams at them, at the unjust world, 'you ████████ ████████████,' I catch a taxi.

'Salaam aleekum,' I say.

The driver is Afghani and charming.

20

Choose Your Goat

'Build me a school,' said Sheikh Rashid in May 1978, 'right here,' and jabbed his finger at Plot B141, down by the sea. And they did. They built Dubai College.

Plot B141 aggrandizes it a bit. In 1978 this area was just sand and a coastal track and a sprinkle of shacks. Now a six-lane highway, an irrigated lawn and an ornamental flower bed separate the school from the beach. And out from the beach stretches the Palm Jumeirah with David Beckham's mum securely lodged amid its fronds.

Only a few yards from the ceaseless traffic a bird is bearing down on a flower bed, an egret. It is as white as a medieval virgin and shaped like a stretched Chianti bottle.

The egret seems unfazed by the roaring vehicles, but when it spots me, the sole pedestrian in vehicle land, it stands still. I stand still. A few seconds and it resumes its progress, picking its deliberate way on huge splayed feet, reaches the edge of the bed and studies the ranks of plants, peering under leaves and flower heads and swaying its head like a charmed cobra. It freezes momentarily, then strikes. In its beak a lizard, gripped across the belly. From only a few yards away I can make out the tiny reptilian claws, grasping at the nothingness of air. The bird tosses the lizard twice to align it with its gullet, then points its beak at the sky and lets gravity do the rest. What started as just another day for the lizard has come to a drastic end. I can see the slight bulge in the bird's throat. The bird moves on and I cross the road. Perhaps five minutes later I've made it across all six lanes. I look back. The bird is hunting again.

'Here's something to read while you're waiting,' says the school secretary, and hands me the Dubai College yearbook. Having taught for too many years, I've seen school yearbooks. They don't vary. The same upbeat glossiness. The same snaps of kids running, jumping, playing musical instruments, grinning and clowning, going on field trips – the officially sanctioned version of adolescence. No record of the moodiness, the sudden swings of love and dread. Every yearbook is advertising.

Framed paintings by the kids line the walls. The names tell the story of the place: Finn Harceaga, Katy Hassall, Anisha Senaretne, Priyanka Patel, Alia al Ghussain, Sofia Vyas, Melissa McWhirter, Rafae Ali. Is there a more cosmopolitan school any-where? Perhaps, but of the one hundred and ninety or so nationalities available on earth, Dubai College has representa-tives from more than a quarter of them.

'If you can't teach here,' says Graham Penson, my twinkling guide around the school, 'you can't teach.' We pass through an area where senior kids are supposed to be engaged in private study. Almost all of them *are* engaged in private study. I don't think I've ever seen that before.

'Six applicants for every place,' says Graham. 'And the kids want to get ahead.'

He pushes open the door to the new performing arts block. A girl of sixteen or so is singing something classical. A pianist accompanies her. Her singing coach listens intently. A sound technician fiddles with a board. Three adults attending to the one child. The voice fills the conditioned air. We tiptoe past and Graham opens the door on an auditorium with an orchestra pit, a huge stage and seating that can be rearranged by laser.

'Nice,' I say, thinking of the cold school halls where I used to put on shows. Yes

'Yeah,' says Graham, 'not bad, is it?' Originally from Birmingham, he's been here many years and plans to stay a few more to see the last of his kids through school. After that, retirement somewhere, though probably in neither Dubai nor Brum.

'You don't sound Brummy,' I say, and he smiles and launches beautifully into his native accent, though beautifully may not be the most apt of adverbs. That rising intonation. Those vowels that spring straight from the bridge of the nose. Though Birmingham is England's second city, its accent rarely makes the national airwaves. Even as in Chaucer's day, the Oxford-Cambridge-London triangle still looks down its vowels at the rest of the country.

'In Dubai,' says Graham, 'class is money. But the place grows on you, and I like to think it's got a bit of integrity to it, a certain tolerance and courtesy.'

So saying, he leads me into a class of tolerant and courteous sixth form kids who have been corralled to listen to the visiting writer and who seem tolerantly and courteously unexcited by the prospect. I tell them about the egret and the lizard. I thought it would make a provocative opening. It doesn't. The kids seem either puzzled or politely uninterested.

I fire out questions about growing up in Dubai, whether it seems like home to them, whether they expect to spend their lives here, whether they think it's a fair society, what they see as the future of the place, but I get only polite platitudes back. Perhaps what seems remarkable to me about the place is just to them the way things are.

But as I sit on a bus heading downtown a while later I acknowledge the truth to myself. And that truth is that I've been too long out of the classroom. I've lost the knack. In the half hour I was in front of them I made no connection with them. So why should they give out? Ah well, I won't be returning to teaching. But they were good kids.

The bus drops me outside the Al Shindagha Carrefour hyper-market, huge and air-conditioned and selling everything from toasters to toasted sandwiches. It's got a display of New Zealand lamb, its rich purple muscle fed on grass half a world away and butchered into neat chops, shoulders and legs. The Indian lamb in an adjacent chiller is half the price, less meaty and apparently butchered by the blind. The cleaver has just hacked through the bone in arbitrary places, and the resulting chunks of animal have been piled unsorted into a thick plastic bag.

Near the shop entrance there's a board of small ads like the ones in sweetshop windows when I was a kid. They are all for accommodation.

'Bedspace available in villa for working ladies. Filipino only. 700 dirhams month.'

'Bedspace available for Indian executive bachelor.'

Executive here means anything other than a construction worker. Bedspace means access to a bed for certain hours of the day. The rest of the time someone else will have it.

Al Shindagha is the spit of land that curls across the mouth of the creek and would close it were it not dredged. And it was on this spit that Sheikh Mohammed's granddad was born. His palace has been duly restored for tourists and is as much a fort as a palace, built of coral blocks from the sea, with tall thick walls and low windowless rooms and wind towers designed to catch the slightest breeze off the Gulf and funnel it inside the building to relieve the heat of summer. One room holds a display of photos of Dubai in the mid-twentieth century. There's a snap of a souk, all shade and heaped goods and men idling in the heat in rag-tag clothing, and another of Dubai under siege from locusts. A single anonymous long-dead insect is immortalized as it loomed against the lens seventy years ago, like an out of focus UFO. Behind it, its trillion brothers and sisters resemble a blizzard. Dibba is apparently the Arabic for locust, and possibly the origin of the name Dubai.

But the photo that strikes me hardest is an aerial shot of Dubai. Just a cluster of white buildings clinging to the mouth of the Creek and giving way almost immediately to the bleaching desert behind.

I fetch a juice and take a seat by the Creek. Where I sit I'd be in the middle of that photo. I face towards the Gulf with my back to the modern world and try to imagine how it was. The place would have been quiet, especially in the heat of summer. The little abras that ferried people from Deira to Bur Dubai and back would have had oarsmen rather than engines. The people passing by would have been dressed not in Chinese cotton casual or in suits, nor probably in dishdashes, but in the universal robe of Arabia. The vast yellow straddle cranes of Port Rashid would not have been there to stab the skyline. There would have been only the ancient horizon of the Gulf's bright waters. And fishing boats. And heat.

I swivel in my seat, and there's the twenty-first century. The glass tower of some money-shifting banking giant, a huge hotel, and tall electric letters spelling ROLEX in English and Arabic. I amble off and find an abattoir.

'You want?' says a Pakistani in loose blue pyjamas, sitting on the rail above a pen of goats.

'Where are they from?'

'Iran,' he says. 'Iran very good meat.'

'I see,' and I appraise his goats in a manner that I hope suggests carnivorous interest. White goats, brown goats, black goats, black brown and white goats, horned and hornless, floppy-eared, straight-eared, straight-haired, short-haired or hair in ringlets, and all of them doomed. If not today, then tomorrow or the day after. The kids pile all over each other to get at a bowl of food scraps. Their efforts, within yards of the eternal cleaver, seem just a little pointless. Though you could argue that the difference between them and us is merely span.

The abattoir has a viewing area. You select your beast, pay for it at the little window, and then toddle up the ramp at your leisure to watch the beast being butchered. One end of the viewing platform is reserved for ladies. At the other end, there's a display of diseased bits of goat. Here's a parasitic cyst, nicely preserved, and beside it a gall bladder that's suffered a haemorrhage. But the glass is misty with condensation and the ink has run on the typed descriptions. There's also a sign saying Suggestions Box but the box is missing.

Inside the abattoir three fittingly swarthy men are sitting on a stainless steel table and chatting and waiting. Two men of Middle Eastern aspect arrive in a Toyota Ute. With them are four happy little boys who have clearly been here before. They rush to the pens and clamber on the metal fencing. The adults swiftly select a good-sized goat with curly hair the colour of milk chocolate.

The herdsman seizes it by the horns, drags it from the pen, holds it for the customers' final inspection, then wrestles it through a doorway in the back of the slaughterhouse. The boys run round to the viewing area while the adults light cigarettes.

The goat appears in the killing shed, borne by a metal conveyor belt with sides that clamp against the animal's flanks. It can move only its head and neck. I watch it striving to make sense of this new and alien place, its head swivelling, its eyes as wide as a goat's eyes go. When it reaches the top of the belt, two men seize it by the legs and lay it on its side on a stainless steel table. The man at the front end draws a knife from a holster at his waist, says a prayer invoking the greatness of Allah and slashes the beast's throat, once, twice. There is no noise. Blood spurts onto the killer's plastic apron. The goat performs a few spasms of the legs then is goat no more. It merely twitches, involuntarily I presume – I hope – as the other man hitches it by the rear hooves to an overhead line, and the killer hoses the blood from his apron. The corpse's head swings beneath the line at an angle no living goat could achieve, the wound across its throat is a ruby chasm, a hugeness.

They cut off the horns with a circular saw and toss them into a bucket, then peel the skin from the animal's head. The head now resembles a Hollywood alien. A man runs his knife up the scrotum and belly, then hauls the skin off the back end of the beast as if peeling a wetsuit off a child. He clamps the loose pelt to a swinging hydraulic device that stretches the carcass as if on a rack, until the whole pelt comes off with a rush. The chain moves the carcass on to be eviscerated. The beast has shrunk to a frame of bones and edible muscles.

The stomach is tossed down a chute. Other organs are put aside. The chest cavity is hosed out. When the blanched and simplified carcass reaches the end of the chain it's unslung, laid on the block, and the butcher asks the customers how they want it dealt with. A few deft cleaver hacks and the whole lot, which fifteen minutes ago was shaggy bleating goat, a goat that could see and hear and run, is tipped into a carrier bag and handed through the hatch. Two boys take a handle each and carry it to the Ute.

I find the whole business gruesomely compelling. I watch half a dozen goats butchered. One is a white kid, little bigger than a spaniel. By the time it's been finished with, it's snack-sized.

Another evening, another party in Arabian Ranches. Is this the residual effect of Christmas, or is the ex-pat life an endless round of such gatherings? The hostess is Iranian. 'In Iran,' she says, 'we like things clean. We don't like animals because they are dirty. This dog,' and here she pats the family mongrel, a mute and docile creature, 'is the first animal I ever touched. Except with a fork.'

The dog looks up with the brown-eyed hope that we mistake so readily for love. I've watched the dog for a while. It's been doing what dogs do at parties, which is to cruise for food. It hung around the kitchen until shooed out by one of the Filipina maids, since when it has sat patiently at the feet of anyone who is eating. It targets women. By sitting patiently it hopes to melt their hearts. And if the woman fails to notice the dog, there is always the chance that when she gets up she will trip over it and food will spill.

I cycled here on a borrowed bike. I haven't cycled in years. And I enjoyed it, despite the residual sensation that someone has gently but insistently taken a cabinet-maker's hammer to a point just behind my scrotum. The route took me past a billion dollars of Arabian Ranches real estate, the houses all subtly different and effectively identical, and in the whole half-hour ride through the warm evening I saw nobody on foot, bar security guards and a single jogger.

But I did see an accident. It was lovely. A woman emerged from her front door and spoke a few brisk words to her maid. The woman was dressed to go out in a tight white dress. She lowered herself into a black Audi, reversed out of her drive, swung across the road and ran smack into the side of a parked Mini Cooper.

Because it happened at low speed I heard every expensive detail: the crack and tinkle of the rear lights shattering and the deep graunch of sheet metal buckling. Apart from the maid, whom I imagine could be relied on to keep schtum, I was the only witness.

The woman got out of the car, inspected the damage, looked

around and saw me on my bike. Her already tight features tightened further. She went into the house and I rode on. I didn't have an exact address for the party but it wasn't hard to find. A whole fleet of 4WDs was drawn up outside it like piglets on a sow.

There's food and drink in abundance, and the real-estate cliché of indoor–outdoor flow is actually happening, all the doors being wide open and there being no temperature difference between in and out. The garden is lush with forced vegetation. The pool sparkles under lights. The bar's a thatched hut, round which the men have gathered to laugh heartily. The women stand in knots. Children frolic in the pool or play games of electronic murder in the television room. And as usual, there are no old people to cater to.

A man who refuses politely to tell me what sort of business it is that he runs is less reticent on the subject of race. 'Indians are OK,' he says, 'but don't give them authority. They immediately establish a caste system. Pakistanis have a chip on their shoulder. Filipinos start well then slowly decline. It's hard to get Africans to do any work at all. Egyptians are ~~fucking~~ hopeless. *FILTH* But the Nepalese, now, I just can't get enough of them. Great workers. Great people.'

'And Kiwis?' I ask. 'Ever had any of them work for you?'

'A dozen or so,' he says, to my surprise. 'And I've sacked the lot. They get bolshy.'

There's a table football machine on the patio, its ranks of players impaled on rods, like kebabs. I tell the host about a bar in my home town that was owned by a laid-back German. He turned the table football machine in his bar into a game between Jews and Nazis. His action caused a furore and was condemned in newspaper editorials. And in direct consequence business boomed. The host laughs and disappears into the house to re-emerge with the *Victor* annual. He opens it to show me line drawings of square-headed Boche shouting '*Achtung, hande hoch und Britische schweinhund.'* The year of the annual is 1973, twenty-eight years after the war ended.

Kids who think 1973 is ancient history are playing with a Wii machine. I've heard the name and puzzled at it, but never seen the beast itself. The kids remarkably, and I suspect atypically, are engaged in some interactive fitness programme. Seeing me watching they urge me to have a go. I have to stand on a box like bathroom scales. 'Hi,' says the machine in a voice that it would be hard to imagine anything worse than, 'let's get fit together, shall we?'

I am with children so I say nothing. The machine requires me to establish an on-screen identity. I prove incompetent with the remote, so the kids take over. They create a dumpy figure called Joe, then to universal laughter they make him bald.

The machine ingests my vital statistics, then informs me that I am 'rather overweight'. Again I say nothing. The screen leads me through some balancing exercises on the little box, at the end of which it summarizes my fitness. And it transpires that as a fifty-one-year-old who still plays a fair game of squash or cricket and who walks miles on the hills with his dog every day, I have the athletic capacity of a sixty-three-year-old. 'Would you like to set some fitness goals, now?' asks the machine.

'Yes,' I say to myself. 'I would, after a fashion.'

The first of them would be to throw this intrusive and patronizing irrelevance of a machine through the window. The second is to fly to Silicon Valley and find the pot-bellied Coca-Cola-drinking slob who programmed it, thrash him at squash, drink him under the table, and while he is unconscious debag him and strap him to the ground in some region of the world that is known to be popular with soldier ants. 'Thanks, kids,' I say, 'I think that'll do me,' and I retire to the lavatory where there is a cage of entertainingly active hamsters.

When I'm cycling back late in the evening, and pedalling with a vigour that is not entirely unrelated to my discourse with Mr

Wii, a Jeep pulls up alongside me. Two of my fellow party-goers want to give me and the bike a lift. They are insistent.

The woman of the couple is wearing a skimpy leopard-skin dress to show off her boob job. Despite the dress she is, by her own confession, hopelessly sentimental about animals. So sentimental indeed that in response to an appeal last year she flew to Borneo to work as a volunteer in a camp for orphaned orang-utans. She lasted a week.

'So I don't suppose I need to ask how it was.'

'I'll tell you exactly how it was,' she says. 'It was ~~fucking shit~~ AWFUL.'

21

'Bye Dubai

Last week was the third anniversary of Sheikh Mohammed's accession. The local business paper marked the event by printing a special bumper twenty-four-page lift-out super souvenir colour supplement. They called it Tribute to a Visionary.

It consisted of pictures of the Sheikh and opinions about the Sheikh. The pictures varied – Mohammed in a hard hat, in a top hat, in traditional costume, in Shanghai, at a construction site, a playground, Ascot. The opinions didn't vary at all. Everyone liked the Sheikh a lot. The chairman of Emaar Properties, the company that built Arabian Ranches, called him 'a great example of a successful leader'. The Secretary General of the Dubai Executive Council said, 'He has established new standards of good governance and wise leadership.' Yahya Lootah of Lootah Real Estate, and there's a name to revel in, said, 'We are blessed to have Sheikh Mohammed at the helm.' And the director of Sheikh Mohammed's office at the Ruler's Court let us know, endearingly, that 'Sheikh Mohammed always provides happy surprises that make each and every one of us proud of him.'

Now, there are three possibilities with this publication. One is that it's all true. The second is that it's the most blatant piece of up-sucking, lickspittle puffery since Stalin died. The third is that it's a bit of both. And I'd go for number three.

There seems little doubt from what I've read and heard that Sheikh Mohammed is a good man. But it would take a very good man indeed to read that sort of thing about himself all the time and not be affected by it. History abounds in leaders who have come to believe flatterers. Africa abounds in them still.

The only two defences that our species has found against such leaders are democracy and a free press. Democracy and a free press are the first things that any would-be tyrant abolishes. Dubai's got neither. It is not a democracy. And neither, for all its protestations to the contrary, does it have a free press. To recognize that truth you have only to imagine a Fleet Street supplement celebrating three years of any British prime minister. Dubai is an autocracy with censorship.

Autocracies, though, get things done. That's their great advantage. Right now, for example, Dubai is building a metro system. Some of it will run underground, the rest on stilts. The trains will be driverless. The project will cost about fifteen billion dollars. It will make a big difference. It will be wonderful. And it has happened because the Sheikh said it would happen. Nothing has been allowed to stand in its way; no resource management acts, no piddling planning laws, no ratepayer protests, nothing.

The simple fact is that had Dubai not been autocratically led – and well led, far better led than many of its neighbours – it could never have come so far so fast. It owes its success to its ruling family. And that ruling family owes its position, historically, to the colonial patronage of Britain. Whether democracy will come one day, I have no idea. Meanwhile I just hope Sheikh Mohammed can keep his head amid the flattery.

Autocracies are common, but Dubai is unique. What makes it unique is the nature of its population. Only around five per cent of its denizens are citizens. The rest are guests, sixty per cent or more from the Indian subcontinent, the remainder from every country on earth. Almost all of them are here of their own free will. Every one of them is on a visa. And every one of them can be hoofed out on a whim. They have no comeback.

The streets of Dubai must be among the safest in the world. This is not because of a vast police presence, nor is it because there are no criminals in Dubai. Organized crime has found Dubai a convenient base. But the streets are safe because petty criminals can be instantaneously and irrevocably got rid of. The two hundred and sixty-two vendors of fake watches that I mentioned earlier, along with the thirty beggars, sixty-nine car washers and fifty-eight unlicensed butchers and fish cleaners, were deported. Gone. Never to return. It makes for safe streets, though I doubt that the fish cleaners were much of a threat to life.

The only people who can't be deported are the Emirati citizens. But very few of them take to crime because most of them do very nicely, thank you.

I doubt that any country in history has housed as high a proportion of foreigners as Dubai does. That makes it odd. But I am not sure that it deserves to be hated, as it clearly is hated by many.

It is certain that some of its workers are duped and exploited. It is also true that there is no great system of legal protection to which the exploited have recourse. But you will find exploitation in any city in the world and you will find greater exploitation, and greater poverty and greater injustice in hundreds of third world cities, the cities that many of Dubai's workers came from. Which is why many of them choose to stay. Home is worse. And I suspect, in the end, that what makes some people hate this place is that it brings the third world into view of the first world.

If African, Indian, Chinese and Filipino poverty stays in Africa, India, China and the Philippines then it is more seemly, and easier to ignore, than if it comes to live in an ostensibly first-world city alongside western businesses and western tourists. To say that is not to defend the exploitation. It is merely to try to explain the reaction to it.

But it doesn't explain the hatred expressed by such writers as Simon Jenkins who, if you recall, wrote that Dubai is 'the last word in iconic overkill, a festival of egotism with humanity denied.' I'm not sure what he means by this. Does he simply dislike the skyscrapers? Does he loathe Dubai just because it's new, rich and cocky?

Dubai is indeed new, rich and cocky. With its seven-star Burj and its world's tallest building and its ski slope in a mall, it has deliberately drawn attention to itself. It has strutted and boasted as a marketing ploy. But that isn't the nub of Dubai. The nub of Dubai has always been, and continues to be, trade. Dubai isn't a playground. It's a port, a hub, a place where people come to do business and make money. Exactly the same is true of New York, or of Shanghai, or of Simon Jenkins's London. Cities exist to do business. It's how they become cities. The rest is fiddle-de-dee.

Architectural show-offery has not made Dubai what it is, and neither has tourism or oil. Indeed, oil now accounts for less than five per cent of Dubai's GDP. As I have tried to show, Dubai has used such oil as it had to create something else, and it is a something else that business has flocked to. In the end, if you hate Dubai it is because you hate the nature of global business. You hate the advertising and the executives and the consumption and the manipulation and the ruthless self-interest of the corporate world. None of which is unique to Dubai. Dubai's leaders merely built a city to accommodate it. They built a place to do business. And the people came.

In my trip round the rest of the UAE one fact stood out everywhere. The smaller emirates had been more selfishly led than

Dubai. They had not thought ahead like Dubai. They now envied Dubai, and they were all in their own way trying to get a slice of the action that Dubai had created.

I choose to spend my last day in Deira, where the streets teem and where, if I were to live in Dubai, I would make my home. Though I won't be coming to live in Dubai.

I watch a Muslim baker in a shop the size of a wardrobe. He squats on a shelf at shoulder level to pedestrians. With swift dexterity he takes a blob of dough and shapes it over a mould to the size of a kiddies' tricycle wheel, then lowers it into a cylindrical oven at his feet. At the same time he fishes into the oven with a giant toasting fork and flicks out the cooked loaves. They land unerringly on a shelf behind a pane of glass where another man collects them, bags them and sells them ten at a time, hot.

'I'd like one, please,' I say.

The man offers me a bag.

'No, one bread,' and I hold up a single explanatory finger. He fishes one out of the bag and waves away my offered money. On the street, I tear off gouts of the warm bread as I walk. It's tough, bland, simple. The last time I ate bread like this was in Xinjiang, the most westerly province of China, which a millennium and a half ago was the most easterly province of the Arabian Empire. And it remains Muslim. Islam's a durable faith.

A butcher's shop nearby is little larger than the bakery, perhaps three metres by two, hung thick with carcasses on hooks. And in among them, like a fat child in a meat forest, stands the butcher, swarthy and sweaty, with forearms like legs of lamb. I watch him unhook a mighty yellow haunch, hack twice, three times through a joint, strip the flesh from the bone, cube it with the same vast cleaver, barely looking at what he does; then reach across, pluck two kidneys from a pile, dice them in seconds, sweep the whole lot from the block to a bag, and pass it to the customer. He takes the money with bloodied hands. When he notices me still watching he suddenly swings the cleaver round his head as if in some tribal dance, then grins with golden teeth.

The barber's got a David Niven moustache and a dapper self-assurance. His menu of services includes earwax and blackhead removal. I have a haircut and shave, the haircut with tiny chattering scissors, the shave with a cut-throat. He tenses the skin between finger and thumb before each deft unhesitating stroke of the blade. When I scratch an itch on my nose, he dabs the spot with a tissue soaked in eau de cologne. I feel pampered by a craftsman. He's from Gujarat. His grandfather established the business here in 1955. The shop back then had no electricity. Now he and his four brothers each have a shop of their own here.

'So this is home for you then?'

'Oh no no no, sir,' says the barber, pausing with his cut-throat in mid-air above my throat, 'my home is Gujarat, sir.' And everything about that story and that exchange, from the grandfather to the sir, seems to me to encapsulate something true about Dubai. He finishes me off with a scalp massage and perfume.

I leave the barber's smelling nicer than usual and feeling braced. And five minutes later, when I'm watching a ragged game of cricket on the standard makeshift pitch, a wish comes true. Perhaps it's because of the perfume.

'You are bowling?' asks a chubby Pakistani, and he offers me the ball. Over his pyjamas he wears a thick quilted vest. On his chin, a wispy beard. On his head a little embroidered cap. His manner is charming, his teeth terrible. Greeny-brown stumps, they are all but gone with rot. His name is Zachariah.

'Are you sure? I am not very good. Too old.'

He grins. 'You are very good.'

It is hard to bowl in flip-flops. I would like to kick them off as most of the other bowlers do but I know my feet couldn't cope with the gravel. I bowl off a couple of shuffling paces. The tennis ball is wound round with red insulation tape to make it resemble the real thing. The batsman, who is dressed like a shop assistant and probably is one, takes the standard mighty swing. He makes clean contact and the ball strikes the window of a dry goods store on the first bounce.

'Very good,' says Zachariah. 'You are very good bowler.' His tone betrays no hint of irony.

An astonishingly skinny Indian youth biffs the ball back to me. It strikes a lump of rubble and shoots off sideways. Zachariah trots cheerfully after it.

I have to wait for a woman in a turquoise sari to cross the pitch from cover point to straightish midwicket before bowling again. The batsman repeats his extravagant and only shot, misses, and the ball strikes the lower of the two concrete blocks.

'Howzat,' scream twenty young men. Several of them are playing in a neighbouring game. You take your joys where you can.

Shop boy flails the air with momentary annoyance, then grins and offers me the bat. I pretend to hesitate.

Its handle is held together with tape and oddments of string. Its bottom corner is worn away from repeated thumping against gravel. I take guard.

Zachariah is keen to bowl at me. He runs in at high speed, bare foot, his green pyjamas flapping, stops dead at the rock that denotes the bowling crease and then simply throws the ball. I play it defensively with a straight bat, sending it back towards mid-off along the ground. There is silence. I'd like to think it is awe. I know it isn't. This simply isn't batting as they know batting. As far as they are concerned, it's just not cricket.

Zachariah comes down the pitch. 'You are having very good health and fitness,' he says.

'Thank you,' I say.

I clip Zachariah's next throw neatly off my legs, through the other match and against the wall of a mosque. This shot draws the attention of the players in the other game. One of them picks up the ball, deserts his team and insists on bowling at me. I have novelty value. He runs in like Shoaib Akhtar. But I have struck a vein of form. The ball flies high and beautiful over long on. I feel the surge of joy that only a well-hit shot can bring. Now half a dozen lads squabble over the ball in their eagerness to have a crack at this bald white man.

Then shouting. Shouting of a different tone. Gruff. Bitter. A policeman has appeared at third man in his olive uniform and beret. He wears stripes on his sleeve and a gun on his belt. He is waving an angry authoritarian arm. The games stop. The Indians stare sullenly at their shoes and mill around. The cop shouts again, makes dismissive gestures, and the lads begin resentfully, sulkily, to disperse. The wicketkeeper kicks over the concrete block stumps. They fall with a puff of dust.

I hand Zachariah the bat. He takes it without smiling. 'I am sorry,' he says as he moves away.

I don't know why the cop intervened. I go on my way hating him. And not because I was batting rather well. Or at least not just because of that.